THE COMPLETE CAR MODELLER 2

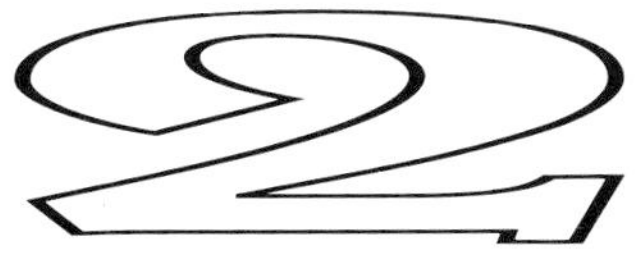

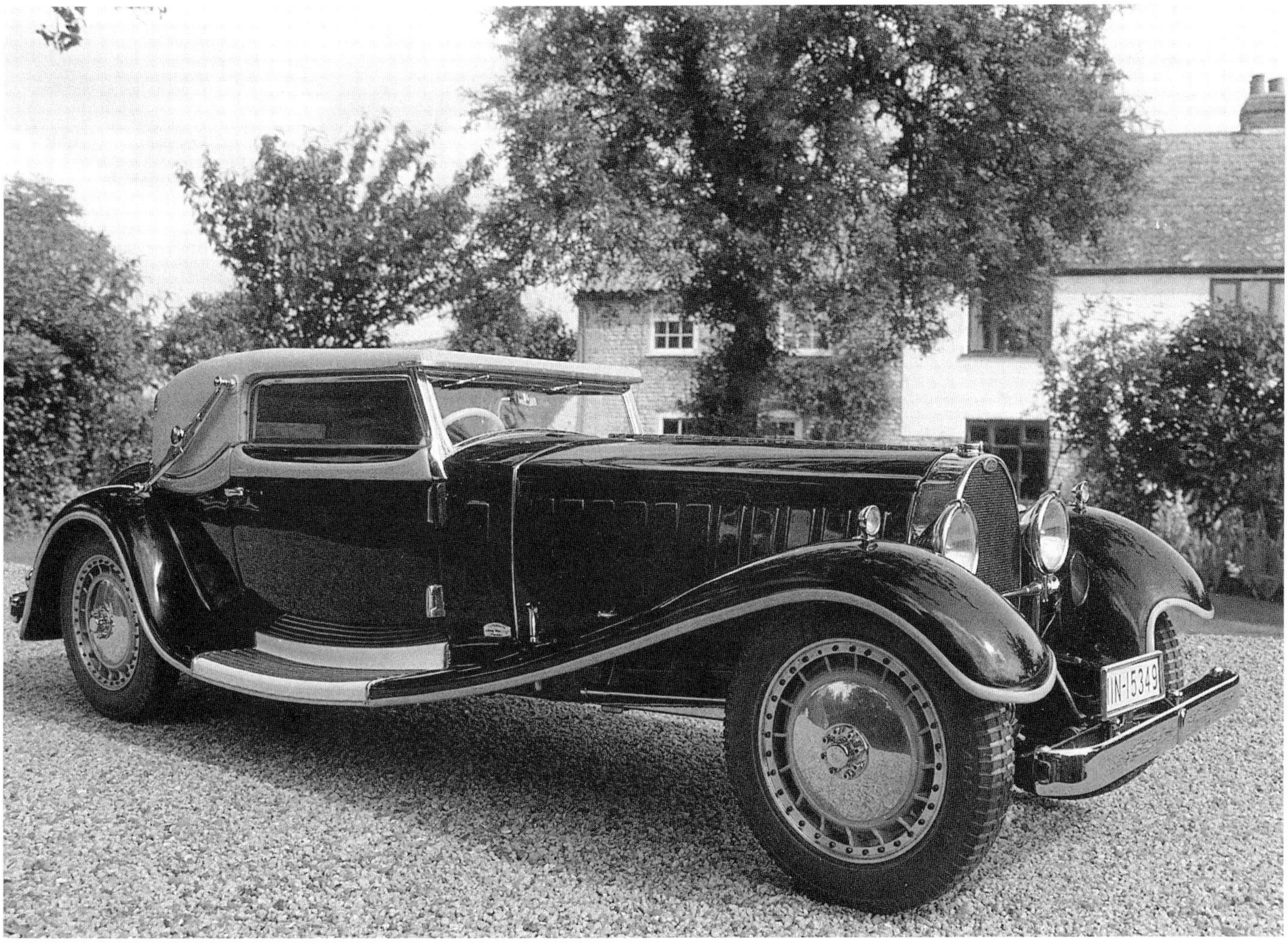

Plate 1

THE COMPLETE CAR MODELLER 2

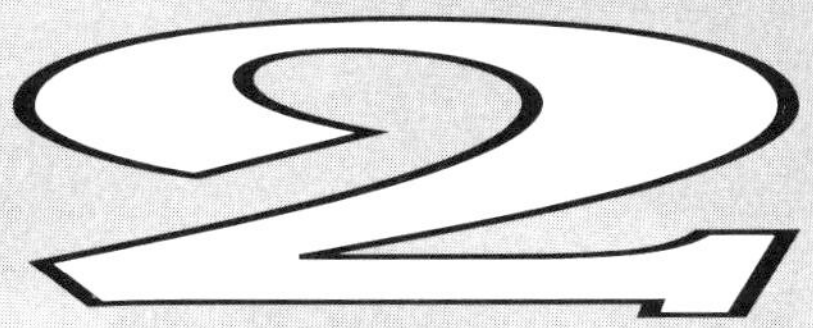

Gerald A. Wingrove

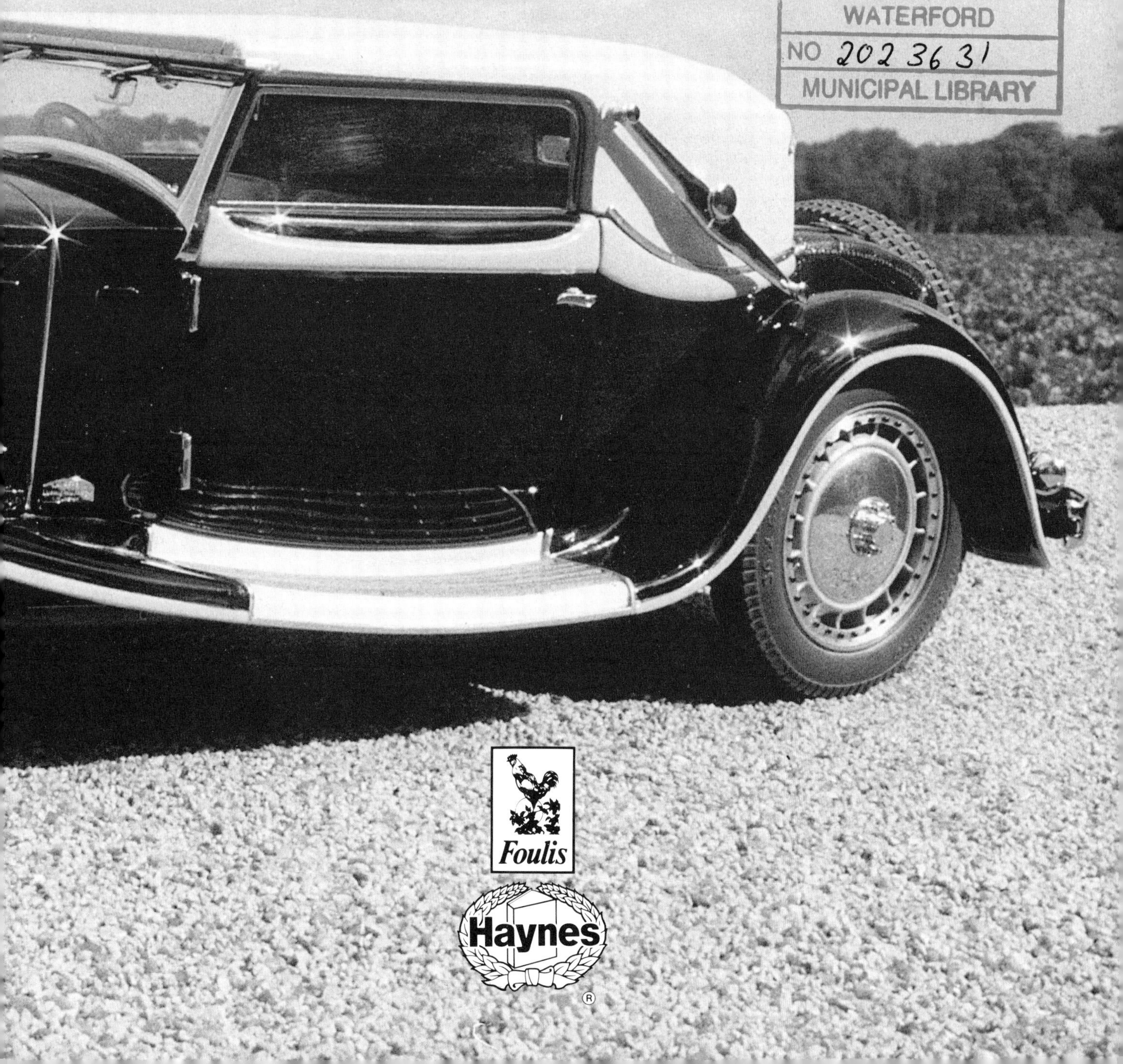

Foulis
Haynes

Dedication

To Phyllis,
For her enthusiasm and unfailing support for all that I undertake.

A FOULIS Motoring Book

First published 1991
Reprinted 1994

G. T. Foulis & Co. Ltd. is an imprint of
Haynes Publishing, Sparkford, Nr Yeovil, Somerset.
BA22 7JJ

British Library Cataloguing in Publication Data
Wingrove, Gerald A (Gerald Amery) *1934–*
The complete car modeller.
Vol. 2
1. Model cars
I. Title
629.2212
ISBN 0-85429-857-6

Library of Congress catalog card number 91-71121

Printed in England by Butler and Tanner Ltd., Frome and London.
Typeset in 10/11 pt Times Roman

Author's notes

The methods and techniques described in this book necessarily involve the use of machine and hand tools which are sharp, heat sources which burn, and a number of chemicals, such as resins and paint, which are poisonous. It cannot be over-emphasised that the greatest care must always be taken when working with all tools and materials, or injury can result. I have endeavoured to bring this to the notice of my readers from time to time, throughout this book. This is something of which one should not be frightened, just aware, as, in most cases, accidents can be prevented if one knows what to expect, and the necessary precautions are taken.

Dimensions are given primarily in Imperial units because even now most modelling material, metal and wire stock is available in these sizes. Exact metric equivalents are given throughout as is customary, but in many instances stock will not be available in the exact metric dimension but only, if at all, in the equivalent metric dimension which will be slightly larger or smaller.

All line drawings were produced on INTERGRAPH MicroStation © by Phyllis and Gerald A. Wingrove.

Colour photographs on pages 67-71 and on the cover are by Clive Friend FBIPP. Additional colour and black and white photographs are by G. A. & P. Wingrove.

Acknowledgements

I wish to express my sincere thanks to the very many people whose help and enthusiasm have made this book possible. In particular, I should like to thank by name the following:

Randy Mason and the Staff and Administration of the Henry Ford Museum & Greenfield Village in Dearborn, Michigan, USA, for allowing Phyllis and me to visit and collect the necessary data of the Weinberger Bugatti Royale, from which the model was made. Also for allowing us free access to the Museum archives to add to this information.

To the Staff of what was the Harrah Collection, in Reno, Nevada, USA, now the William F. Harrah Automobile Foundation, for the help and assistance with Bugatti Royale data.

Also the late Mr Briggs Cunningham, of the greatly missed Cunningham Collection, who also allowed us free access to his Bugatti Royale as a source of original Bugatti data.

To my many collectors, whose encouragement and enthusiasm have made it possible to produce this work and share it with others.

Last, but no means least, my wife and partner Phyllis, who not only built almost half of the model that illustrates this book, but who also typed, read, and retyped the manuscript.

Gerald A. Wingrove

Contents

Foreword

No motor museum can hope to display every car that it would wish to display to tell the history of the automobile. One approach is to display models of those cars which are missing to fill in the gaps in the story. It was therefore in the early days of building up the Museum at Beaulieu that I decided on a policy of displaying models to tell the history of the Grand Prix car and also the sports car. I was fortunate in starting the collection by buying a set of model Grand Prix cars which had been constructed by the British model maker Rex Hayes, but when his contract finished I was looking around for another model maker to take his place. It was by pure coincidence that, in 1968, I received a letter from Gerald Wingrove, who later arrived at Beaulieu with some beautifully modelled bits and pieces of a Duesenberg. I was immediately impressed with the excellent quality of Wingrove's work and commissioned two trial models: the 1967 replica Repco-Brabham and the 1913 Prince Henry Vauxhall. These two models set the foundations of an excellent relationship between Beaulieu and Gerald Wingrove. Over the years I have watched with admiration how he has perfected his craft and has rightly become world famous as a model maker of automobiles.

But that is not all. In his early days Gerald Wingrove was more attracted to ship modelling and he engrossed himself with all the details of life aboard the great sailing ships and those engaged in record voyages. It was therefore only natural that when I wanted to create for the Maritime Museum a large scale model of Bucklers Hard, the 18th century ship-building village on the Beaulieu River, I should turn to Gerald Wingrove. He executed a magnificent five-square-foot scale model of the village in 1803, including the 36-gun HMS *Euryalus* which, together with other ships built at Bucklers Hard, fought at Trafalgar.

The enormously painstaking research which Gerald Wingrove carries out for each model is amazing and his models can be seen in many famous collections around the world. So often, however, great craftsmen are unwilling or unable to impart their knowledge and skill to others who may follow them. One of the most admirable aspects about Gerald Wingrove is not only his willingness but his ability to impart through his books so much of the knowledge, skill and enthusiasm which he puts into his models. I have no doubt that there must be many budding model makers who one day will owe their successful careers to reading such books as this. As far as we are concerned at Beaulieu, we are proud that we commissioned his very first car models and are delighted that they are on display to the more than half a million people who visit Beaulieu every year.

Montagu of Beaulieu

Lord Montagu of Beaulieu

Introduction

It has now been some thirteen years since the highly successful book *The Complete Car Modeller* was first published. I gave much thought to whether I should embark on a major rewrite of this or produce a completely new work on the subject, particularly with a view to incorporating the new ideas, techniques and materials that have manifest themselves over the intervening period. I decided that because the earlier work is still largely relevant to current model makers' needs, a completely new book would provide much more space and so allow me to elaborate further on my techniques in general, and the new ones in particular. So I have taken the plunge and started again at page one with a completely new book.

This book should be looked upon as complementing the earlier work rather than superseding it, because the answers given to the problems posed then are still valid, but with a further ten years of experience behind me, I now feel I can offer some interesting and equally valid alternatives as well.

Another distinct advantage with a completely new book is that one can approach the subject from a slightly different angle, and so give much more meaning to the original philosophy. The aim of this book is to give the subject a new perspective. To assist in this I will be using a single model to take my reader through the various stages, unlike the previous book that used a number of different cars to tell the story. In that, my aim was to stress that the techniques so described were relevant to the building of any type of automobile miniature, rather than just the one being dealt with. Having now made that point, we can devote the new book to working with one subject from beginning to end. This will allow us to see in the finished model the consequences of making any part in the specific way that we did. With the space available in a completely new book, I am able to devote more of it to the construction of new tools and their uses, as well as to tools in general and our studio workshop in particular, none of which I was able to cover in much detail – if at all – in the first book.

The single subject that is used here is the 1932 Weinberger Bugatti Royale, on public display in the Henry Ford Museum and Greenfield Village complex in Dearborn, Michigan, USA. This was built as a one-off custom body on a Bugatti Type 41 chassis, which is one of only seven built. The fascinating story of the life of this car, the most travelled by far of all the Bugatti Royales, is the subject of another book *The Anatomy of a Bugatti Royale* to be published by G.T. Foulis & Co., which gives not only the car's complete history and how the research into it was undertaken, but also includes a hundred or so photographs and copies of the scale plans from which this model was built. The 'Anatomy' book is intended as companion edition to the two 'techniques' books, so eliminating the need here to elaborate on why Bugatti or Bentley made their parts in the way that they did, which, in my experience, will be of little interest to the reader who is looking for ways to build his Rolls-Royce or Packard model.

So, although this book covers the techniques of building an exact scale miniature of the Bugatti Royale, it is expressly not a detailed 'how to' account of building it. My aim is still to use the subject solely as a vehicle to take you through the various stages of building a miniature, and to discuss the techniques and tools used at each stage.

Another reason why I do not write the 'how to build by numbers' type of book, with pages of dimensional drawings, is that my approach to model making is not that of an engineer – even though I may use an engineer's tools – but that of an artist. If one did work to the exact scale equivalent of every last dimension of the original, one could still miss the effect that I endeavour to achieve, this being to show the character of the original. To do this successfully, we may in fact be producing, albeit sub-consciously, a caricature of the vehicle, by reducing some part and enhancing others. What I actually do is produce a three-dimensional artistic impression of the subject, based not only on my knowledge of it from photographs and dimensions actually collected from it, but also on my personal feeling for it. It is for this reason that I prefer the style of model photograph that I use exemplified in Plate 1. If I have captured the essential character of this subject, your first impression from the untouched straight-from-the-camera photograph will be of looking at the car. If I have not, you will immediately recognise this as the 16-inch-long model that it is.

My feelings have always been that, for me to provide dimensions for someone else to work to, to build a subject such as this, is to deny them the ultimate satisfaction of actually creating their own artistic impression of it.

However one approaches scale modelling, there is no practical way that anyone can produce an exact scale one-fifteenth size replica without using licence to change sizes somewhere. Having accepted this, whatever is then made must of necessity be an impression of the original.

If my technique books assist my reader to achieve their artistic ambitions in this field, then I will have achieved all I have set out to do.

Gerald A. Wingrove
Digby,
Lincoln,
England.

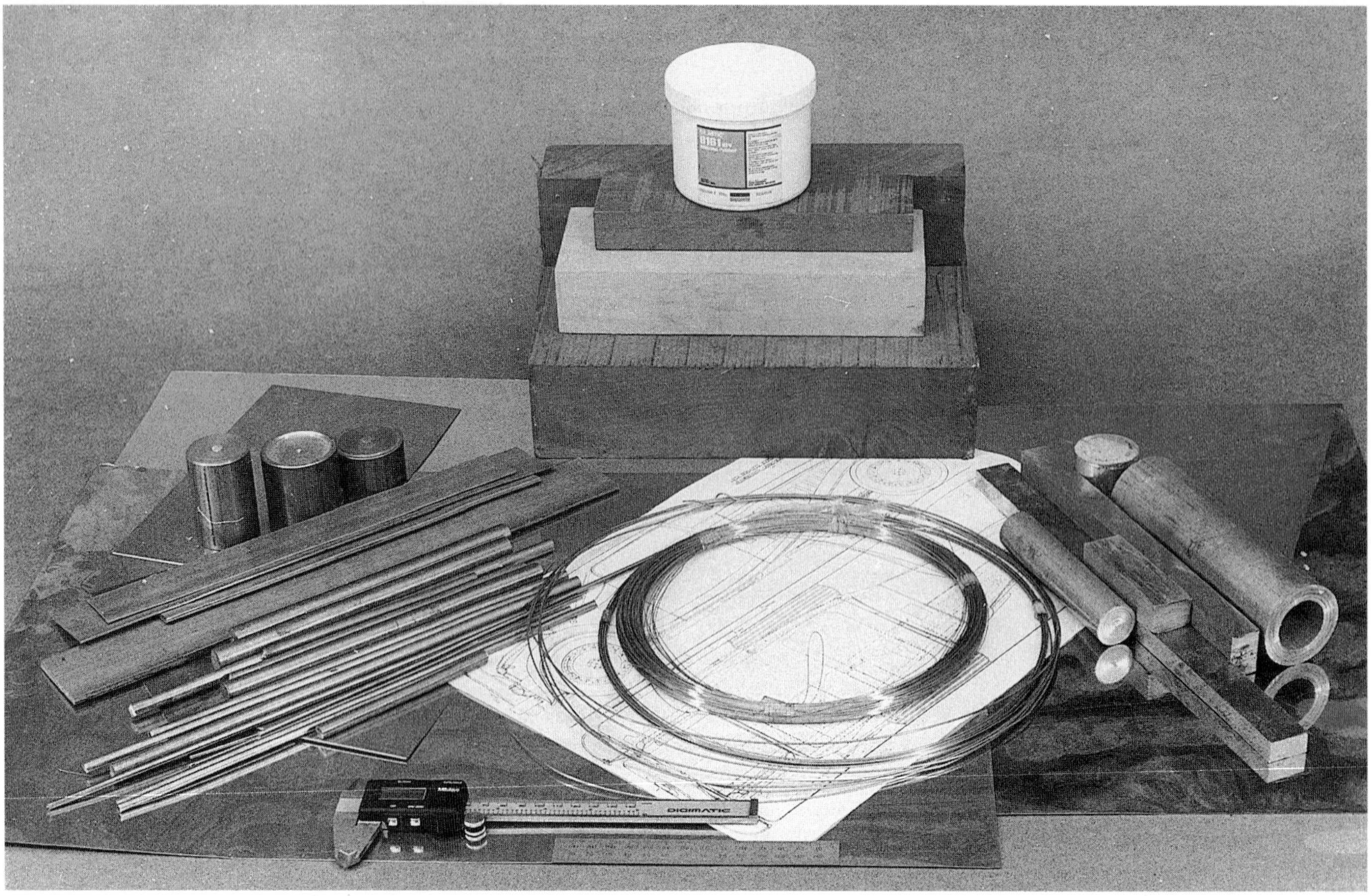

Plate 2

Plate 3

PART ONE
Tools & Materials

THIS BOOK is about scratch-building scale model cars. For those not familiar with the term, it means building from basic materials, which, in my case, are mostly metals. You can, of course, use whatever you choose, the essential point being that you make every part, using nothing bought off-the-shelf. Plates 2 and 3 illustrate this point, while Plate 1 shows the finished model the 1932 Weinberger Bugatti Royale, the building of which is the subject of this book.

Plate 2 illustrates our starting point: the material. From top to bottom are a canister of silicone rubber, blocks of hard wood and brass, copper and aluminium bar and sheet, together with nickel silver wire in several diameters. Because most of our work will be with metals of various sorts, with brass the principal one, let us consider this first.

For our purposes, there are two basic ways of changing the shape of a piece of metal. With a thin sheet, one can form shapes with the aid of a hammer; with a block of the material one can change the shape by removing metal with the aid of cutting tools. Unfortunately such is the difference between these two processes that we need two distinctly different types of brass to accommodate them with ease. Keeping this in mind, let us now consider the materials.

BRASS is an alloy of copper and zinc usually with small amounts of other ingredients added to cater for particular needs. The material that we need for hammer work called 'cold working' is a straight alloy of copper and zinc, and is bright yellow in colour. This is obtainable in large sheet form of various thicknesses, and as brass tubing. In sheet form it can also be purchased as soft, half-hard, and hard, the difference being not in the composition of the metal, but, in layman's terms, its bendability. Such is the structure of the metal, that by squeezing it, either as a sheet passing between two rollers as in manufacture, or by the application of a hammer, it can be made to change its shape. One of its characteristics is that of getting harder in the process of being worked (termed work-hardening). Also, if it is left for any length of time, it will harden itself, which is called age hardening. To reverse the effect, which is caused by stress within the structure of the metal, we use a process called annealing. In this, one raises the temperature of the brass sheet (usually with the aid of a gas flame) to almost red heat and then lets it slowly cool. When cold it will be found to be in a soft pliable state.

Brass sheet purchased for our needs should be in the half-hard or hard state, for reasons that will be explained later.

Another characteristic of this type of brass is that when it is worked on with cutting tools such as drills, it will be found to produce a waste (called swarf) in the form of a long spiral, (which, incidentally, will be found to have very sharp edges). As a result of this the cutting tools get very hot, which can reduce their cutting ability. Although this may not seem very important when drilling holes in thin sheet, it would soon be found to be a distinct limitation should one attempt to work a large piece by normal machining processes. For this a machining-quality brass is produced which includes in its composition a very small percentage of lead, making for a lighter shade of yellow. This additional ingredient is responsible for the very crisp little chips that are produced as swarf whenever a cutting tool is presented to the metal. This in turn helps to dissipate the heat from the cutting edge of the tool, making for longer tool life and easy working with all forms of hand or machine tools.

It is machining-quality brass that is sold in long lengths of various forms, principally round, hexagonal and rectangular, in innumerable sizes, from very small to extremely large. Its only disadvantage is that it is brittle and will not bend to any great degree. Annealing has little or no affect on the bendability of this grade of brass.

Other characteristics common to all brasses, which particularly recommend them for use in this work, is their ability to accept a range of solders that work at different temperatures, the ease with which they can be electro-plated, and the ability to hold a high polish. The brass sheet is used for flat or slightly curved bodywork where its stiffness will be used to advantage. The machining-quality brass is used for all machined parts. Brass is used for almost all fabrication of parts, and when the finished piece is to be painted or electro-plated.

COPPER is a base metal, that is, a pure mineral as against an alloy, and is reddish in colour. It is the main constituent of brass and is responsible for most of that metal's versatility. Its main difference is that it can be annealed to a much softer state, and it can be worked for a longer period before it rehardens. It is obtainable in sheet and bar form, but for our purposes only the sheet copper is of interest. A variety of thicknesses is available and, like brass sheet, it is available in three grades of hardness. Again, for our requirements, half-hard or hard are the most useful for our needs. When annealing, heat to a dull red colour with a gas flame, and cool directly by placing in a tub of water.

Copper sheet is used for those parts of the bodywork that are extensively shaped, such as the rear section, and for producing wings.

ALUMINIUM is a base metal refined from the mineral ore bauxite, and is silvery white in colour. In its pure state, it is very soft and ductile with little strength. To overcome this it is alloyed with very small amounts of a variety of other metals to produce a range of alloys under the collective name of aluminium. It is possible to obtain it in both sheet and bar form as soft and bendable as copper, and as hard and brittle as machining-quality brass. Because there is a whole range of reference numbers denoting all the different grades, and these may differ from country to country, I will not include them here. All you need to know is that there is a wide range of characteristics available which are not readily discernible by colour to the untutored eye. For our purposes, if it is a large block or bar for working with cutting tools that you need, then ask for high-speed machining-quality aluminium alloy. If your requirement is for a soft sheet for shaping with a hammer, then ask for a cold forming aluminium alloy. The latter will behave in a similar way to copper in that it will work-harden, at which point it should be annealed with a flame. Unlike the case when heating copper, where you can actually see the correct temperature by a dull red glow, with aluminium the melting temperature of the metal is much lower and it gives little visible indication of when the critical temperature is being approached. The method I use depends upon having a gentle gas flame which is kept moving over the surface of the sheet. Heat the metal a little, then take a strip of wood (any wood will suffice) remove the flame and just pass one end of the wood across the surface of the aluminium. Repeat this – first applying the flame and then the wood – until the tip of the wood leaves a black line on the surface of the metal sheet. This is the correct temperature for annealing. Remove the flame and let the metal cool. Heating beyond this on thin sheet is likely to cause blistering and then disintegration of the metal.

Aluminium can be soldered; it is, however, not easy to do until one has mastered the technique, and because it is not a process we will need to use, I do not propose to cover it here.

Aluminium is used in our work where we are producing in miniature a part that is also made of this metal in full size, and where we wish to show the surface finish that is characteristic of aluminium.

NICKEL SILVER is an alloy of nickel and copper, and is also known as German Silver. The mention of silver in the name is not a reference to a silver content in the alloy but to the colour of the metal which is a bright silver with a very slight tendency to yellow. Like aluminium it is also obtainable in cold-working sheet form and machining-quality bar material. As a sheet material it is even harder than the cold-working brass and cannot be softened to any great degree by annealing. Its use in our work is for making very small or inaccessible brightwork parts, that on the original might have been either nickel or chrome plated.

One could, of course, write a book just on metals, their make-up and uses. I have of necessity restricted myself here to the barest essentials, just sufficient for my reader who has had little or no previous experience with them, so that he can at least recognise a piece when he sees it, and so understand more fully how they can be worked and what we can do with them at a later stage. As we move on to the tools and the actual making up of the various parts, I will discuss further the particular qualities of the different metals that make them desirable for the individual items and the techniques involved in their use.

HARD WOOD. Rather than give a list of timbers here, most of which you may never have heard of and would find impossible to obtain, I will restrict myself to saying that if the wood you have in mind for use is hard, has a close grain with no knots, is dry and available, it will probably fulfil you needs. The wood is used for making the pattern blocks needed to work the sheet metal on, in order to form the body and wing parts. The size is not too important because thick sections can always be made up by gluing smaller pieces together. Thicknesses of 1 inch (25 mm) or more with widths over 3 inches (75 mm) and lengths by the yard (metre) should be sufficient for all your needs.

The final item of materials in Plate 2 is the canister of silicone rubber. This is a thick liquid, often white in colour, although it is now available in black and other colours, and is sold with a small bottle of transparent liquid called catalyst. When the two are mixed together and allowed to set, the result is a hard silicone rubber. This is used for making moulds and for producing the model tyres. When I wrote *The Complete Car Modeller*, one needed to find a specialist supplier from which to obtain this; however, it has now become better known and should be obtainable from most craft tool suppliers.

This concludes our material needs with the exception of one or two small items that will be dealt with in detail as and when their need arises.

Let us now consider the tools with which we are going to manipulate these materials and the place in which this will be undertaken. Plates 4 and 5 illustrate our own working environment, the studio workshop in which the Weinberger Bugatti Royale was created.

This assembly of tools and their placement in relation to the hand that is reaching for them was developed in the first six or so years of my work as a professional model maker. It has now served me almost unchanged for a further fifteen years, so I do now consider it the ideal, and very relevant indeed to the quality of work that Phyllis and I now produce, and the time that it takes to complete it. This is not to say that I recommend that you need to set yourself up like this before you proceed to the next chapter, but I do think one or two points are worth a passing mention here.

The first point concerns lighting: the most important factor governing how and what you produce is how well you can see it. The need for and provision of good lighting seems so obvious one wonders why anything need be said about it: all you need is a bright light and you are on your way. However, the brighter the light the darker the shadows, and the more strain on the eyes moving between the two. The ideal is a bright but not brilliant 'shadowless' light. I have achieved this by mounting two 24 inch fluorescent tubes 5 inches apart on a white board. Aluminium sheet is used to extend the front and back down to form a reflector which prevents glare into the eyes. With the aid of screw hooks, this is suspended on chains from the ceiling and can be raised or lowered. For very fine assembly work the light unit will be down to within 18 inches of the bench top, which is just below eye level, and the illumination given is perfect. In Plate 4 this can be seen in the raised position. The lighting unit seen over Phyllis's bench (Plate 5) is in the form of a circular fluorescent tube on an angle poise stand, which proved quite successful, but this has now been replaced by a commercially made twin-tube light unit, almost identical to my own, that has just become commercially available.

Next in importance to the lighting comes the workbench. Whether you stand against it or sit at it, as we do, the ideal height for the top should be equal to the height of your elbow. If you are building a bench to stand to, measure the distance from your elbow to the floor; this will give you the correct working height. If it is a ready-made desk that you intend to sit at, then procure an adjustable height chair that will allow you to rise to the occasion, or fall, as the case may be. Although the desk should be placed close to a window, and as much window space should be available as possible, it is not a good idea to actually have it in direct sunlight because of the hard shadows that go with this.

Plate 4

Plate 5

Our own benches started life as oak office desks purchased from a second-hand shop. Each has a top size of 30x54 inches and came with two side drawers. I noticed that when sitting at them, one's feet and legs take up less than half of the 30 inch depth available, so I recessed the inside of the oak legs to take a $\frac{3}{4}$ inch veneered chipboard panel on each end, and then glued and screwed another large panel between them down the centre of the underneath of each desk. With a floor piece, shelves and sliding doors fitted to the other side, I now had some very useful storage space.

Plate 6

Plate 7

Under the original drawers on each side of the seat position, I have also fitted various sliding trays and racks to add even more storage facilities. Some of these trays and racks can be seen extended from the benches in Plates 6 and 7, and in more detail in Plates 8, 9 and 10.

Both of the benches are 'live'; by this I mean that a single electric cable from the mains supply leads to a junction box fitted to each bench. Several sockets and some power tools are wired directly into these, including a small red neon light fitted to one corner of each bench to indicate when the power is on. This we have both found to be a most convenient arrangement, for it provides all the power where it is wanted without yards of cable everywhere, and with a fused master switch at the input end of the mains power cable, one is able to switch off or isolate the benches at night, or whenever they are not in use. Considering that such items as electric soldering irons, etc, are used repeatedly at the benches, the ability to make a quick visual check at night to see that the neons are not illuminated does give some peace of mind.

Plates 8 and 9 illustrate the power side of my

Plate 8

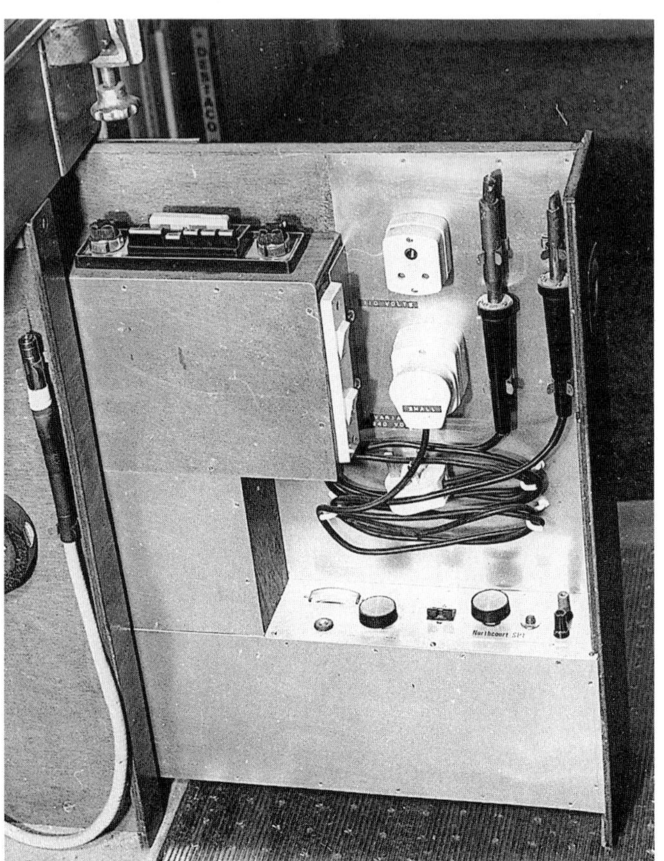

Plate 9

bench. No, this is not an electrician's nightmare; only half of the cabling in the first is mains electric, the others are for radio aerial, stereo speakers, gas and compressed air lines, etc. All of these have been left long because they are connected to movable items. Plate 8 shows a motorised flexible drive as used in the jewellery trade complete with foot control. This is equipped with a collet attachment at the business end that will accommodate tools from about 0.008 in (0.2 mm) up to $\frac{1}{8}$ in (3.2 mm) in diameter. Above this is a small canister of propane gas with a controller as used in the very small camping stoves, and to the left of this is a miniature air compressor. The twin piping for both leads to a burner, stored when not in use in two clips to the left of the flexible drive head. This is used for silver soldering. Another example of the same apparatus, but this time made up as a free-standing unit, can be seen in Plate 15.

The rack shown in Plate 9 is fitted on runners so that it can be extended for use, or slid out of sight under the bench. In the top section is contained a small car radio and cassette player for in-house entertainment, and switches and sockets to accommodate the large and small electric soldering irons. Concealed in the bottom are three transformers, one to feed the car radio with 12 volts, while the second, via a variable resistance, provides power to the sockets, and thence to the irons. The reasoning for this will be dealt with later, as will the use of the third transformer providing stepped DC voltages from 6 to 12 volts.

Plate 10 illustrates one of the two sliding racks on the bench, the second being just visible on the right and holding coils of nickel silver wire of various sizes. The extended rack contains a selection of small hand tools, files large and small, a range of pliers, hammer and punches, etc, all readily available to hand when needed.

Plate 11 shows the milling machine, with all its accessories and cutting tools kept close at hand in the extended drawer beneath it. The two closed racks shown extended in Plate 12 hold most of the basic bar materials that are used in our work. Note the floor covering between the machines on the left and more particularly under my work bench on the right. As 30 per cent of my time is spent on my knees looking for that vital piece that has just been dropped on the floor, which is inevitably one of the smallest, I decided quite early on to invest in a section of plastic floor covering. The floor of the workshop is laid out in a

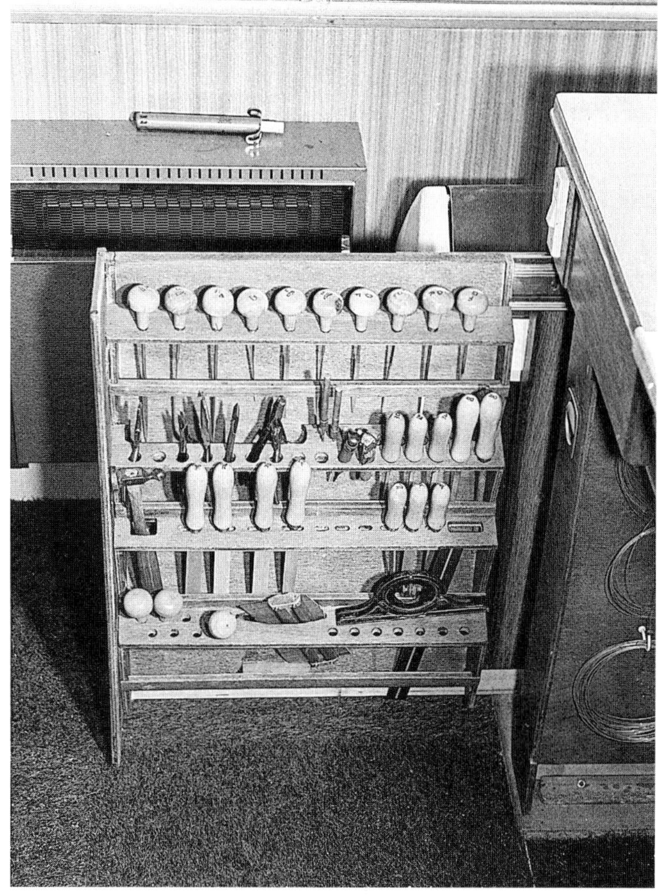

Plate 10

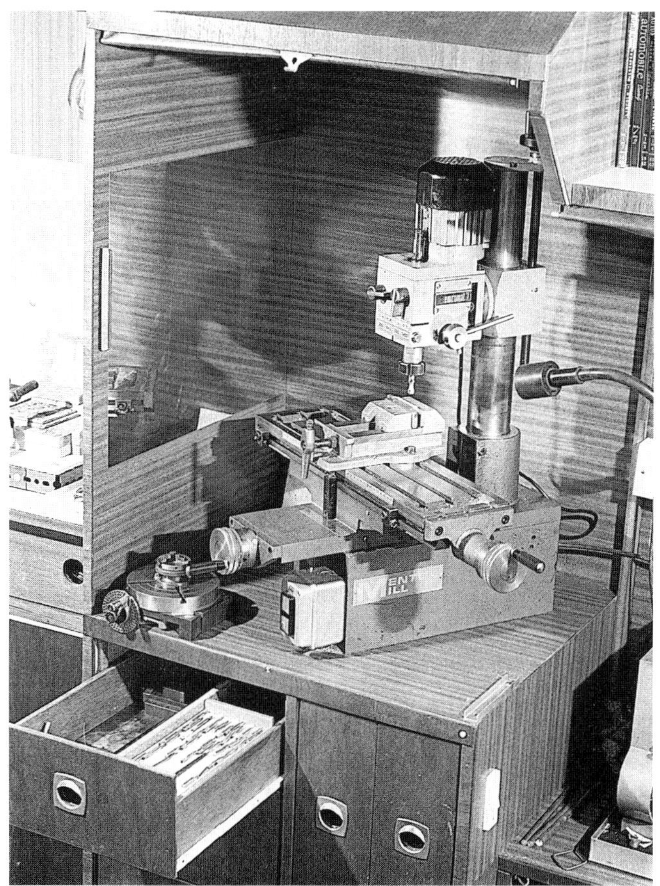

Plate 11

Plate 12

dark green felt tile, which is good on the eye and warm on the feet, but its disadvantage is that it is the very devil to locate anything smaller than a brick in the pile. This transparent plastic carpet overlay is sold for hallways where a lot of tramping feet may be expected, and it has moulded on the underside a series of points to anchor it to the existing floor covering, the top surface being lightly ribbed. This not only makes it a simple matter to locate whatever finds its way on to the floor, but also makes life easier for keeping the floor area around the bench and machines clean of swarf and waste from both. Plate 13 illustrates

Plate 13

the position of the lathe and storage for all its accessories and tools close at hand. The milling machine is set up for 'standing' work height, while the lathe, being positioned directly opposite my work bench is set at the same height as the bench and is operated from the same swivel chair. From this one seat, I can not only work the lathe and work at the bench, but I can also reach all my hand tools, files, drills, taps, lathe tools, abrasive papers (stored in drawers below the open ones in Plate 13) also the motorised flexible shaft, gas torch, soldering irons, stock of materials and radio cassette player. If one is engrossed in detailing some minute piece on the latest project, the most distracting thing is to have to stop and look for the next tool.

I have already mentioned one safety point, that of being able to isolate the 'live' benches from the power supply when they are not in use. A second one, and of primary importance if you intend to make a 'live' working bench such as those shown here, is to consult a qualified electrician on the limitation and safety aspects of what you are intending to do before you start.

Having shown, to our minds, the ultimate working studio, perhaps a few words on what went before would not come amiss, particularly if you are now considering available space with what you can do. My model making started with a small table with drawers underneath. With this I could work on the top and store my tools and materials within. From this I progressed to the back end of a garage which provided a long bench to which I added the underbench storage. From this I moved through several home-built workshops from 6x10 ft up to our present studio of some 400 sq ft area. One thing has manifest itself throughout: the more space you have the more space you fill – there appears to be no ideal size.

To assess the space you might need, let us first consider what it will contain, and at the same time take a look at the tools we will be using to work the materials already discussed. Before I do, I should emphasise again that Phyllis and I do work here full time making models such as the Weinberger Bugatti Royale for museums and private collectors, the point being that the machines and tooling that we have equipped ourselves with have been chosen for maximum efficiency, and are not what I started with when building models as a hobby in the back of my garage.

The lathe is probably the largest and most

Plate 14

expensive piece of equipment that you will need. I say 'need', because if you intend to produce your own wheels and tyres it is essential. I have read of people producing the most wondrous things on the end of an electric drill, but there are now so many small lathes on the market, at quite modest prices, that to my mind it is the essential piece of equipment. The size of the lathe is determined by the height of the centre of the spindle from the lathe bed. If you double this figure it will tell you the maximum diameter that you can hold in the lathe. A two inch lathe will hold a four inch diameter component, just. As a guide, the largest diameter required for one-fifteenth scale car modelling that I have encountered is the 2½ in diameter wheel on the Bugatti Royale, so if this is your aim, then a minimum size of lathe to accommodate that would be a 1½ in lathe which would leave a margin to allow room to work on the outside of the diameter. The general rule is to go as large as your accommodation and purse will allow. You can do minute work on a large lathe (6 in) but you cannot do large work on a small one.

The milling machine, while it is essential for our work, I would described as merely very useful for hobby work. The lathe is used to produce round work in different forms, which is difficult to achieve in any other way; the mill on the other hand, produces flats and squared work, which can be achieved by other means, albeit not as accurately, but work is possible, nonetheless. Some lathes have among their accessories a milling head, this being a motorised tool holder with mounting column, and these can be ideal. In a milling attachment one immediately saves about half the cost of an equivalent machine because when the milling head is fitted to the lathe, it utilises the lathe bed for its base and the cross slide as the table on which the work to be milled is mounted. The other major advantage is that it will take up very little additional space because it is mounted on the side of the lathe.

Next in line for our consideration is the hearth (Plate 14) because of the space it takes up in our set-up. This consists of a large gas torch mounted on a base made from slotted angle and asbestos sheet, the requirement being a fireproof area where pieces of sheet metal can be heated for annealing purposes, and for silver soldering. The gas torch consists of a handle and burner which produces the flame. A good quality torch will have a range of different size burners for it, from very large ones down to very small ones called needle-flame burners. If you have room for this size of torch, then two burners, one of medium size and one small would be ideal. Incidentally the hottest part of the flame is the outermost quarter, and the coolest part is that closest to the burner. My torch is held in an adjustable holder, two spring clips being used to secure it in place. This arrangement allows the torch to be used in a fixed position on the hearth or hand-held. Because asbestos has now generally become out of favour, there is a range of substitute materials taking its place. One of these is vermiculite slab insulation which has the texture of fine fire brick. This will take temperatures up to 1100°C without harm, so it is an ideal material from which to build a hearth.

The gas used is propane held in a rechargeable cylinder outside the workshop and piped in via the flexible pipe visible in the photograph. A word of warning here; go to a specialist supplier for this equipment, one who will stock the torch, hose, cylinders, valves and accessories. We are dealing here with high-pressure gas that is extremely flammable: do not try to set this equipment up on the cheap. I once connected a cylinder to a torch with a reinforced rubber, high-pressure compressed air hose, because I happened to have a length available. In about a week it had split, not because of the gas pressure but because the gas had attacked the rubber. Luckily, one of the fittings required to set this all up is a pressure reducing valve, which is so designed that if there is a hose failure, it will shut off the gas supply automatically. Perhaps a word or two on safety in general would be appropriate here; although these points do all look rather obvious, it is sometimes the obvious that is overlooked. Remember that a gas torch, particularly one with a large burner, will throw out an enormous amount of heat, and heat can travel further than you may at first anticipate. Always ensure that you have several layers of heat resistant material behind the area that you are working on. Keep combustible materials away from the hearth area, or at least behind a fire resistant partition, and make a habit of switching off the gas supply at the bottle, cylinder or mains after each session or at night. Note that the fire bricks do not change colour with heating, consequently moving one with your hand when hot is not to be recommended. The heating of materials and fluxes can cause fumes particularly if they are overheated; assume that all are harmful so avoid inhaling them. Particular attention should be paid regarding fumes produced by the acid pickle bath. Although this will not give off anything of note while not being used, should something that is not properly cooled be placed in it, then steam and fumes will be produced which are most unpleasant.

The shelf at the top (Plate 14) contains a number of pieces of shaped fire brick for use in packing or supporting work being soldered. To the right of the hearth, protected by a piece of asbestos, are two plastic containers, one holding clean water, and one (the pickle bath, mentioned above) a weak solution of sulphuric acid (1 part) and water (10 parts). When making this up, remember always to slowly add the acid to the water, it is most dangerous to add the water to the acid. Use of the pickle bath will be explained later. On the left is an electric light to illuminate the proceedings, and to the left of that is the fire extinguisher, something that should be in every workshop (this is also true for a smoke alarm in case something is inadvertently left on).

Plate 15 and 16 illustrate two further examples of gas torches suitable for silver soldering. The first is a most useful tool, and as you have seen, we have two in the workshop for soldering smaller parts. This is a commercial torch made in the UK but not readily available even here. It is most interesting in that it has its own air supply provided by a miniature air compressor. This little compressor is also sold for supplying air to oxygenate tropical fish tanks. For the more adventurous of my readers who would find this tool of use in their work but cannot locate a supplier, the above information may lead you to some parts from which you could build your own. Incidentally, the gas canister is not sold as part of the original equipment, the equipment can also utilise the ordinary domestic gas supply.

Plate 16 illustrates the very latest in miniature gas torches. It is one of an increasing number that are now appearing in the craft catalogues, although I did

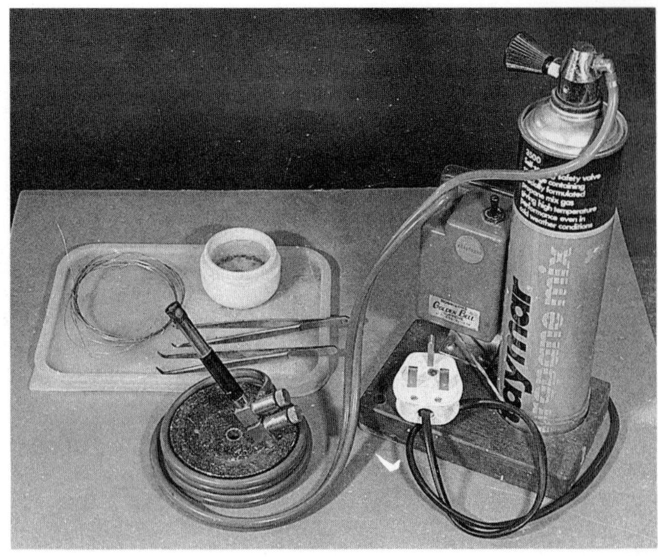

Plate 15

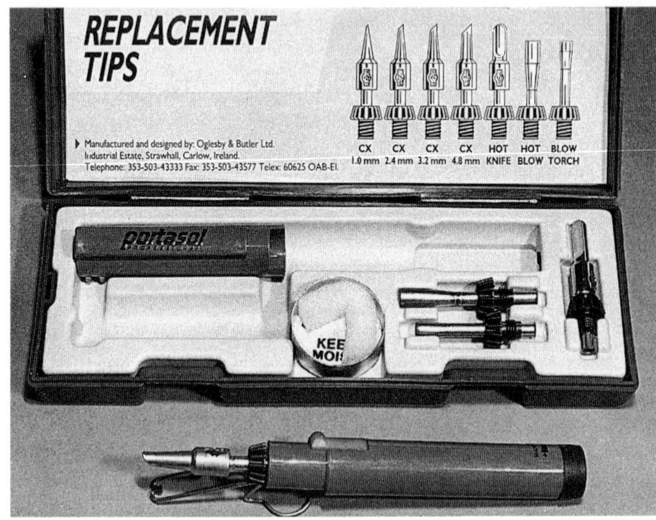

Plate 16

find this particular one advertised with computer accessories, which must be an indication of just how widely they are being used. The gas supply is provided by a large pressurised can of the type sold to refill gas cigarette lighters. This is used to charge or fill a small tank in the handle. One charge probably lasts about half an hour, depending, of course, on how you use it. The blowtorch is ideal for very fine silver soldering, and the range of soft soldering 'bits' can also be most useful, particularly as the whole unit is independent of any power cable or hose. We will also see later in the proceedings how the 'Hot Knife' and 'Hot blow' can also be utilised in this particular project.

Having now made mention of soldering a number of times, I should perhaps stop here to elaborate a little on this, possibly the most important of all the techniques associated with the type of metal work we will shortly be involved with.

We will be working with two different types of solder for joining together parts made in brass, copper, and nickel silver, and combinations of these. They are known as hard (silver) and soft (lead) solders. Hard, or silver solder, is an alloy of silver, or more

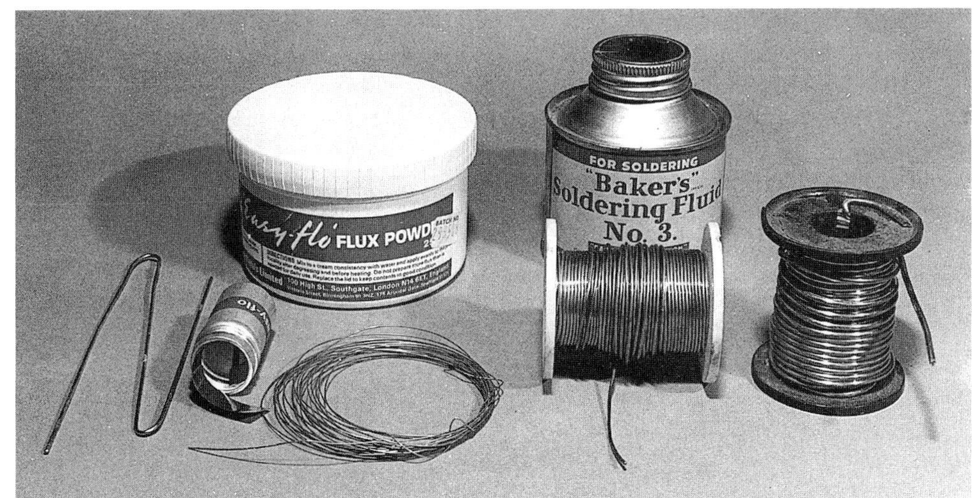

Plate 17

importantly a range of alloys of silver blended with other metals to provide a stepped series of melting temperatures. Particular manufacturers produce their own range of these, but in general there can be as many as six with melt temperatures from around 600°C up to over 800°C. This temperature range is the reason for the gas burner rather than the soldering iron for applying the solder. The latter is restricted to the application of soft solders which we will deal with later.

Of the range of silver solders available, the most useful for our needs is the one with the lowest melt temperature (608–617°C) listed in most UK catalogues as Easy-Flo No.2. This is available in many forms. The ones we use are two sizes of wire 0.030 in (0.75 mm) and 0.060 in (1.5 mm), and a very thin sheet or strip of about 0.004 in (0.1 mm) thickness, or thinner if available. Also required from the same supplier will be flux. In relation to hard solders the flux is chosen to match the melting temperature of the solder concerned and will indicate by its reaction the correct soldering temperature for that solder. Its main use, however, is to prevent oxides forming in the joint area while the metal is heated. 'Prevent' is the operative word; all joints and areas to be soldered must first be cleaned with an abrasive of some sort back to bright metal before flux is applied and the piece brought up to soldering temperature. The flux to be used with the above named solder is called Easy-Flo Flux and is usually purchased as a powder. Just prior to starting some silver soldering, take a small amount of this, a teaspoonful if it is small work, and mix with a little tap water to a thick paste consistency. This is then applied to the parts to be soldered before heating with the flame. The manufacturers recommend mixing fresh flux for each sitting, and it will tend to dry out into a solid block if left for several days, but if you do manage to maintain it as a workable paste, it will do the job. If you can work it, use it. Silver solder can also be obtained in a semi-liquid form as silver solder paint. This consists of fine particles of silver solder suspended in a liquid flux. Before using this, make sure that it is thoroughly mixed as the silver does tend to separate out to the bottom of the container very quickly. The actual technique of silver soldering will be covered in detail when we get to our first work example.

There are, like hard solders, a range of soft solders. All are basically an alloy of lead and tin, and the more of the latter there is the brighter the colour, which is a silver grey. The melting temperature of all soft solders is below 350°C, and the ones we will be using will have a working temperature of between 185 and 240°C. These can be worked either with a soldering iron or gas flame. Of the fluxes to be used with soft solder, we need only to consider two basic varieties, corrosive and non-corrosive. The former is a liquid containing zinc chloride and is mainly used for soldering such metals as iron, steel, stainless steel and zinc, but it is also ideal for joining our three basic metals. Being corrosive, it is easy to get a perfect soldered joint with it, but it is essential to wash off any residue left after soldering. The alternative is the rosin-based flux developed particularly for the electrical and electronics industry where it would be difficult or impossible to remove the corrosive residue after soldering. They are found most commonly in 'cored' solders sold on small reels where the solder has its flux combined with it. Although it is essential not to start soldering on anything other than bright clean metal, it is even more important for good joints when using rosin fluxes. Soft solders can be obtained as 0.060 in (1.5 mm) or 0.093 in (2.3 mm) diameter wire on reels, as well as in short bar form without a rosin flux core. Plate 17 shows examples of the solders we have discussed. On the left are the silver examples together with the flux powder, and on the right are the soft solders, rosin-cored and solid, together with a liquid flux. I have purposely given a description of these items rather than rely on trade names which may not be available in your particular locality.

There is another soldering device that I have kept until last, because it uses neither flame nor heated bit, yet it can be used for hard and soft soldering. This is sometimes called an electronic soldering machine, the technique being described as resistance soldering. I have only recently become aware of this apparatus, mainly through a series of articles from a very old, now out of print, modelling magazine sent to me last year by a friend in the USA. This describes the building of a most fascinating machine from old war surplus bits and pieces (and that will give you an idea of its age) for about $25. Having perused a number of tool catalogues to see if a similar commercial device was readily available today, I was disappointed to learn that in the UK at the time of writing, it was available only from specialised jewellery trade catalogues at a very exorbitant price. I believe the situation in the US may be somewhat better as I have seen one electronics tool catalogue listing a range of these, that appeared to indicate a variety of prices somewhat lower than in the UK, together with a range of tools for use with them. However, the voltage difference between the US and UK precluded my looking any further along that road for the time being.

The essence of the machine is a transformer to drop the mains voltage down to about 6 to 10 volts and give a current up to 30 amps. A variable resistance and foot switch are added to this, as are the tools that actually facilitate the soldering operation. In Plates 18 to 21 can be seen the resistance soldering equipment that I built for myself. Although it appeared to work perfectly right from the start, I did have the presence of mind to take it to the manufacturer of the transformer for testing. It so happened that this was made locally, and although they were quite fascinated with the device, they were somewhat perturbed by the readings from their test gear. They have since made certain recommendations and supplied me with the correct parts that now make up the perfectly safe and very useful machine illustrated here. It is most

Plate 18

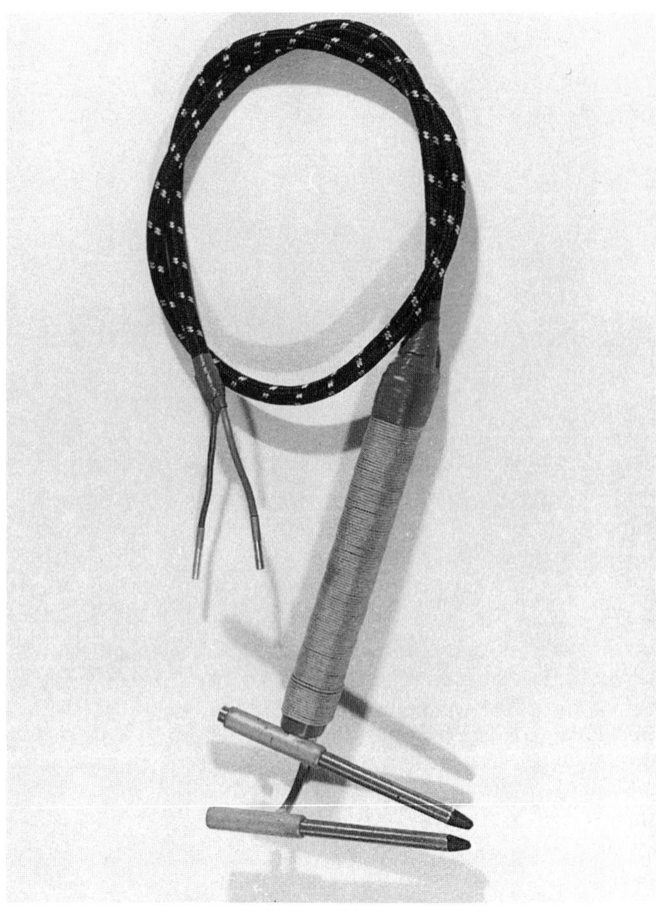

Plate 19

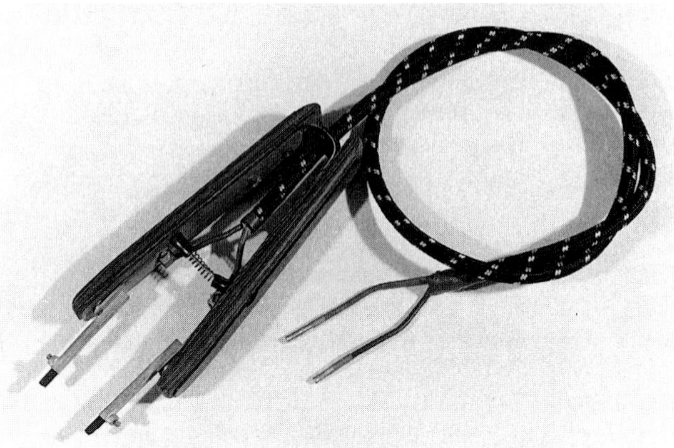

Plate 20

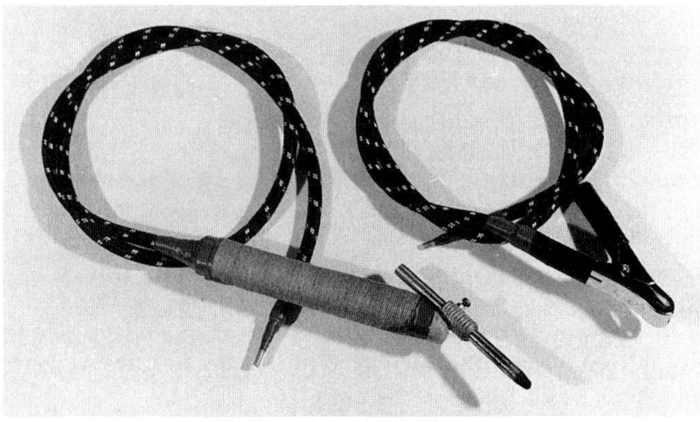

Plate 21

necessary always to find a qualified person to test any such equipment. My experiences in building this equipment prompt me to describe it in general terms, rather than try to explain in detail its construction.

In use resistance soldering works like this. Two carbon rods, as used for arc welding, are provided at the output ends of the low voltage leads. These are then placed in contact with the fluxed metal to be soldered. When the power is switched on via the foot operated switch, heat is generated at the contact points of the carbons. The amount of heat and the speed at which it is produced depend on the power setting of the device. It is this characteristic that gives the system its great advantage over other forms of heating, because the heating time varies between instantaneous and several seconds. Although a flame is ideal for the uniform heating of large areas, when it comes to very localised heating, the problem with both flame and conventional soldering iron is that one needs to apply heat at a faster rate than that at which the object will conduct the heat away. As with the other forms of soldering, we will return to the subject and illustrate its use when we reach the construction stage of the model.

Plates 19, 20 and 21 show the three principle tools used with the machine. All are basically holders for the carbon rods, the first being a single non-adjustable holder with insulated handle for retaining the two rods in close proximity. In use the points would be placed on each side of the fluxed joint. When power is supplied the points and the local area are immediately brought up to soldering temperature, solder applied, and the joint made. In Plate 20, the two carbons are held at the ends of a tweezer-like device with insulated handles. This is ideal for very small work that can be held together between the carbon tips, ready fluxed and with solder in place. One on/off press on the foot switch can bond them together in the proverbial flash. Plate 21 illustrates the most versatile of the three tools because it can be used in the most inaccessible places. This consists of, on the left, an insulated handle holding a single carbon rod and, on the right, a cable terminating in a heavy-duty crocodile clip. With these connected to the soldering machine and the clip clamped to any convenient part of the item to be soldered, one only needs to place the carbon tip at the exact spot where the heat is required to make the most effortless soldered joint of your life.

I propose to give a brief tour of the small tools department, mainly for those who are not familiar with things engineering, starting with the precision end. Plate 22 shows the tools in question. Were we building the actual vehicle, unquestionably the principal tool would be the one on the right, called a micrometer, which can accurately measure to 0.0001 in (0.0025 mm). From my remarks earlier you will remember, however, that we are going to produce a small scale artistic impression. For that work one is better advised to invest in one of the two 6 inch long vernier calipers shown centre and left. Accuracy can be down to 0.001 in (.03 mm) when you have got the feel of the instrument, which is all that is needed for our work. Price-wise, the one on the left with the dial indicator can be obtained for a third of the price of the one showing a digital read-out. The digital vernier does, however, have the facility of instant conversion from inches to millimetres. This can be useful in some work.

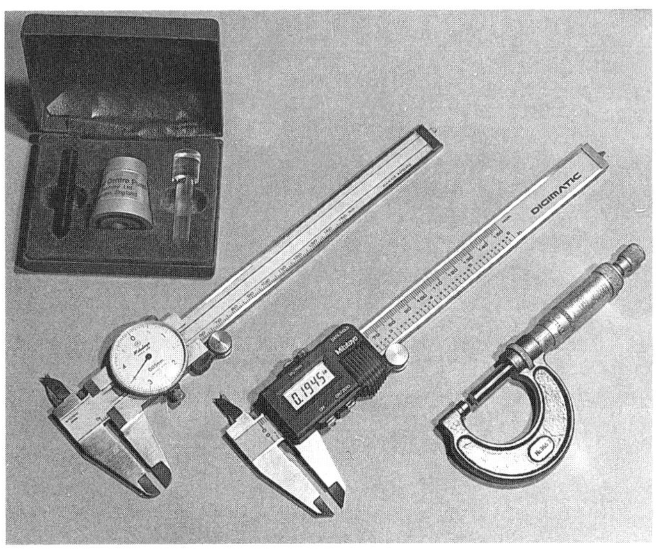

Plate 22

Although the micrometer gives a more accurate and reliable reading, it is only good for one inch. For dimensions greater than this, you will need to purchase a larger micrometer. You will also need other instruments for the accurate measurement of internal dimensions and depths, all of equal importance to the first. The one instrument giving all of these is the vernier caliper. The jaws on the bottom are used for outside measurement, the two crossed blades above are used for inside dimensions, while just visible at the other end is a square pin provided for the measurement of depth. At the top left corner of Plate 22 is a box containing another recent and most useful acquisition, an optical centre punch. To make a hole in an exact position the procedure is to scribe lines on the piece of metal, crossing them at the precise point that you wish the hole to be. One then makes a small indent in the metal with a centre punch to act as the start for the point of the drill. It is obvious that no matter how accurately one has scribed the lines, the crucial part is to make certain that the indent is placed where the lines cross, which is not easy. This device uses a block with a hole in the centre that is placed over the crossed lines. A length of clear plastic with two crossed lines on one end and a magnifying glass at the other is inserted into the block and lined up with the scribed lines. The block is then held firm while the magnifier is replaced with a steel punch that is then smartly hit with a hammer, so leaving an indent placed in the exact centre of the scribed lines. I should say that it takes much longer to describe the operation than to accomplish it, but it does bring to your notice a most useful tool, obtainable from engineering tool suppliers.

Plate 23 illustrates the remaining measuring and marking-out tools which, from top to bottom, are a depth rule, a 6 inch rule shown millimetre side up, a protractor for marking out angles, a steel scriber, a spring-operated centre punch (no hammer needed), and at the bottom left dividers, and at the right, a small engineer's square. Most will be available at craft, DIY and good hobby shops in some form or other.

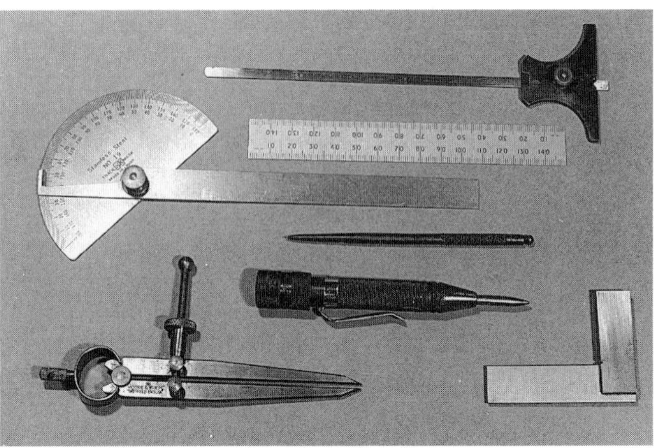

Plate 23

Plate 24 shows holding devices from various sources. At the top left is shown a hand vice, made to my own design. The principal aim of this – arrived at by the provision of three pivot points – was that the jaws remain parallel throughout all its movement. Similar ones are available commercially with a single pivot point, that will also be found of use in holding small parts, square or round, while working on them. The top centre shows another type of vice called a 'pin vice'. This is provided with small collets (round jaws) at each end for holding small pins or drills, etc. At the top right is a small packet of aluminium spring loaded clips sold for use in ladies' hairdressing. Provided these are of the large variety and fitted with strong springs, they are ideal for holding small parts together for soldering. Being made of aluminium, the solder will

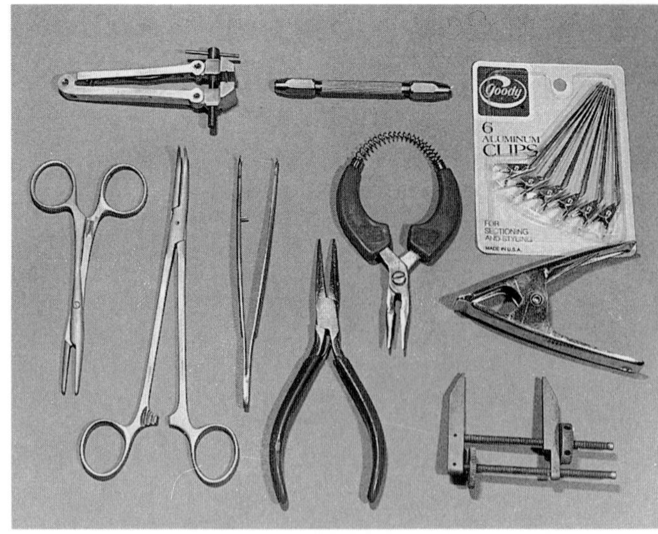

Plate 24

not stick to them. Below these, and to the left, are two medical forceps, made of the finest quality steel and provided with notched grips on the handle. They can be locked in the closed position and have many uses in the workshop. They are becoming more readily available from second-hand and surplus tool suppliers. Next come tweezers which, if you can obtain them from the same suppliers, should be of the long, strong, medical variety. In the centre are two sorts of pliers, both most useful for their different applications. If you can afford them, several shapes should be included in your tool kit; pointed, flat-nose, round-nose, and side-cutters in a small size is a good start, with larger ones added later. Lastly, on the right, is a medium-size spring clip with very wide opening jaws, also useful for holding things together for soldering, etc. At the bottom right-hand corner is a small engineer's clamp, one of a pair I made up many years ago to hold parts together for further working. They consist of two rectangular blocks of steel, fitted with two threaded rods which are in turn provided with a large threaded locking nut each. With a work piece between the jaws, the lock nuts are used to exert a very strong restraining force to prevent the movement of the workpiece.

In Plate 25 can be seen a selection of machine tools, although some, as we will see, can be hand-operated. On the left are two sizes of twist drill, the workhorse of hole drilling. The smaller has a cutting edge just 0.010 in (0.26 mm) in diameter. Because of its small size, this type of drill is provided with a shank of larger diameter so that it may be more easily held in a chuck (as its holding device is called). Next come two taps which are used to put threads in holes. The larger one of the two has a squared end which allows the use of the tools immediately above it, called a tap wrench, to be fitted for hand operation. The second tap has had soft soldered to its shank a length of brass with a knurled or roughened end for grip. These very small taps are quite expensive and very prone to breaking with normal usage. By fitting mine with this hand piece, I find that they are much easier to use by hand and last considerably longer. The two round tools are called button dies, which, with the holder

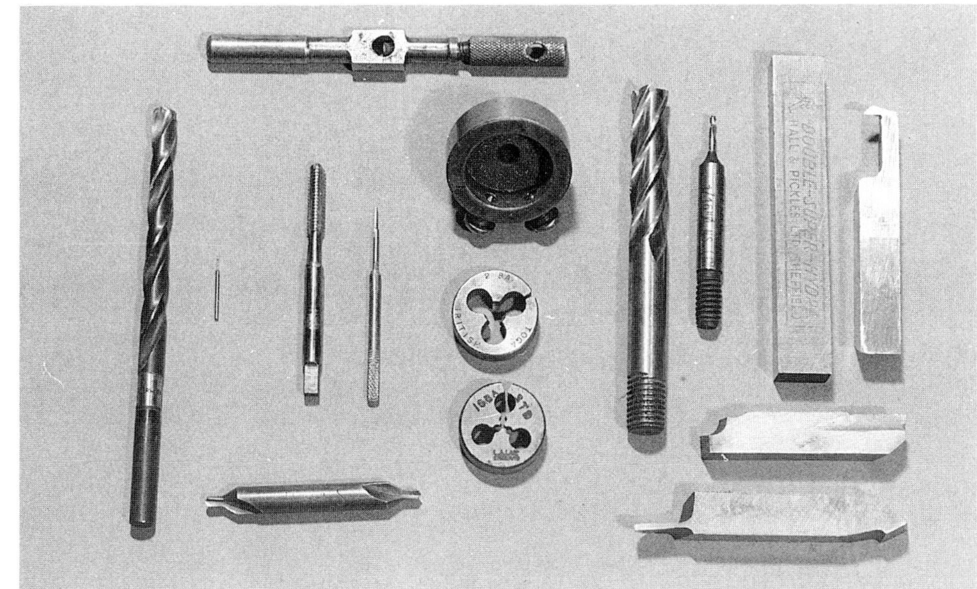

Plate 25

Plate 26

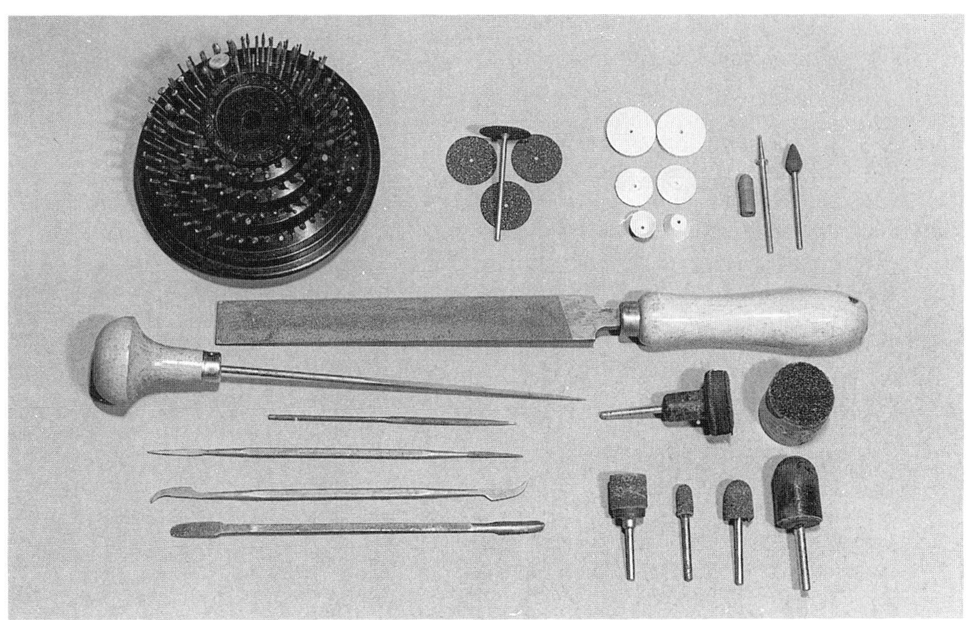

above them, are used on the lathe to make external threads on round bar materials. To the right of these are two cutters that are used on the milling machine, called end mills. These are obtainable in a variety of sizes and shapes and, as with all these tools, will be readily available from an engineer's supplier. The rectangular pieces on the right illustrate a range of lathe tools which are shaped with the aid of a tool grinder from solid pieces of rectangular high-speed tool steel; one unworked piece is also shown.

Plate 26 illustrates another range of cutting and shaping tools. At the top left is a stand of dental burrs. You may well be able to collect together a number of these of various grades, sizes and shapes from your dentist, all of which will be found invaluable. The white discs, called polishing wheels, come from the same source, and are a form of rubber impregnated with a very fine abrasive. Shown here are three of the four basic shapes: large disc with square edge, small disc with knife edge, and cup. In use all are mounted on a small mandrel, like the cutting disc on the left, which we will be coming to shortly. The fourth shape of impregnated rubber wheel is shown on the far right, and comes in two forms called 'points'. The larger ones use a separate mandrel with a tapered thread for mounting, while the small ones are moulded directly to their individual mandrels. Points are available in a variety of shapes, sizes and grades of hardness and texture. These points, together with the cutting discs, are from the jewellery trade. The latter, properly called separating discs, are made from bonded abrasive grit, and are $\frac{7}{8}$ in (22 mm) in diameter and just 0.030 in (0.74 mm) thick. As shown, they are used on a small mandrel in conjunction with a flexible drive, as are all these small tools. As the name implies, they are used for cutting items such as very small pieces of brass that would otherwise be too small or difficult to get at with a saw. One word of caution though; the discs can cut to a depth of $\frac{1}{4}$ in (6.5 mm), but as they are made only of bonded grit, they are prone to shatter if great care is not used. Formerly, I used a grit-impregnated steel disc of similar dimensions. When getting near to its maximum depth it was prone to stick, and then jump out of its groove and run around my fingers which were holding the workpiece. It was quite a painful experience. In this respect, breakage of the discs may act as an intentional safety feature, but, as when using any cutting tool look out for the flying pieces. Wearing some form of eye protection when using any form of cutting tool is always to be recommended.

On the bottom right in Plate 26 is a similar range of rotary abrasives that are from the pattern-making trade catalogues. In the main these are abrasive grit bonded to a paper backing that is then stuck on to a special mandrel. This consists of a steel stem with a shaped rubber head specifically made to take a single

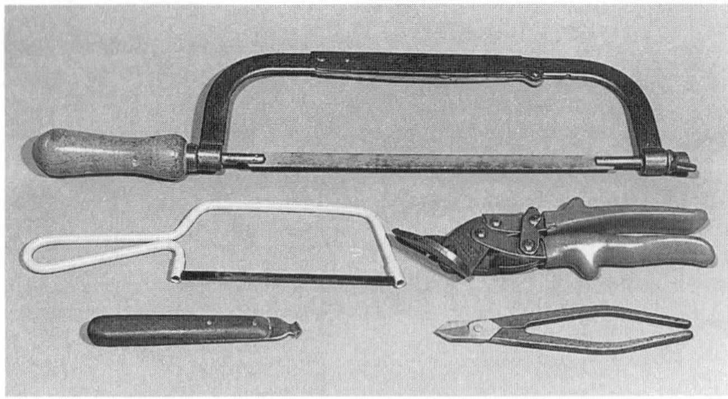

Plate 27

size. The caps and discs that form this range of cutting tools are very varied in type, not only in size and shape, but also in the grit size (coarse or fine). A small selection can be most useful for a number of jobs because they can be used on all manner of materials, from hard metal to soft wood. The remaining tools here you will probably be familiar with. Files are obtainable as round, half-round, square, three square (triangular), flat (tapered sides), hand (parallel sides), and knife edge. The large one illustrated is a smooth, 6 inch hand file, the length being the distance from the shoulder to the end of the file; the tang that takes the handle is not included. They can all be obtained from about 4 in (100 mm) up to 14 in (350 mm) in length, and in three different cuts: smooth, second cut (medium) and bastard (rough). I keep a selection of the 6 in size and renew them as soon as they start to show signs of wear. These are used exclusively for working with brass, copper and nickel silver. If I am working with steel for jig and tool making, then I use a second set that are used exclusively for harder metal.

The second file down with a mushroom handle is one of a range of miniature files known collectively as needle files (or Swiss files). These are available in two lengths, three cuts and twelve shapes. Although they can be obtained singly, many craft shops stock them in selected packs of various shapes and cuts, which is the best way to purchase your first examples. Lastly in Plate 26 are the double-ended files shown at the bottom left, which are collectively called 'riffler' files. There can be as many as forty different shapes in this range. They are much more expensive than normal files, but a few selected ones in the tool box will always be useful usually in working on the most inaccessible corner of a job. These and the needle files can be found in the jewellery trade catalogues.

In Plate 27 we come to the principal separating tools: the hack-saw, junior hack-saw, heavy-duty compound snips, and below at the bottom right, jeweller's snips or shears. Note the shape of the compound snips which allows for the cutting of metal without buckling it. The small tool on the bottom left is another of my own devices. This is the 'grooving tool' and is made from a flat plate of tool steel fitted into a handle. The end is ground to a 'V' shape coming back to form a hook on each side. The two ends thus formed are also ground to a 'V' shape. Using a steel rule as a guide, the tool is drawn across sheet metal, and after several passes, the groove will be

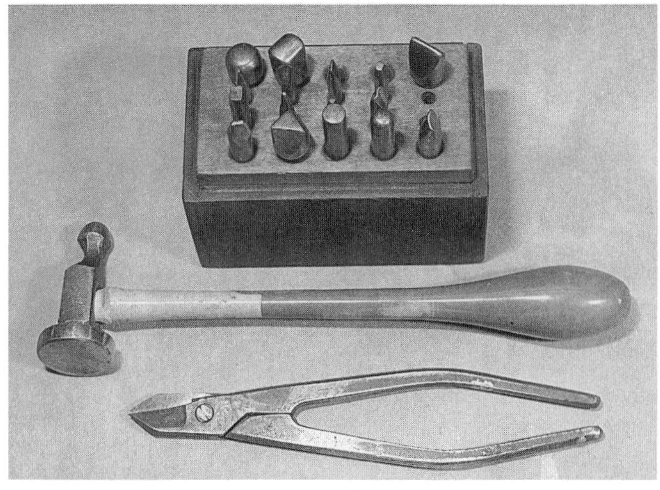

Plate 28

deep enough to allow the sheet to be bent along this line. A sharp corner at the bend will be the result. Should separation of the sheet into two pieces be the aim, then bending back and forth will accomplish this.

Plate 28 illustrates the main tools for working sheet metal into the shapes we will be needing for body and wings. Again there is a pair of jeweller's snips, and above them a jeweller's hammer known as a repoussé hammer. These are available in 4 oz and 6 oz sizes, mine being the smaller of the two and excellent for my needs. With this is needed a flat block of metal; my own is a 1 inch thick by 6 inch square block of iron obtained from a scrap yard many years ago. This is the anvil on which the sheet metal is worked with the repoussé hammer. The box shown at the top of Plate 28 contains a number of steel punches with heads of various shape. These are all made from tool steel in the workshop; some will be seen in use through our project.

Plate 29 illustrates the type of vice that I have fitted to the right-hand corner of my workbench. It has two working jaws that can be swivelled into position. The body of the vice can also be swivelled around to any position to suit the work in hand. There is also a flat area on the top of the vice to act as a small anvil. The reason for the illustration is to show the machine held in the vice, which is a rolling mill. This is home-made, but serves the purpose quite well of changing the cross-section of wire and strip material. Such jobs might include transforming a round nickel silver wire into a flat of a given thickness, or taking a strip of brass of rectangular section and forming a radius on one side for making car bumpers. Whatever shape is cut on to the rollers will form the opposite shape on the material passed between them. A very wide range of rolling mills will be found illustrated in most jeweller's tool catalogues, together with an enormous array of shaped and patterned rollers.

A number of years ago I came upon the problem of pressing out louvres, those small slits on the bonnet side of almost every car from the twenties and thirties. How to form a number of louvres of different widths without making a special tool for each one had been a recurring problem. Because there was nothing on the market at the time that would provide an answer, I

Plate 29

decided to design and build something that would. In Plates 30, 31 and 32 we see the result, a small yet quite powerful press. It consists of a base, a column, a ram to hold a tool, and a handle connected to a cam mechanism that lowers the ram when the handle is

Plate 30

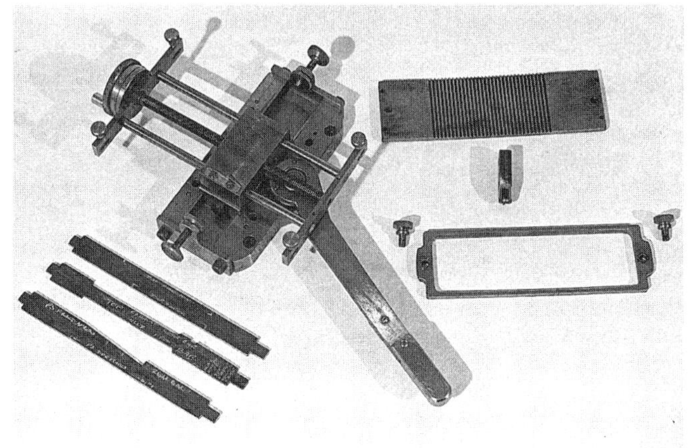

Plate 31

brought over to the front position. Plate 30 shows the basic machine, the small block standing on the left being a blank from which the press tool can be made or to which the press tool can be attached. In Plate 31 we see the mechanism that I produced for forming tapered louvres, and in Plate 32, the machine is set up and a complete set of louvred panels has been made on it for a P3 Alfa Romeo. Although we will not require tapered louvres on the Royale, the machine will be used with another device especially made for it to produce the rectangular door-type louvres that are the feature of the Weinberger Bugatti Royale.

All that we have so far seen has come from our main studio workshop. Outside this is another room, aptly named the 'dirty' workshop, for those operations producing excessive amount of dust. The main occupant of this is the woodworking machine (Plate 33) which is a combination machine of circular and band saw. The need is to cut wood, so if space is at a premium, money short and time in plenty, then a good handsaw will do the same job.

In Plates 34 and 35 are my own particular answers to two serious dust problems. At one end of the room I replaced an outside window with a thick plywood board, in the centre of which was mounted a large enclosed extractor fan. In front of this I built a large box from the ever-useful slotted steel angle and sheet aluminium (Fig 1) with a vent at the back facing the suction side of the fan, and a door at the front.

Plate 32

Plate 33

Plate 34

This front door has a window in the upper half formed by a sheet of glass, and in the lower half two large holes in which long rubber gloves have been secured. The door is also fitted with a positive catch to hold it securely closed when in use. The complete box, which forms a 24 inch (600 mm) cube, is mounted away from the wall holding the fan by some 6 inches (150 mm), with the top, left-hand side and bottom being boxed in. The right-hand side is provided with a large door that gives access to the back of the box and fan.

Inside the box, which is fitted with a light, stands a special type of spray gun which is connected via an air hose to an air compressor. The apparatus is for sand-blasting, which is a most effective way of cleaning metal parts. Plate 34 shows the spray booth, to give it its proper name, with the door open, and Phyllis holding the spray gun with a rubber-gloved hand. During operation, the door is, of course, closed and one would view the proceedings through the window in the door, while holding the part being cleaned in the left, gloved, hand. Sand-blasting spray booths can be purchased ready made, but they are very expensive. The special spray guns with integral container are not

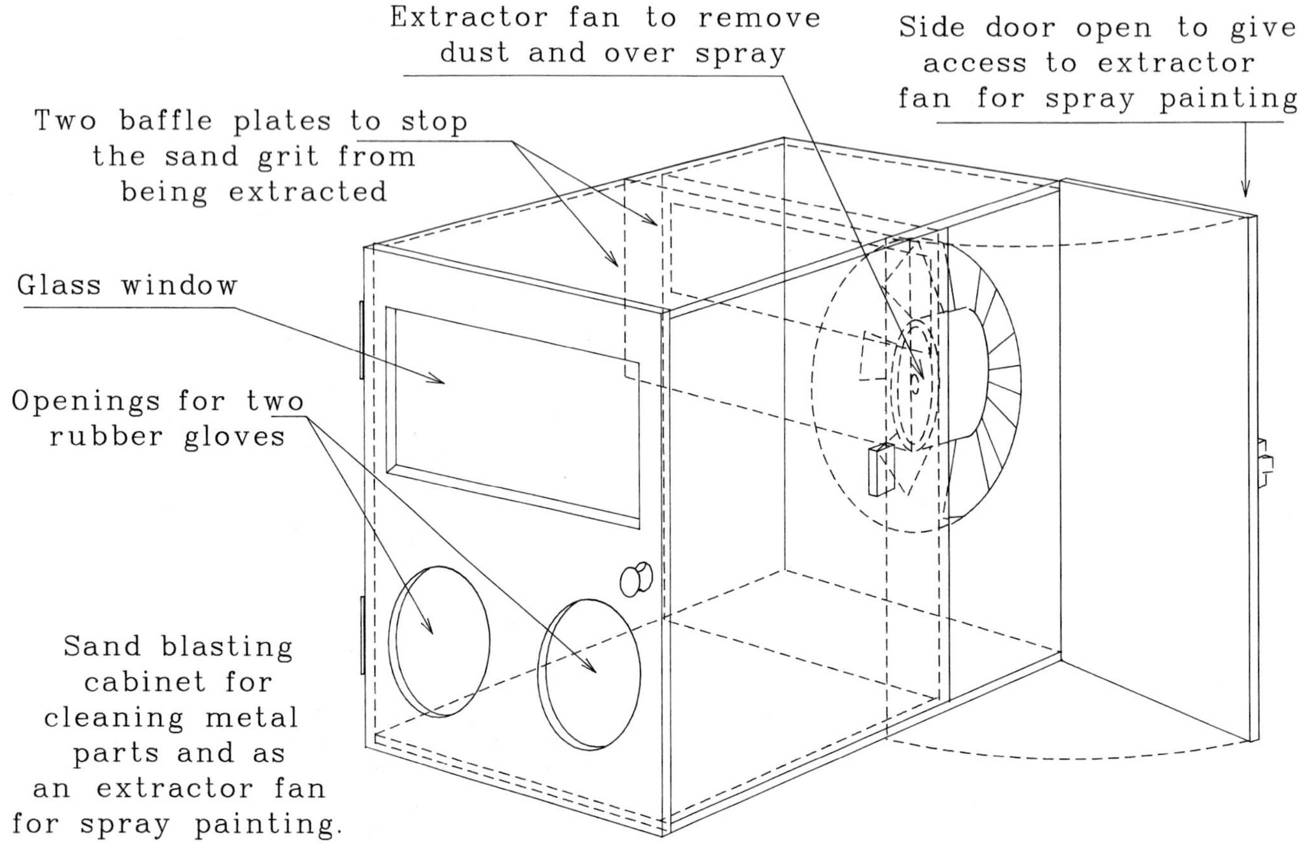

Fig. 1 Extractor cabinet for sand blasting and paint spraying.

Plate 35

so expensive, and can be found at some specialist suppliers to the motor trade, as also the special sands made for this purpose. The very thick rubber gloves with 16 to 18 inch (400 to 450 mm) arms can be obtained from safety equipment suppliers. The use for the large second side door, Plate 35, is to act as a baffle and to allow the single fan to take away the fumes and overspray when painting the finished model. This door would, of course, be closed against the spray booth when sand blasting is in progress. The paint spray gun is an altogether smaller affair called an airbrush. These have become very popular in the last few years and there are a number of them on the market. Choose a medium-size one with a good size bottle and a small paint cup among its accessories. Air compressors come in many shapes and sizes from the minute one we saw supplying air to the burner, to machines the size of your car. When you have decided what tools you need to run off it, seek advice from the supplier of the tools as the size needed will be determined by the air capacity of the tools to be used with it.

Having discussed the materials, together with the tools that we use to manipulate them, and the environment in which this takes place, we are left with one last aspect of our basic work that may be of particular interest. This is the collecting of data for drafting the set of scale plans.

As I stated in the Introduction, the aim of this book is to assist the reader with ideas on how to make this or that part, and to integrate this into the model of whatever subject he has chosen to make. As such, I have intentionally left out of this book a complete set of working drawings for the Bugatti Royale. These, together with its history and a hundred or so photographs, are the subject of a separate volume *The Anatomy of a Bugatti Royale*. I believe, however, that the tools we use to collect the data and produce these scale plans may well be of interest to those who would like to undertake their own research and photography.

Each subject that we choose to make, we first visit to collect the necessary details from which the 1/15-scale plans are drafted. This can be anything up to a twelve thousand mile round trip, as many of our subjects are in California in the USA. The Weinberger Bugatti Royale, for example, is in Michigan, some four thousand miles from our studio in Digby in England. As many of these subjects are also in museums that are, without exception, not illuminated with the photographer in mind, I needed to give considerable thought to the minimum photo kit I could put together to bring home the maximum amount of data. I have always been interested in photography and have always run my own darkroom for processing black and white material.

The determining factor was space, and having seen the results of what airport baggage handling can do to some people's luggage and their contents, I decided early on that the case holding this gear would be travelling with me on flights as carry-on luggage, the point being that this determines a maximum size of case. My own measures 18x14x6 in and is well within the regulations for carry-on luggage.

The contents, like most things over the years, have multiplied, although I should say that we do now seek to bring home a wealth of information whenever we set forth, as anyone reading the story of the Weinberger Bugatti Royale will appreciate. Plate 36 illustrates the current contents of our camera case, while Fig 2 identifies the items. The camera (out of the case while taking the photograph) is a 35 mm single-lens reflex which I feel is essential if you want to come home with the picture that you *think* you have taken. With this type of camera, one views through the same lens that is taking the picture. Other types of camera use a separate view finder which, particularly if it is situated to one side of the taking lens, will not show you the same view that the camera film will see. This condition becomes more apparent the closer one gets to the subject. Because most of the shots we need are close-up ones of mechanical detail, one can see how important this can be. While the normal lens for my camera is 50 mm, the most useful one for the confines of a museum display and for inside car shots is a wide-angle lens of 28 mm. There is some distortion in a picture taken with this lens, but for our needs it is not important because we take care of the relative position of parts from the dimensions we also collect, the photographs in the main being used for detail information only. The electronic flash is essential for inside work. It is worth obtaining the most efficient that money and space will allow. Note that for use with a wide-angle lens one also needs a wide-angle diffuser for the flash or the outside edges of your picture may be lost. Spare battery packs are also necessary; museums are the last place in which to shop

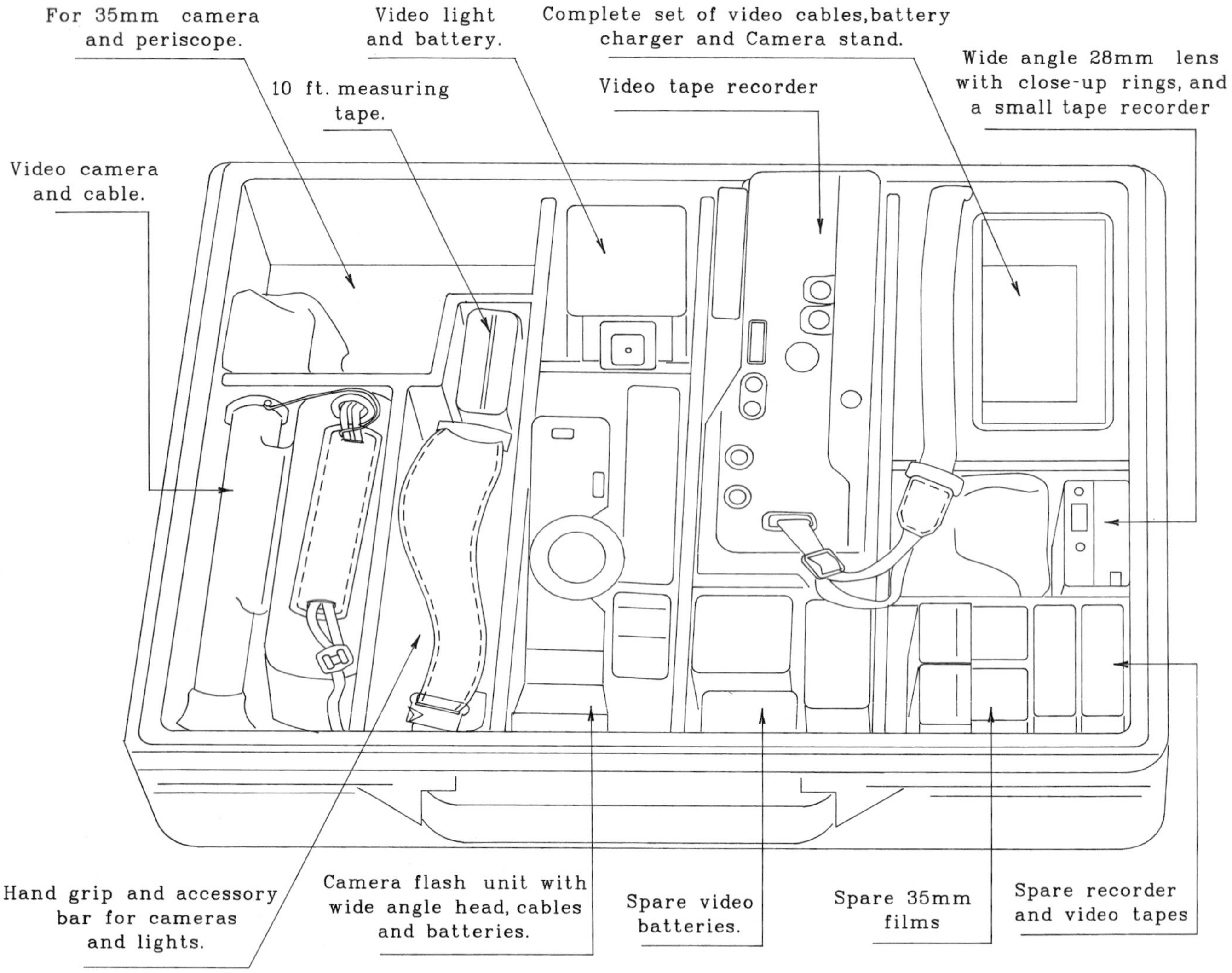

For 35mm camera and periscope.

Video light and battery.

Complete set of video cables, battery charger and Camera stand.

Wide angle 28mm lens with close-up rings, and a small tape recorder

10 ft. measuring tape.

Video tape recorder

Video camera and cable.

Hand grip and accessory bar for cameras and lights.

Camera flash unit with wide angle head, cables and batteries.

Spare video batteries.

Spare 35mm films

Spare recorder and video tapes

Fig. 2 Camera case contents.

Plate 36

for replacements. There are some types of plastic 35 mm slide boxes that can be most useful, as they will very conveniently hold four 35 mm film cassettes. I keep a number of these fully stocked, two in the camera case for immediate use.

Eight films at 36 exposures each, plus one in the camera, will give a very useful 324 pictures. Two close-up rings for use with the 50 mm lens are included, in case we have a chance to copy diagrams from manuals, etc. The most useful accessory by far, however, is a periscope attachment that allows one to look through the viewfinder from above, below, or from the side of the camera, rather than the normal position of directly behind it. The advantage will become apparent when one considers taking photos of the underneath of the vehicle, and from high above it. One can place the camera on the ground, viewing the pictures from above, or one can have the camera above one's head and look up into the viewfinder to see the vehicle from a height of, perhaps, seven feet.

In use, the camera is mounted on one end of

Plate 37

an accessory bar, the other end having a large hand grip attached, with the flash unit mounted on an accessory shoe that is bolted in the centre. The same assembly can be seen in Plate 37, but with a video camera replacing the 35 mm one, and a video light replacing the electronic flash.

The video camera and video cassette recorder (VCR) were added to the kit because of their portability and the usefulness of being able to wander at will around the vehicle with the camera, and record the subject in the round. After more than twenty years I am firmly of the opinion that, however many photographs one takes, it will always be found that more should have been taken, because this or that is still hidden behind some other component. The video camera's ability to move over and around items has, I hope, provided the answer to yet another problem. As can be seen, the case accommodates the VCR and the camera, which, incidentally, uses an optical view-finder. The alternative is a camera with an electronic view-finder which uses battery power all the time you are setting up the picture, but usually allows you to play back the recording through the view-finder. A battery charger plus the necessary cables and fittings to allow the camera and VCR to run directly off mains power (110 and 220 volts) or a car battery, are all fitted into the case, as well as a small camera stand. Three video tapes are included giving a possible filming time of 4½ hours, as are battery packs giving 2½ hours of running time. Finally, a miniature tape recorder with 2 hours of tape is included for interviews; this proved invaluable in recording the Bugatti Royale story.

In the lid is a large clipboard with a plentiful supply of paper, this together with a 10-foot rule, being used to collect a dozen or so rough sheets of notes and dimensions of the vehicle. The 10-foot rule has been marked up on one side into 2 inch segments, each alternate one being painted black. This is useful in some instances when included in a detail photograph, where the rule can be laid against or held in contact with a number of items.

With this type of photograph one can then take off actual dimensions. The crucial point is, however, that the parts being photographed must all be on the same plane. Should this not be so, errors in measurement will be inevitable.

Having collected as much information as possible, the next task is to interpret this into a set of 1/15-scale drawings. For this Phyllis uses a modern drafting machine (drawing board). First, each of the measurements is translated into its scale equivalent. These are then plotted on the drawing board with the aid of the digital vernier calliper (Plate 22). Then, with constant reference to the detail photographs, the various dots are joined together using the straight edges of the drafting machine, or as in Plate 38, one or a set of large plastic sweeps called french curves. When all the basic shapes are in place and match in different views, the smaller detail is added to complete the process. Until earlier this year, all our plans were drafted by this process, which entails copying and recopying many items several times before we can arrive at a complete set of detailed chassis and body drawings.

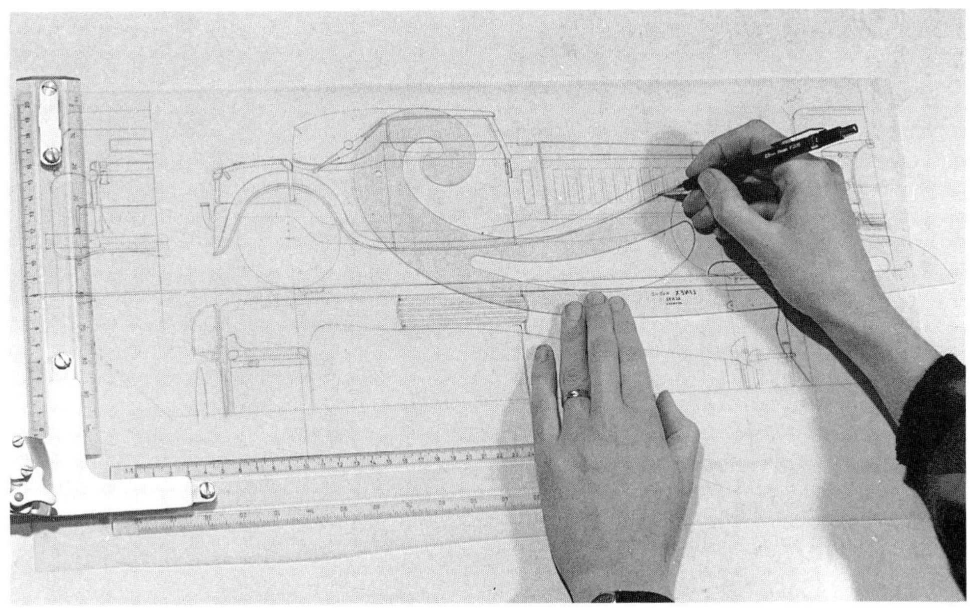

Plate 38

Plate 39

Because we decided to rest our modelling hands for a while and return to writing with this book, and since we also like to keep abreast of modern technology to see if we can bring it to our aid, we acquainted ourselves with the world of CAD (Computer Aided Design), in the form of the INTERGRAPH MicroStation (Plate 39). This, we believe, has improved the accuracy and detailing of the plans we use.

This concludes the tour of our studio workshop, and a review of tools and materials that we use in our work in general, many of which were used in the building of the Bugatti Royale, in particular. It has, of necessity, been only a brief visit, but I hope it will be sufficient to add understanding to what is to follow, and perhaps give some food for thought regarding your own workshop now or for the future. I will make the point again, however, that what you have seen has been accumulated over twenty years or more, and for our purposes is the ultimate, if only because it has to pay for itself. I started with a small second-hand lathe, an electric drill, a couple of files, a hammer, chisel and hacksaw to produce my first models. The amount of tooling that you have is no indication of what you can make, for it is not the tool that determines such things but the hand that controls it.

I have endeavoured to drop markers throughout the first part to assist my reader in where to look for further information. In my early years, I was an avid enthusiast of my local library, particularly for books on craft subjects. Of interest was what one could do with the different tools, and how I could utilize them, rather than the actual topic. The craft of model making can and often does use the tools, materials or techniques of almost every other creative occupation.

PART TWO
The Chassis

THE SUBJECT that will take us through the various stages and techniques of manufacturing a typical car is the Weinberger Bugatti Royale. Before we start, though, a few notes on this outstanding vehicle will certainly add to the interest.

The Weinberger Bugatti Royale is almost twenty feet long with a wheel base of 169 inches (nearly four and a half metres), and weighs in at 7035 pounds (3197 kilograms) or 3.14 tons. The eight-cylinder engine is 56 inches long (1.4 metres) with a capacity of 784 cu inches (12,847 cc). Originally this was 12,763 cc but the engine was rebored when it was repaired after frost damage in the winter of 1937/38. It was reputed to have a top speed of 125 mph, although most authoritative writers consider that 100 mph is probably a more realistic figure. Given that weight, and the fact that the car has cable brakes and is now nearly 60 years of age, no one is likely to attempt to prove a point on the matter.

The Weinberger Royale was built on a Bugatti Type 41 chassis, one of seven made, although eleven different body styles were fitted to these. The Weinberger is built on chassis No.41121 and has the original body, but the prototype, 41100, received five different styles, the final one being the Coupé de Ville designed by Jean Bugatti which is now resident in the Musée National de L'Automobile at Mulhouse in France.

The Weinberger Cabriolet was built for Dr Josef Fuchs by Karosserie Ludwig Weinberger of Munich in Germany. Dr Fuchs was a well-known citizen of Nürnberg. A surgeon and gynaecologist, he had also made a name for himself in motor racing and as a concert pianist by the time he placed the order for this, one of the most expensive cars ever made. One could have purchased four Phantom II Continental Rolls-Royces for the price paid for this, and still have sufficient change to add three SSI sports saloons to the collection.

In 1933, just before Hitler came to power in Germany, Dr Fuchs moved to Switzerland, from where, in 1934, he took himself and the Royale to Shanghai in China, which was then in turmoil in the north, because of an invasion by the Japanese. From here, after much trouble clearing himself from a charge of narcotics smuggling, he managed, in the nick of time, to get himself and the 20 foot Bugatti on to a ship bound for Canada. Just a few weeks after he left, full-scale war broke out on the streets of Shanghai.

In the winter of 1937/38, having driven three times across the States from coast to coast in the previous few months and travelled over 21,000 miles with the Royale, Dr Fuchs brought the big car to New York. Here it was left in Fuch's backyard unprotected when the first frosts arrived. The water in the engine froze and cracked the cylinder block, damage that Dr Fuchs could find no one to repair. The car was put on the market but remained unsold even for the lowest offer price of $350 (£87). As a result, it was sent to a local scrapyard in the Bronx district of New York. Within a short time, however, the Royale was spotted by Charles Chayne, a wealthy enthusiast, who purchased the now almost derelict car and put it in store until after the war, when he had time to rebuild it back to something like its former glory. Chayne made many changes to the car (none of which, in my opinion, were improvements), and it is to him we owe a debt of gratitude for the fact that we can enjoy this car's fabulous proportions today. It is presently in the Henry Ford Museum & Greenfield Village, Dearborn, USA.

Plate 40 shows the Weinberger Royale on the day it was collected by Dr Fuchs from the workshops of Ludwig Weinberger in the spring of 1932. Plate 41 was taken in about 1940/41 shortly before being consigned to the New York scrapyard. Plate 42 illustrates the reborn Weinberger Royale with Mr and Mrs Charles Chayne in 1959, when they presented it to the Henry Ford Museum & Greenfield Village complex in Dearborn, Michigan.

My aim, however, is to concentrate on how we solve the problems presented by a project such as this, rather than the actual making of this particular model. In this way the answers will be equally valid for any subject dealt with.

After collecting all available data on the subject that is to be your project, the first task is to find a place to start and then produce the working drawings. This not only gives one the opportunity for deciding the actual dimensions, but also exercises the mind with regard to how one can actually make a particular part. You will be producing your own rough dimensioned drawings from which you will work and also, possibly, your own scale plans. Once you have become familiar with the technique of interpreting undimensioned scale plans, you will be able to use it to interpret scale plans from any source. Apart from the pleasure actually gained by doing this from the beginning, in the process you will be deciding how you want to build the project with the capability and tools that you

Plate 40 (Photo courtesy of Horst Lattke and Henry Ford Museum & Greenfield Village)

Plate 41 (Photo courtesy of the Charles Chayne Collection, National Automotive Collection, Detroit Public Library)

Plate 42 (Photo courtesy of Henry Ford Museum & Greenfield Village)

have available, and whether, say, it is to be a simple, no internal detail, kerbside model, or a full working example. We choose to restrict our working parts to door catches and door and bonnet hinges, which is sufficient to allow access to see all of the detail that we customarily include in our work.

It has always been my practice to start building from the ground up, so the first consideration here then is the wheels and tyres. The wheels on the Bugatti Royale are cast aluminium and peculiar to Bugatti. Ettore Bugatti used a similar wheel, though slightly smaller in dimension, on the Type 46 and Type 50 models as well, so the particular details will be good for an interesting range of vehicles. I described the techniques of making spoked wire wheels in *The Complete Car Modeller*, so it is my intention to deal only with the cast wheel here.

Figs 3 and 4 show a portion of the Weinberger scale plans for the wheel and tyre. They show the basic shape and the context and setting of the piece we

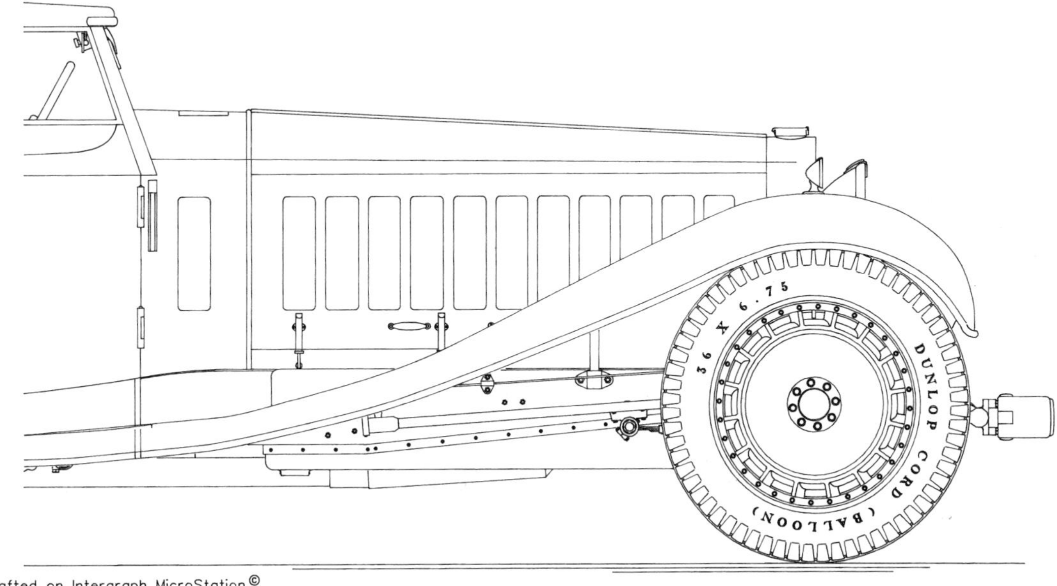

Fig. 3 A typical side view of a wheel as shown in the scale plans.

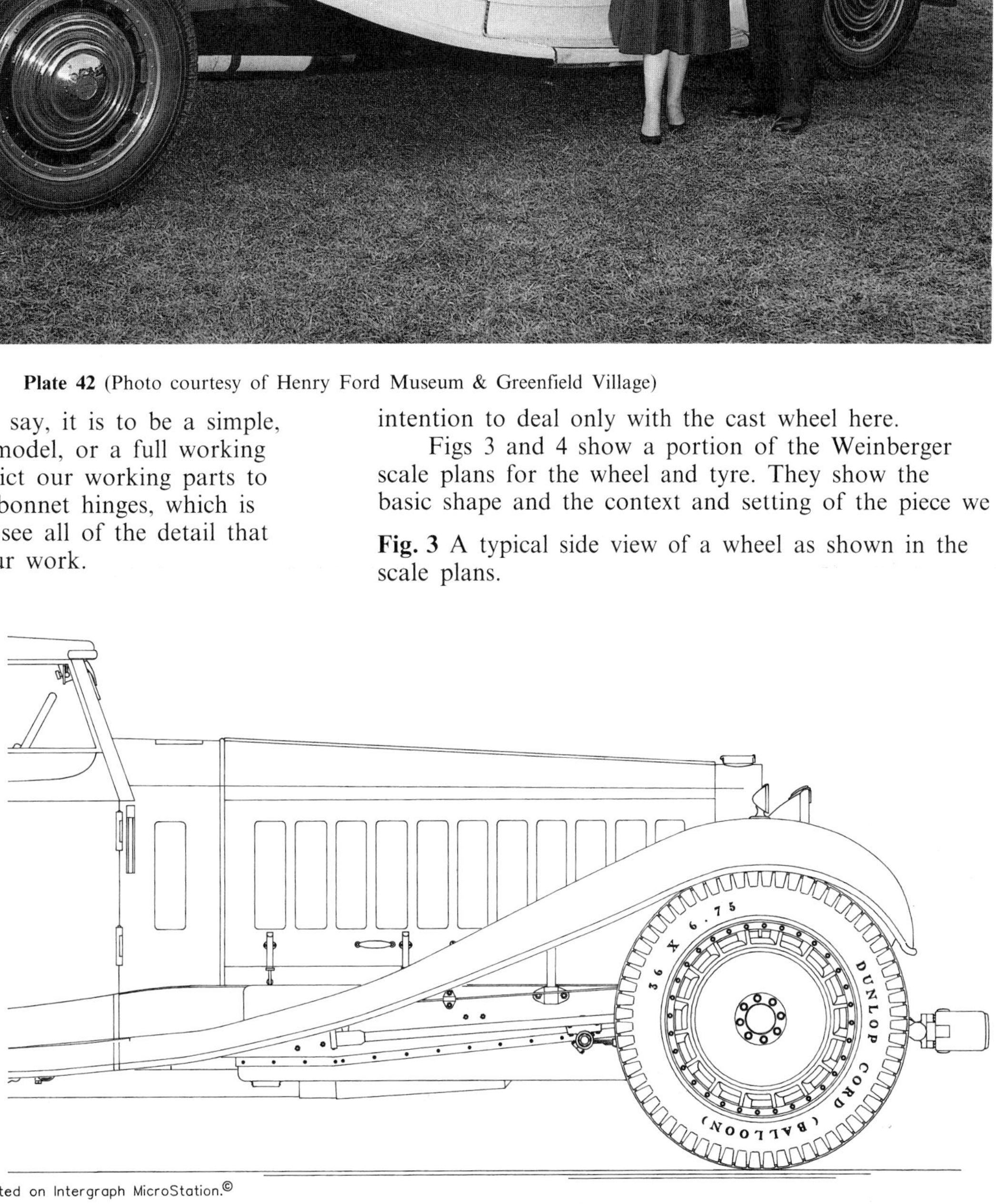

Drafted on Intergraph MicroStation.©

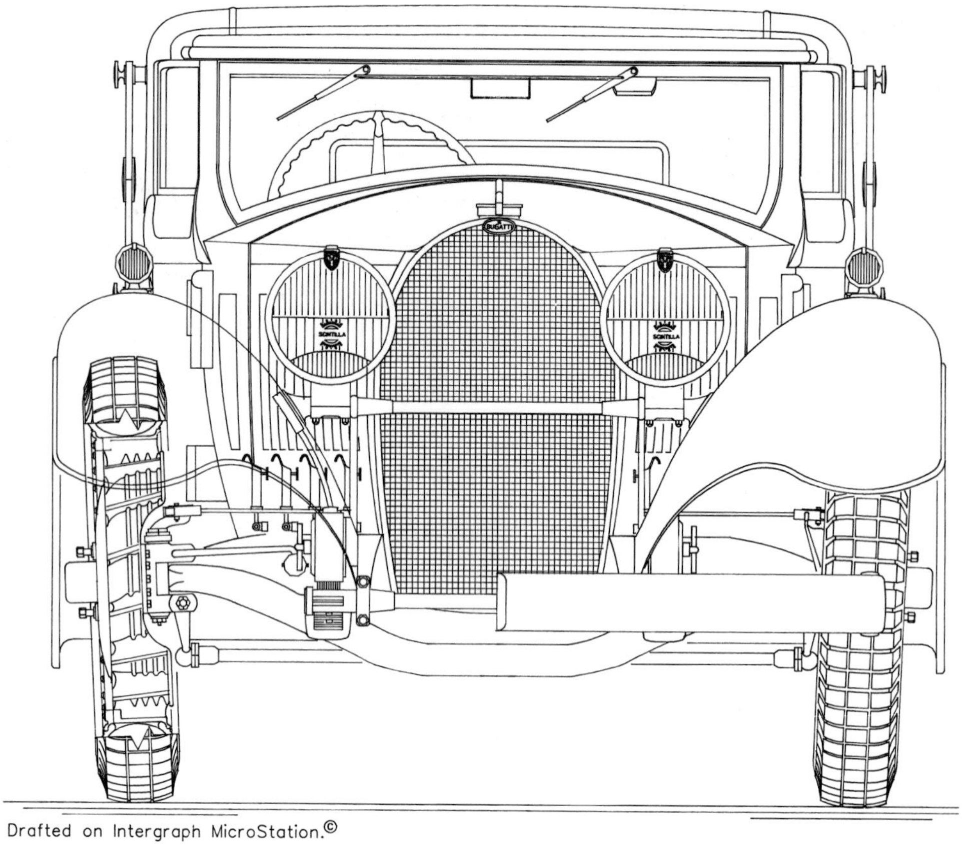

Drafted on Intergraph MicroStation.©

Fig. 4 The front view of the wheels with one opened up to show the cross-section.

are considering. These, together with any photographs, will give you a feeling for the piece and its relative proportions as a whole, as well as of the individual parts. This is the essence of the design process, for you are not about to duplicate a part from the same set of dimensions, even scale ones, that produced the original. What you are about to do is design and build a part that resembles in miniature the full-size object of real life. In most cases for vehicles of this vintage, the original drawings just do not exist now. Even if they did, I would still recommend working in this way, for I feel that to capture the character of the original on this small scale, one will inevitably, even subconsciously, use some licence. Never consider any item in isolation when determining its size. I am amazed, as you may well be, that the model in Plate 1 actually looks like a twenty-foot-long Bugatti Royale, and not a model that can be held in one hand. In considering the picture, if the ring of bolts around the wheel rim had been provided with heads twice or half the size shown here, the illusion of size would have been destroyed. Yet the size of the bolt heads was not one that I made a note of when I collected the dimensions for the plans. The size of these was determined by what I felt 'looked right' in the surroundings, ie the rim of the wheel. Because they do look right in the wheel, they also look right on the finished model. It is important to grasp this point, for as we will shortly be seeing, many of the dimensions we will need will be taken directly off the scale plans. There is a limit, however, to the size that one can go down to, if only because of the thickness of the pencil line. The actual size of detailing such as this I leave to my intuition at the time of making the parts. When you get into the swing of things, you will soon get the 'feeling' for it and will intuitively know that it has to be this size or that to look right. It is only the attention to detail of the smallest parts that will assure the correctness of the completed model.

Working drawings need only be in the form of notes and rough sketches made on a pad. No drafting tools or drawing board are needed because the drawings do not have to be scale or even correctly proportioned, one with another. They are simply used as a visual method of dissecting the part into manageable pieces, and then adding relevant dimensions. The dissection need not necessarily be in the same place as in the original. The Royale wheel is a good example of this. The outer flange on the full size wheel is detachable, hence the ring of bolts, so that the tyre can be fitted, this rim having no well in it unlike a modern one. To make the wheel in the same way on the model would mean a great deal of work that would offer no advantage over my own method in the look and feel of the finished wheel. Since the reason for the problem of fitting the tyre in this way, can be eliminated in the model, we can redesign the wheel to suit our convenience, always providing it gives the same impression as the original in full size.

Fig 5 illustrates how I have chosen to do this for the full set of Bugatti Royale wheels. This is the time to look ahead so that one can visualise how it is possible to put things together, not only so that they will look right, but to allow for any further working on them. This also goes for their ease of assembly, should anything need to be removed to assist the fitting of other parts at a later date. In consideration of Murphy's Law, I always feel it prudent to make as few parts as possible into permanent fixtures. Even with the best laid plans there always seems to be one piece in the way as one nears completion, the removal of which would make life so much easier.

Of equal importance when putting together the

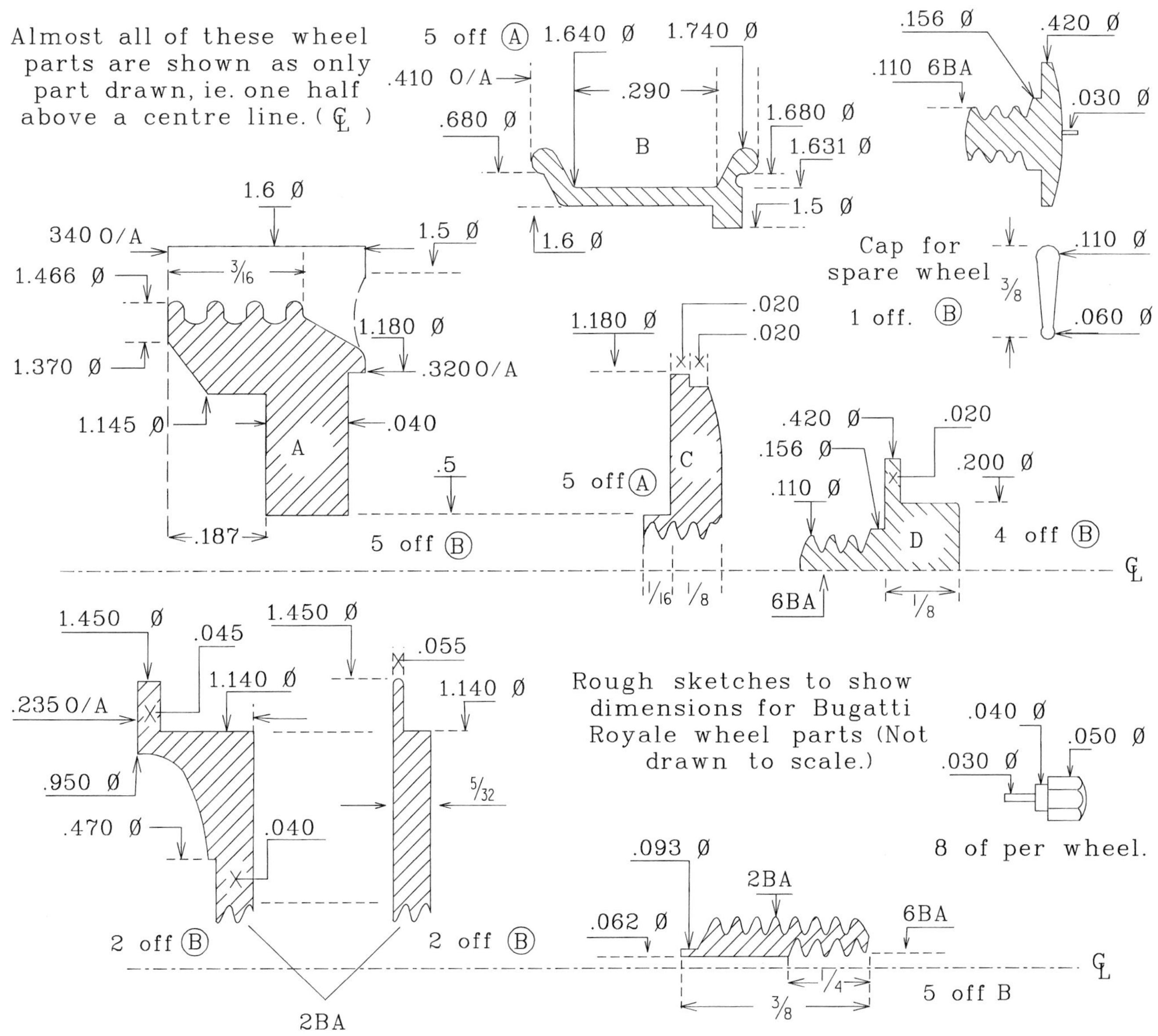

Fig. 5 Rough sketches for dimensions. Almost all are part drawn as one half above a centreline.

working drawings is giving due consideration to the order and number of operations that are going to be necessary to produce the part.

All this may sound most complicated, but the more experience one has, the more alternative solutions one will have available to answer the problems of making each piece. The piece in question will actually direct you to most of them. By this I mean that you are not starting with nothing. You know the size, the shape and finish. The size and shape will give an indication of how it can, or cannot (just as important) be made. The finish will often dictate the material from which the piece will be made.

The original Bugatti Royale wheel was an aluminium casting; one, I might add, that was extremely complicated for the foundry men to produce. This tells us that the final finish required will be aluminium, either as a paint, or in solid metal, in part at least. In considering the next stage – how do we make it? – we need always to be aware of our machining options. Basically, this means that on the lathe we can produce any shape provided it is round, and on a mill we can produce any shape provided it is a combination of flats. If we find, when looking at the wheel, its production cannot directly be accommodated by either of these methods, then we mentally adjust the shape of it until it will. This thought process will eventually lead to the number of operations needed to make the piece.

The wheel in question can clearly not be made on a lathe (because of the spokes) or a milling machine (because of the radii) as it is. If we mentally remove the spokes and ring of bolts, however, we now see that there is first an outer ring, then an inner diameter, both of which can be turned on the lathe without problems. If we were to make these two parts on the lathe, the question then is: would it be possible to add the bolts and spokes to them? The answer is yes, by drilling holes for the bolts and milling slots for the spokes to sit in. In fact, if the spokes were to be soldered in place, they would appear to become one with the rim and hub, and thus the wheel would look as though it had been cast. However, here we have our first conflict. Aluminium is not easy to solder, particularly when it comes to fitting sixteen tiny plates (spokes) around a relatively large block such as this.

It is apparent when viewing the full-size wheel, that there are two distinct surface finishes: the typical dull 'grainy' silver, denoting a casting in the immediate area of the spokes, and the 'shiny' machined finish of the outer rim and the centre dish. Also of relevance is the small groove just inside the spoke diameter that is often painted to match the body on this type of wheel.

From this, a clear road to follow is emerging for we are now getting indications of the materials to be used. The finished wheel needs to look like turned aluminium; the centre and outside rim should look like machined aluminium, while the spoked diameter could in fact, if placed between two aluminium parts, look quite acceptable if painted with aluminium paint, thus giving the grainy finish of a scale version of a fine cast finish. We have now arrived at three pieces: two in aluminium, and a third – one needing a lot of parts soldering in place – in brass, with a paint finish.

The materials having been decided, we now look at the pieces in close proximity to the wheel, to see if they can offer any suggestions regarding the shape of the three parts and how they can be assembled. We find two items: the brake drum backing plate, and what I will refer to as the hub cap. The brake drum is attached to the axle and carries a number of small items. It is painted, which again suggests the use of brass. The hub cap is also made up of a number of small parts and is chromed; here, too, brass would seem to be the best material. The method of fitting the wheel to the backing plate and axle together with the hub cap will determine the inside shape of all these parts. At this stage, pencil and paper would be taken up to sketch out one's ideas. When they look reasonable, add the dimensions to see if there is enough metal to actually achieve what is wanted. The initial sizes will be checked from the scale drawings with the aid of a vernier and marked on the sketch, the remaining sizes being determined by what the piece is expected to do. The stub axle will need to be as large as possible for maximum strength, but not so large as to interfere with the visible detailing of it.

As our work is made for display only, and not to play with, I have never seen the advantage of making wheels turn. When one considers that the finished Bugatti weighed over seven pounds, about three and a half kilos, and considering the fine detail built into it, free-turning wheels would seem to be a distinct liability. For this reason it has always been my practice to thread the stub axles and screw the wheels in place. As a very simple locking device, I also drill and tap the stub axles to take a male thread projecting from the hub cap. These two threads not only differ in size but also in the pitch of the thread. Once the hub cap is screwed home, the difference in thread pitch prevents the wheel from being unscrewed. The final consideration in setting out these pieces is economy of materials. Metal can be quite expensive, particularly brass in large sizes. For this reason, and because we have the technique of silver soldering at hand, I would not, for example, machine the stub axle in Fig 5 from the same piece of brass as the backing plate. The same result can be achieved by turning the backing plate from the large diameter brass stock necessary and then drilling and tapping the centre hole. The short threaded stub axle can be made from a piece of brass just fractionally larger than the thread diameter, which is then screwed into the backing plate and secured with a small spot of silver solder.

Having determined the sizes for the various parts, metal is selected to suit and a start is made on the lathe. Plate 43 shows the first operation (on part A of Fig 5). The first operation should always be the one

Plate 43

which requires the greatest amount of work on the piece, subject only to the fact it should, if possible, provide the means for holding it for the second operation. For those not familiar with lathe work who I may just have lost, let me explain. For a piece of metal to be machined in a lathe, it first has to be fixed in some way to the power that is to turn it. The securing method in this instance, is by means of the jaws of a lathe chuck. Whatever fixing is used, however, only the outside and the front 'face' can be worked on with tools. Should a piece be removed from the lathe and then put back, it can be very difficult to replace it in exactly the same position, for various reasons, so that it will run true, (not wobble). It follows that the least number of times a piece is taken out and replaced (operations) in the lathe, the better. It is also for this same reason that the maximum amount of work, ie turning (removing metal from the outside), forming (making the grooves), facing (turning the front), chamfering (the angle on the inside), and drilling, be done before removing the piece from the lathe for the first time. Because only one side at a time can be 'got-at' with the tools, almost all parts made on a lathe from bar material (round-section brass) will need at least two lathe operations to complete.

To return to Plate 43, a block of brass bar is held on its outside diameter in a three-jaw chuck. This is then drilled to provide the hole in the centre and is bored to give the large inside diameter that, on the second operation (Plate 44), will provide the means for holding the piece, by having the tips of the three jaws on the inside of this diameter. The three grooves are

Plate 44

formed with a pointed tool, one at a time, then with the same tool the diameter is reduced behind these to give less work for the second operation. At this stage the piece is cut off the bar with a thin tool called a parting tool and the next piece is turned on the remaining block of brass bar. Although one needs quite a large lathe to machine these parts from large blocks of brass bar, it is possible to make them on quite a small lathe by first cutting parts to length with a hacksaw, or having them cut into short individual lengths by the material supplier. With the piece parted from its bar, it can then be fitted into the chuck (Plate 44) to have a small recess bored into the front face and an angle and radius (round corner) formed on the outside. When these two operations have been performed on the requisite number of parts, plus one (always include a spare in case of mishap), then we can proceed to the next step (Plate 45).

Plate 45

This stage will provide the sixteen grooves for the spokes to sit in for silver soldering. These can be cut by hand with a hacksaw; a better plan, however, would be to machine them on a milling machine with the aid of a dividing head. The dividing head allows a workpiece to be rotated through 360 degrees and held consecutively in a selected number of equally spaced positions. Most dividing heads have two methods of selecting the number of positions required. One is through a precision drive for making gears, etc. (which need not concern us here) and the second is using a milling table which can rotate about a central axis and which is marked out in degrees.

In the Royale wheel there are sixteen spokes. By dividing 360 by 16 we end up with a requirement for spoke slots cut at 22.5 degree intervals. The spoke hub can be mounted on the table by means of a chuck and a simple threaded two-piece spigot as shown in Fig 6.

Fig. 6 A spigot with locking bolt and washer used on the lathe and milling machine as a holding device. It can be made in a range of sizes.

The spokes are in the form of turbine blades that draw air in and across the finned surface of the brake drum when the wheel is turning. This means that they have to be left- and right-handed for the two sides of the car, as can be seen from the examples placed on the base.

In Plate 46, we see the individual spokes being fitted in their slots. These are only roughly cut to length, and when fitted will give a larger diameter than is needed. Before final assembly, each spoke or blade is coated with a silver solder paint using a small paint brush. Make sure that the silver solder paint is well mixed because the solder granules do tend to gravitate to the bottom of the container.

The assembly is now placed on a fire brick in the hearth ready for heating with a gas torch up to silver soldering temperature. The aim in this process should be to heat evenly and slowly with a broad clean flame (one that is not smokey). It will be observed that the flux bubbles and the liquid element will evaporate in the early stages. If the parts being soldered are not secured in some way, the agitation will be sufficient to move all but the largest pieces, so it is necessary to put a spare strip of metal or wire around the assembly. The correct soldering temperature will be observed when the flux is seen to have settled down

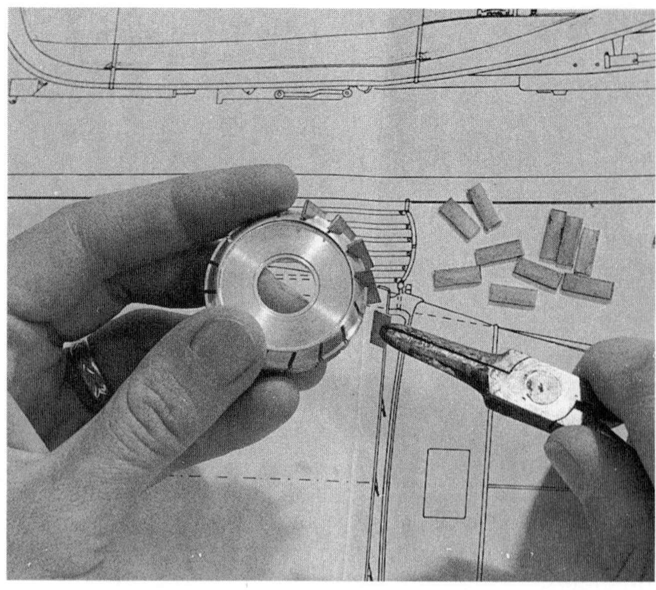

Plate 46

and taken on a clear watery appearance. At this point the silver will glow and start to run to the joints between the various parts. Watch this carefully because as soon as it is seen that all the solder has run, remove the flame from the workpiece. Excessive heating above the first melt temperature will tend to 'boil' the solder, burning off some of its alloys and producing porosity in what remains. Should the finished piece need chrome or other plating, then this porosity will show as tiny pin holes at the soldered joint, a condition that is very difficult to eliminate.

Another point worth mentioning regarding silver soldering in general, is that it will always take a slightly higher temperature to remelt a silver-soldered joint, because each heating and melting of the solder will tend to make it alloy with the surface of the pieces being soldered. This has the advantage that quite complicated assemblies can be built up through several silver soldering operations without disturbing earlier ones, if care is taken in controlling the temperature by judicious application of the flame.

To return to Plate 47, should it be found that not enough solder paint was used, then a thin rod or stick of silver solder can be introduced to the workpiece

Plate 47

close to the flame where necessary. The aim here is to form a small fillet (a little rounded corner) for the whole width of each spoke where it attaches to the hub. This will give the appearance of the spokes and the hub having been made as a single piece, ie a casting. After soldering, the parts are placed in a pickle bath for an hour or so. This will remove the flux residue which tends to form a hard gloss-like substance when the piece has cooled down. Without a pickle bath the residue is difficult to remove and tends to blunt tools that come into contact with it.

The next operation (Plate 48) is to remount each of the parts on to the spigot and turn off a small portion of the outside diameter down to the given size, and then to turn, or face back, the front and rear surface of the spokes to conform to the dimensions required.

Plate 48

In common with most of the advice that is given here what is described is offered by way of a suggestion and should not be taken as the only answer to a given problem, this section on the wheel being a good example. When I started to produce this first set of wheels, my intention was to proceed as described, culminating in a silver-painted spoke section wheel part. Just at this time, however, I made the acquaintance of a two-man company that specialised in very fine detail investment casting. Although most of their work was with precious metals for the silver and jewellery trade, they also cast in aluminium from time to time. As they expressed an interest in attempting to make a casting of this particular item, we used one of these pieces as a pattern from which to produce a mould. Subsequently, cast aluminium parts were produced for part A, Fig 5 for this particular model.

I should say that companies who can, and of equal importance, who are willing to undertake this work in such small quantities are very few and far between. Investment casting as a process will reproduce the very finest detail and it entails the use of a pattern best made in metal, preferably brass. This is used to make a rubber mould into which molten wax is forced after the pattern has been removed. When the wax has cooled and solidified, the item is taken out and coated with a special grade of plaster. When a suitable thickness has been built up, it is dried, then heated gently to melt out the wax, so leaving a cavity in the plaster mould that will match the original brass pattern. The metal to be used for casting is now heated to the melt temperature, as is the plaster mould, and the metal is poured in. When cold, the plaster mould is broken open, hopefully to reveal a perfectly cast copy of the original pattern. This is a long, quite costly, and highly skilled operation, and aluminium is not the easiest metal to cast by this process in small quantities by hand. So it is not really a job even for the above-average model maker.

A simpler process is to cast in cold-cast metal. This is basically a finely ground metal powder mixed with a resin and catalyst. Various resins are used but the most common are the polyester and epoxy types. The easiest to lay hands on of these is the polyester resin system because it is the same resin system that is used in fibreglass car repair kits. It is easily obtainable, clean to use, and sets quickly, and is the one that I use for casting small parts as we will see later, with various other 'fillers', as the additions to the resin are called.

Some fillers, which can include almost anything you can think of that can be obtained in powder or granulated from, can inhibit the curing of the resin after the catalyst has been added, so if you are not sure, always try a small sample first. Aluminium powder, however (available from most good craft shops) has no effect on the resin system and can be added to the resin (always before the catalyst) until it is positively stiff, if need be. After the catalyst has been added and the mix has set hard, it can be worked with all the normal metal and some woodworking tools to quite good effect. Of interest here, however, is the fact that cold-cast metal can be polished on a buffing wheel like ordinary metal, although it will have a slightly grainy appearance, the character depending on the amount of metal powder in the resin mix.

To see an example of this material, visit your local department store or gift shop and look out for the bronze ornaments. If an ornament weighs less than you think it should (bronze is quite a heavy metal) examine the surface and you will more than likely see that it is made in cold-cast bronze, ie a fine bronze powder mixed with resin. The reason for the light weight is that only a thin layer of the resin bronze mix is used for the surface, the remainder being filled with a less expensive (and weighty) mix.

Let us return to the Bugatti wheel, and in particular, part A, Fig 5. To cast this in cold-cast aluminium it will first be necessary to make a mould from one of the completed parts just made. To do this, first set the part or pattern into a base of modelling clay that has been rolled out flat to a thickness of about $\frac{1}{4}$ in (6.00 mm) and of a size to provide a border all round of about $\frac{3}{4}$ in (19.00 mm). Make a ring of thick card $1\frac{1}{2}$ in (38 mm) larger in diameter than the wheel part to be cast and press this into the modelling clay, providing a wall height of not less than 1 in (25 mm). Take something that is smooth and rounded and make three or four slight depressions in the modelling clay half-way between the card wall and the wheel pattern, and not too equally spaced round the pattern. These are to provide a key so that the two parts of the finished mould will fit together exactly. If the depressions are spaced slightly out of true, it will be much easier to see how the parts fit together.

The mould is made from silicone rubber, the same as that used to produce the tyres. This is now mixed and poured over the pattern, making sure not to leave any air bubbles in contact with it. If a small paint brush is used to manipulate the rubber in, around, and over the pattern during pouring, this will help to eliminate the problem. When this is set, the modelling clay is removed from the underside of the pattern and another card wall of similar size is provided so that the second half of the mould can be cast. A little wax or petroleum jelly applied to the surface of the first half of the mould will prevent the new rubber from sticking to it. When this is set, the two half moulds are separated and the original wheel pattern removed. A stiff mix of aluminium-filled resin and catalyst is now worked into every crevice of each of the two half moulds, after which these are filled to their top edge. The resin mix should be sufficiently thick not to immediately run out of the half mould when it is turned over, for as soon as both parts are full, they should be put together and allowed to set.

When the resin mix has hardened, the part can be removed from the rubber mould. It should be borne in mind, however, that although the catalyst will set the resin quite quickly to an apparently solid state, the resin will in fact continue hardening for several hours depending on the temperature of the room. Because of this the parts are best left to stand for a day before working on them. A pattern of this part produced for this process should be finished complete and polished, except that the spokes (or turbine blades) should be left slightly long so that the individual cast parts can be turned down to the finished edge. This also is true for a pattern made for investment casting, but in addition this should be made oversize on all dimensions by about 4 per cent, because there is always an element of shrinkage at the wax stage.

The outer rim ('B' in Fig 5) and the centre portion ('C') were turned down from aluminium, the former from a large-diameter thick-walled tube, and the latter from solid bar. In Plate 49 we see the set-up for drilling the 32 bolt holes that are a feature of this wheel. Because the outer rim is very thin and quite fragile, the small jaws of the holding chuck would tend

Plate 49

to distort it. To overcome this, I turned up in brass a ring of equal thickness to the rim and of a diameter that will just slip into it. This has a groove formed in the outside diameter that will accommodate a ring of wire. I use nickel silver wire because it is quite hard and will retain its shape. The brass ring is now cut into three almost equal parts, the wire being slipped into position in the groove to hold them together. With this device inside the rim, and the jaws of the holding chuck inside this, it will be seen that the pressure necessary to hold the rim is much more evenly distributed around the diameter and distortion is kept to a minimum. The whole assembly is mounted on a dividing head to facilitate the equal distribution of the 32 holes around the diameter of the outside face.

The inside diameter of the rim was bored out to the same diameter as that used for turning the outside of the spokes, so that with a little pressure, the former can be pressed over the latter. The centre portion, 'C', of the wheel is slightly domed on the outside and provided with a diameter behind this that will be a press fit into the middle of part 'A'. The centre is provided with a drilled and threaded hole to match the stub axle, as mentioned before. Parts 'B' and 'C' are given a very fine sanded finish (dull shine), while part 'A' is painted with a good quality aluminium paint. While the assembly of the three parts is made by pressing one into another, they can be secured permanently after all work is completed by judiciously applying spots of cyano-acrylate (instant) glue to contact points at the back of each wheel where the glue will not be visible.

The last item here is the hub cap ('D' Fig 5) which in life size does not really exist as such. I have combined a number of separate items for my own convenience in such a way that they serve my purpose for locking each of the wheels in place and yet still look correct. An added advantage is that we have eight small individual components per cap, all of which need to be chrome plated. To be able to handle these as a single item will save considerable work at a later stage.

On the full-size wheel, we have in the centre a cup, sometimes painted black, but in our case with a plated finish. This is, in fact, a cover for the end of the stub axle. The wheel is held in place by eight bolts that pass through a plated steel ring, then the aluminium wheel, and into a large flange on the inside that is part of the wheel bearing case. In the model I turned the cup, the ring and the threaded section (for screwing into the end of the stub axle) from a single piece of brass bar. This was then mounted in the dividing head and drilled to take the ends of the dummy bolts, these having been turned on the lathe with short stubs where the threads would be. The stubs are pushed into holes in the ring, silver soldered in place, and the surplus filed flush with the back of the ring. With the wheel threaded on to the outside thread of the stub axle, and the newly formed hub cap threaded on to its inner thread, as previously explained, the individual wheels are held secure.

We have now mentioned bolts twice, with regard to the wheel rim and the wheel locking cap. As will be obvious, bolts form a major characteristic of engineered structures, their distinctive feature being the hexagonal head. This presents one of those recurring niggly problems that can be overcome with a simple quick answer. In full-size practice, this is a job for the milling machine, a dividing head and a pair of rotary cutters separated by a distance piece equal in width to the across flat size of the hexagon being formed. The bolt head is passed three times under this cutter assembly to receive its three precisely placed pairs of flats. This, of course, is one solution, but I would suggest it is used as a method only as a last resort with regard to our immediate needs.

The obvious answer would be to purchase a series of bolts with the hexagon sizes required; these, however, are not available in a range of the small sizes needed, neither is hexagon bar material available from which to make them. I employ two solutions that answer all my needs. The first method can be used for bolts with a diameter up to about 0.09 in (2.286 mm) and requires the use of two pairs of pliers, both of which should have smooth inner jaws. One pair is the size of the bottom centre example in Plate 24, while the second is a size larger. The would-be hexagon which could start life as a $\frac{1}{32}$ in (0.81 mm) round head rivet, or a turned engine spark plug, will have as a minimum, a diameter (from which to form the hexagon) and a smaller diameter of some length that would form the threaded portion.

To form a hexagon, hold the piece in the jaws of the small pliers by the lesser diameter, take the larger diameter in the jaws of the more powerful pliers and squeeze gently. Repeat the operation twice more at equally spaced positions around the head. With a little practice, near-perfect hexagons can be formed on the heads of all but the largest bolts.

Plate 50

Incidentally, the ring of bolts around the Bugatti wheel rims are square headed, not hexagonal, as are some on the engine, but these can be made in the same way by making four flats in place of the six.

The second method, which I use for larger diameters or where a longer length of hexagon is required, is to place the part in the three-jaw lathe chuck. With the machine switched off, hold the chuck with the left hand and one of the three jaws uppermost. With a flat file in the right hand make a small horizontal flat across the top of the workpiece. Twist the chuck around one sixth of a turn so that the next jaw is in the lowest position, and make a second flat across the top of the workpiece with the file. Repeat one jaw up and then one jaw down until all six flats have been made. As with the previous method, practice will make perfect.

Plate 51 illustrates the detailing of the tyre pattern which is used to make the two part mould in which the rubber tyres are made. As this aspect of our work is covered in detail in *The Complete Car Modeller*, I propose to discuss it here somewhat briefly. The aim of the exercise is to produce a fully detailed tyre in rubber, in this case a cold-setting silicone rubber. To do this we need a rigid mould in which to cast the tyre. The foremost problem with this is that to produce a detailed tread pattern, the bottom of the pattern groove is of necessity of a smaller diameter than the full outside diameter of the tyre. This is called an 'undercut', which can, without flexibility in one part, prevent its being removed from the mould.

To produce the mould, we need a master pattern that will incorporate all of the detail required in the finished tyre. This needs to be made from a hard material since it requires several machining operations (Plate 51). From this is made a flexible mould (centre top, Plate 52) into which is cast a flexible tyre pattern (top right in same photo). These, together with the tyre, are made in silicone rubber. At the bottom of this Plate can be seen the two half moulds formed in polyester resin around the flexible tyre pattern. In Plate 53 we have the completed moulds with a newly moulded tyre *in situ* on the right, together with a complete Bugatti wheel and tyre at the bottom.

The method of making the wheel is called fabrication (the building of a completed structure from simple elements) and it is the method used to build all

Plate 51

Plate 52

Plate 53

parts of the model. In Plate 54 we see the start of the chassis frame. At the top is the pattern taken directly from the scale plans. In fact, the pattern is cut from the plans and pasted on to a strip of sheet aluminium (or stiff card) which is then cut back to just remove the outside line of the frame drawing and $\frac{1}{32}$ in (0.78 mm) holes are drilled through at all the points

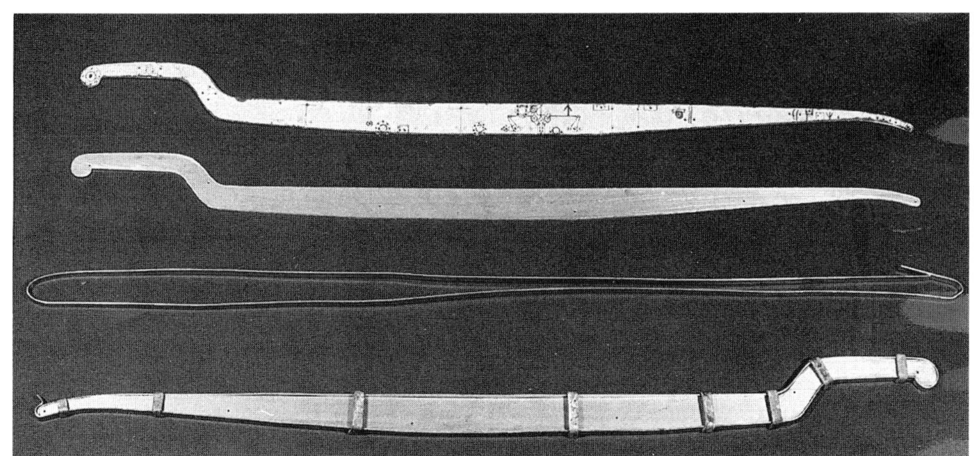

Plate 54

indicating a bolt or rivet. It is then placed over a strip of $\frac{1}{16}$ in (1.57 mm) thick brass sheet, and several of the holes are taken through this also. Only about five or six holes need to be drilled through the brass at this time, for location purposes; put one at each end, with the remainder about equally spaced along the length. If a rivet or piece of wire is placed into the first and second hole during the drilling process, it will assist in locating them all with precision, one with another, which is most important. With the holes drilled and the pins still in place, a scriber is used to mark a line around the edge of the pattern on to the brass. Two brass strips should be marked out and drilled, making sure that when they are placed together, the scribed line appears on the outer sides. The two brass strips can now be held together by placing short lengths of wire through the five or so holes, and lightly hammering the ends over so they are flush with the outside. The operative word is lightly, for the fixing together of these two frame sides is only needed for the shaping process, after which you will need to separate them. The cutting back to the scribed line can be done with a hacksaw for the rough work and various files for the final shaping. As with the pattern, cut back to just remove the marked line so that when the pieces are finished and placed on the scale plans, they appear slightly smaller than the drawing.

A strip of brass of approximately 0.012 in (0.30 mm) thickness and of a width equal to that shown on the plans, is now passed around the edge of the frame sides and bent to conform to their shape, with the two ends coming together at the front end of the frame. Two of these are made and then, with the side-members separated, they are each fitted and held in place with scrap brass strip formed into U-shaped clips ready for silver soldering to form the chassis frame side-members. This last stage is illustrated at the bottom of Plate 54. Before silver soldering, paint flux over both sides of each piece and start heating with a broad flame from the rear end, working forward. As the flux indicates the soldering temperature, remove a clip and apply the silver solder to that part, working forward as you go. In this way, the expansion of the various parts will be taken care of. With all the clips removed and the parts soldered together for their full length, you can reheat and make any adjustments that are necessary. The aim is to form two U-section chassis rails which are a mirror-image of each other with the open side of each rail towards the centre of the car on the finished model. If there are any lugs indicated on the plans, such as the six used on this Bugatti for mounting the engine, then they should be cut out now and silver soldered into place. Cut these larger than indicated, and shape back with files after they are in place.

The two side-frames can now be pickled to remove the flux and then cleaned up with files to their finished size. It should be found that the allowances made by removing the outside line of the frame pattern and the scribed line on the frame side plates will now have been made up by the brass strips forming the U-section.

All the cross-members can now be made up from brass section as indicated by the plans, together with their mounting pieces, which should be apparent from the photographs. Note the rivet or bolt arrangements on the outside of the frame where it is known that a cross-member meets with it, and design a fixing to conform with this. In all probability, the arrangement will turn out to be the same as the original, even if viewing it full-size was not possible.

In Plates 55 and 56, we see the assembly of the chassis cross-members to the side-members with the aid of the carbon-rod soldering tool and a reel of cored soft solder. First, the cross-member mounting plates and brackets will be riveted in place, the holes in the side frames having previously been drilled according to the side frame pattern. Note that in Plate 56 the

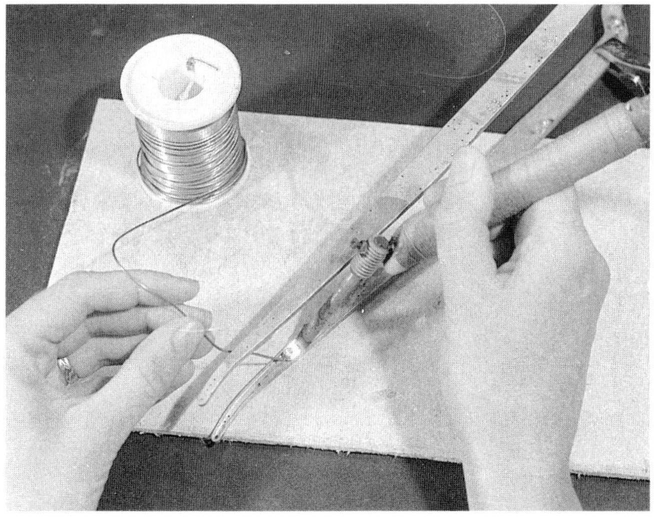

Plate 55

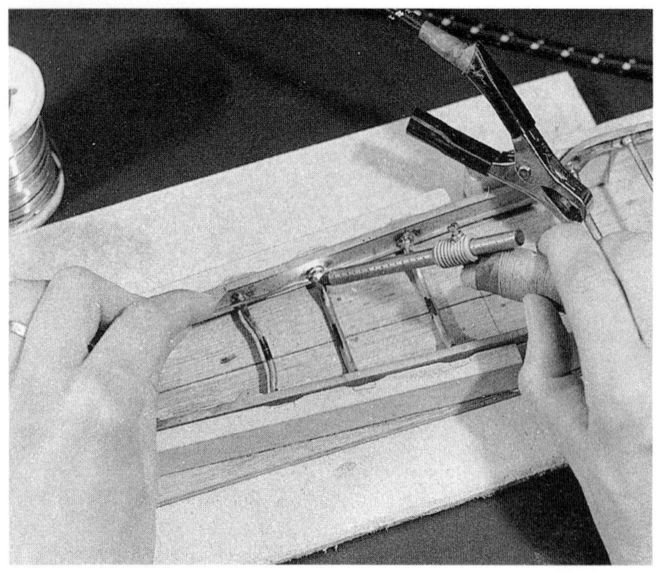

Plate 56

chassis frame is being assembled in a simple wooden jig. This consists of a rectangle of thin plywood with two strips of hard wood tacked and glued to it to correspond with the overall outside dimensions and angles of the two side members. The more accuracy that is put into the making of this, the more accurate the chassis frame will be. This is most important for the correct placing of the later fittings, particularly with regard to the body and fenders. The body will be made around a squared hardwood block, and it can be most frustrating to find that when the body is fitted to the chassis, it will not fit because of some slight inaccuracy in lining up the two sides at this stage. Bear in mind that by the time we get to the bodywork, all the chassis and fitting will be complete.

Plate 57 illustrates the complete chassis frame together with a second set of cross-members and the form tools or dies that produced the various bent parts. With shaped parts, it will often be found to be much simpler to make an opposite shape as a pattern, and then make the actual piece match this. For example, one could bend a brass tube to look like the shape indicated on the drawing, but one would have

Plate 58

no way of knowing whether the shape on one half exactly matched that of the other. By cutting out a small template (in card or thin sheet aluminium) to match exactly half of the shape, one can use this to mark out both sides (of a centre line) on a second template to be certain that the form is correct. One can then either bend the cross-member to match this precisely, or use it to mark out a pair of press tools between which the cross-member is formed.

An example of the template is shown at the bottom left of Plate 57, and the press tools are shown in the centre. This I have made double-sided and is shown with the top plate removed at the far right. The centre part is made to match the outside shape of the clutch housing supports (left side) of which two are required, and the cross-members that pass immediately in front of and behind the engine. Although all of these are different lengths, the two pairs do have the same form.

With the frame complete, we move to the classic Bugatti front axle (Plates 58 & 59). Because of its unusual form this front axle does not immediately suggest a ready means of construction, bearing in mind the facilities afforded by the lathe and milling machines. Bugatti apparently worked the whole piece from a single steel tube, a very time consuming task for a very highly skilled forge master. For our size of operation, we could fabricate it from five basic pieces, ie three round-section pieces for the axle and two blocks to accommodate the front springs. This approach would, however, present some problems in locating and holding the parts together for silver soldering.

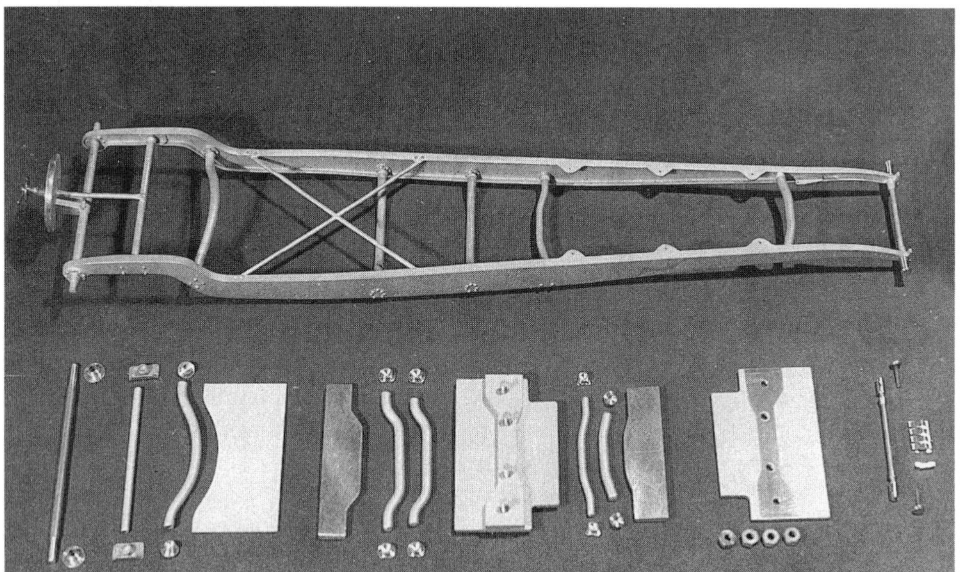

Plate 57

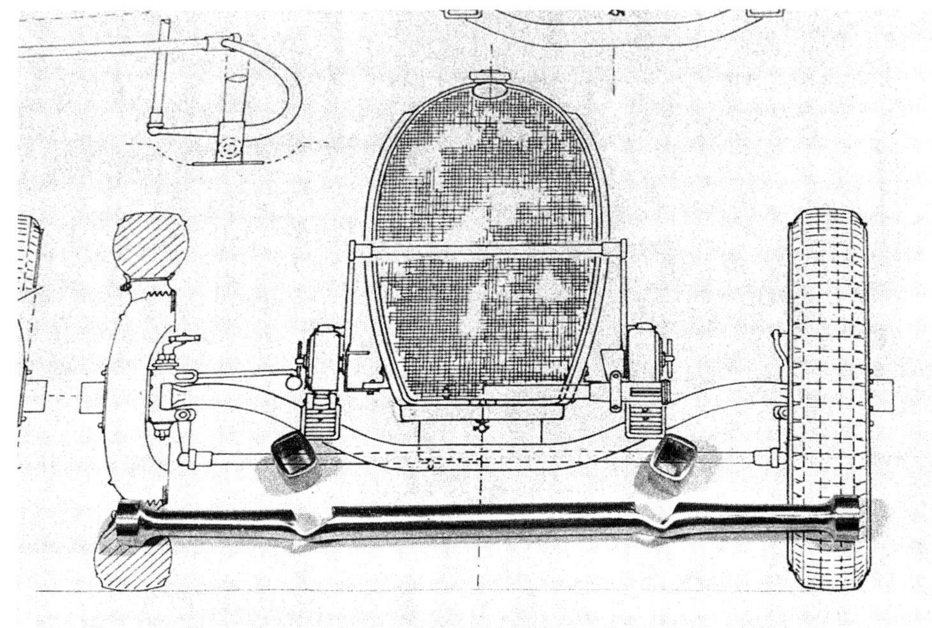

Plate 59

As will be seen in Plate 58, I turned all three portions of the axle as a single piece, with sufficient metal left in place at the location of the spring blocks to allow a slot to be milled through at an angle to accommodate them (Plate 59). The two blocks for the springs are of round brass tube forced over a square steel former of a size equal to the dimensions of the complete spring assembly. These are silver soldered in place after which the axle is bent to match the curve of a sheet metal former similar to the ones discussed regarding the chassis frame. The stub axles and blocks to take the steering arms, etc. are built up from a number of simple shapes produced on the lathe and milling machine with the aid of pins and silver solder. I then silver soldered these to the axle because I prefer to build a static miniature, but it would be a simple matter to provide bearings and a king-pin, should one wish to produce operable steering.

The outer portions of the rear axle present few problems, being a basic fabrication of simple turned parts, as previously described. The interesting part is the large block, or casing, in the centre, which in the Bugatti Royale houses not only the back axle differential, but also the gearbox. Basically, it consists of two halves that are bolted together around the outside edge. The problem with this type of construction, and common to many engineered subjects produced originally as castings, is that the individual bolts often pass through a raised strengthening piece moulded in with the outer flange. These will be of a given size and shape that blends in with the overall shape of the casting and the size of the bolts being used, and with a top surface that is machined flat, no matter what the shape of the casting may be.

All these requirements can be most difficult to achieve without splitting the shape into several pieces. A look at Plate 62 will best illustrate this most clearly. We have here six basic pieces. The lower two form the main bulk of the casing while the top centre two form the centre flange on each side of the two halves. The remaining two are equal in thickness to the former two but are shaped back around each bolt to give the raised strengthening moulded piece mentioned earlier. Plate 60 shows the starting point with four thin plates that make up the centre portion. In this case each is about 0.045 in (1.14 mm) thick with just one being marked out and drilled directly from the scale plans. This is then used as a master pattern to drill the other three. A hole is drilled in the centre of the diameter and two others are drilled through all the pieces to provide for locating pins. The master pattern is also used to assist in marking out the two thick pieces of rectangular brass on the right, and to provide both with the three holes for locating the pins. The centre hole is now opened up with a larger thread clearance drill in this case to take a 2BA bolt of 0.185 in (4.69 mm) diameter.

Plate 60

A short piece of metal is turned, drilled and tapped 2BA on the lathe for use as a spigot to hold these two blocks together on the milling machine, to allow the surplus metal to be removed (Plate 61). The spigot holding the two blocks is mounted in a three-jaw chuck, which is bolted to the centre of the dividing head mounted on the milling table. After the initial shaping with a standard end-mill, a second cutter is used to rough down the general shape, to the

Plate 61

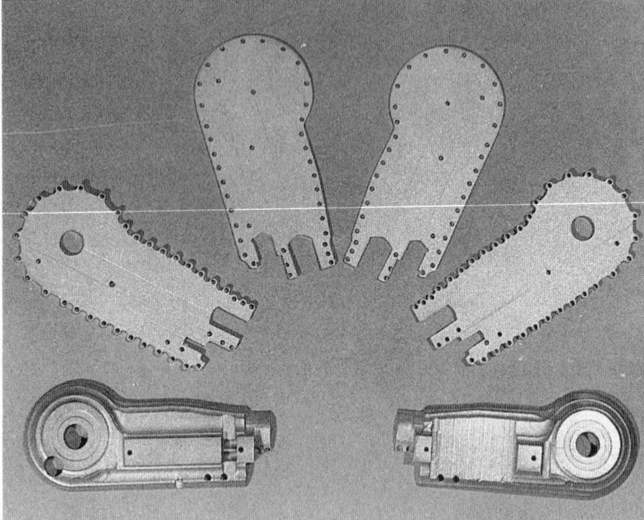

Plate 62

state shown at the bottom of Plate 62. This cutter has the corners ground off to an angle of 45 degrees. As we are working with brass and only using it as a roughing tool, this can quite easily be ground by hand on a standard tool grinder. One just needs to remember to 'back-off' behind the cutting edges as in drill grinding.

In Plate 63, we can see the two main blocks taking on their final shape. The rounding off is started with files and completed with file abrasive paper on shaped cork blocks. Most DIY stores stock thick blocks of cork up to a foot or so square. Small pieces cut from one of these, shaped to suit the work in hand, and used as a backing for various grades of abrasive paper will be found to cover most of one's needs regarding smoothing out the most complicated of shapes. Also in Plate 63 will be seen the additional fittings that make up this complicated item. These are all turned on the lathe first, then drilled and put together as far as possible before assembly with the main parts.

Although there is a cross-hole to take the rear axle through this casing, as mentioned earlier, there are also two holes at the forward end, the lower one of

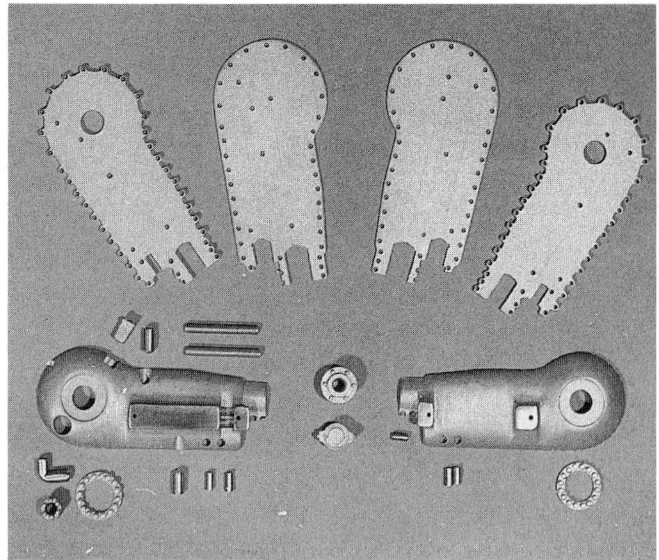

Plate 63

which is blocked off while the upper one takes the drive shaft from the clutch. To drill these, all six pieces are clamped together in a vice with locating pins in place and the assembly treated as a single block.

With all the parts made and able to fit together, these are now painted with flux and assembled to form a single casing. The assembly is then heated with a soft broad flame to silver soldering temperature, and the solder applied where necessary. Plate 64 shows the finished axle fitted between the rear wheels.

Plate 64

Springs are made up from individual strips of brass or nickel silver cut from a sheet. To determine the thickness of individual leaves, divide the thickness of the complete spring assembly by the number of leaves in it. In this case I used a strip of 0.012 in (0.3 mm) thickness for the leaves.

Plate 65 shows the method used for producing the smaller shaped sheet-metal parts. On the left are two blocks of steel shaped to the inside dimensions of the plates on the right. These are drilled out according to the plans with provision made for two bolts (far left)

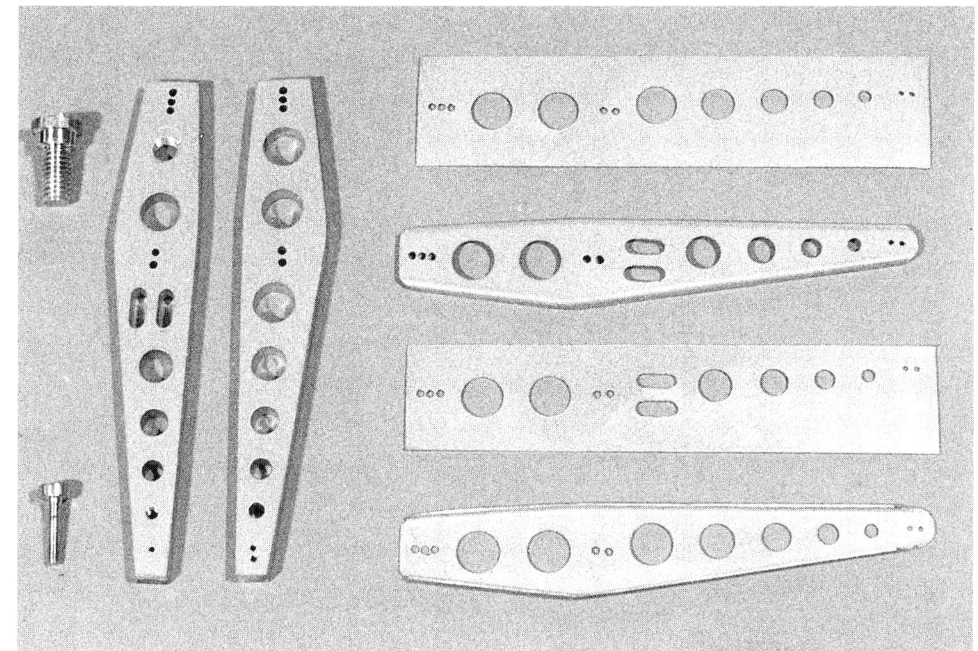
Plate 65

Plate 66

to hold the plates together. One of the steel plates is used as a drill jig to drill the series of holes in the arms on the right which, at this stage, are just rectangular pieces of sheet brass (top and third down on the right). When drilled, the pieces are bolted (one at a time) between the two steel plates, and the outside edge is worked over with a hammer to conform to the shape. After removal, the edge is cut back to the required width with snips. This method allows for a left- and right-handed piece to be made with identical shaping.

In Plate 66, we see the start of the clutch housing which consists of three pieces of brass mounted in the lathe chuck for turning. To do this safely one needs to secure the three pieces together very positively or there is a real chance of the parts separating from the chuck at high speed as soon as a tool is put to it, which would be most dangerous. To do this safely, I first machine, or otherwise provide, a smooth flat face to all the contact surfaces. These are then tinned and soft soldered together with the aid of a low flame. When all of the machining is complete, the parts can be separated by melting the soft solder again with a low flame, all trace of solder removed with a file and abrasive paper, and the parts finally assembled with silver solder. It is most important to remove all trace of the soft (lead) solder before fluxing and hard soldering, because any mixing of the two will make for a very weak joint.

The reason for turning this 2 part as a threesome will become apparent in Plate 69 where again we have a flanged joint bolting two halves of a casing together. This component being the clutch housing, the main part of the casing forms a circle enclosing the clutch, with additions, such as the starter motor and generator etc, attached to it. As with most parts, we again see work for the lathe (turning) and the mill (flats), but neither one can be undertaken with the other in place.

The first task is to determine the thickness of the four centre plates and machine a dummy piece to that thickness. A short length of round brass bar was then sawn down the centre and the two flats cleaned up and made square. These were then soft soldered to the dummy plate, one on each side and turned to size as a single block. With reheating, the dummy plate was removed, provided with four holes for locating pins, and used as a guide to mark out the shape of the four centre plates. The plates and the outer casings were all very carefully drilled to take these four locating pins to facilitate the final assembly of all six parts.

At the top, Plate 67 shows the two halves of the turned casing with the dummy section between, placed on the four centre plates for locating the outer row of bolt holes. On the far right is a rectangular block produced on the milling machine, while in the centre we have the smaller turned parts that form the various fittings. The bottom row makes up into the couplings for each end of the clutch housing.

In Plate 68, a dental burr is being used to carve a depression in the top half of the casing to take one end of the shell to which the starter motor is attached. This may be seen at the lower right of the photo. Note that one side of it has been cut away. The motor fits into this and is held in place by a large collar with two clamping bolts, as can be seen with the motor in place in Plate 69. Again this is a case of splitting

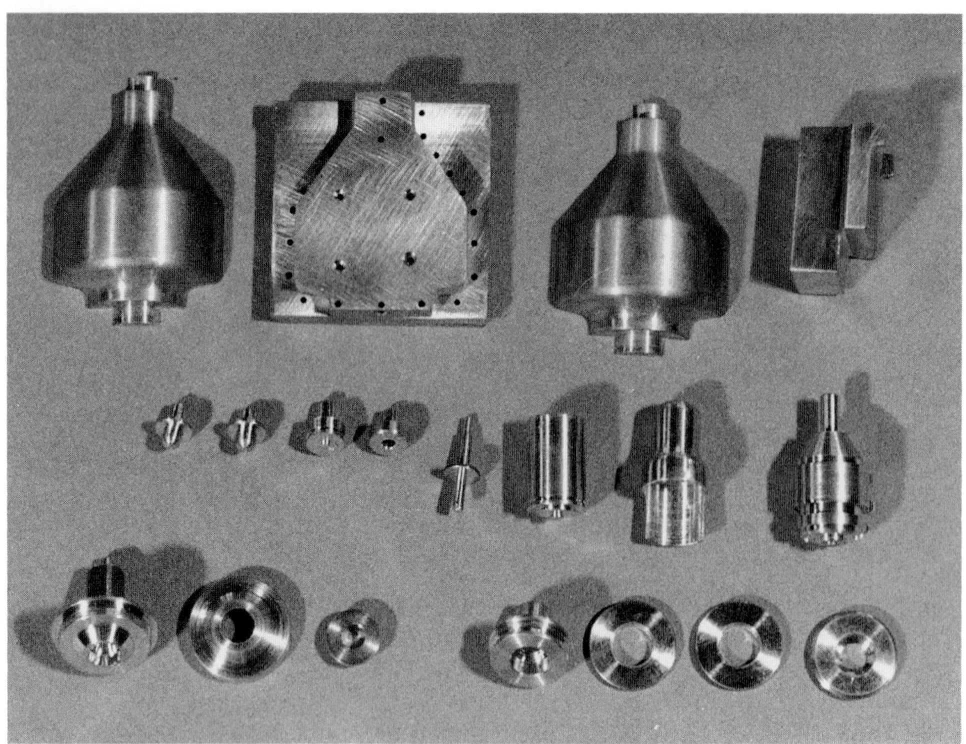

Plate 67

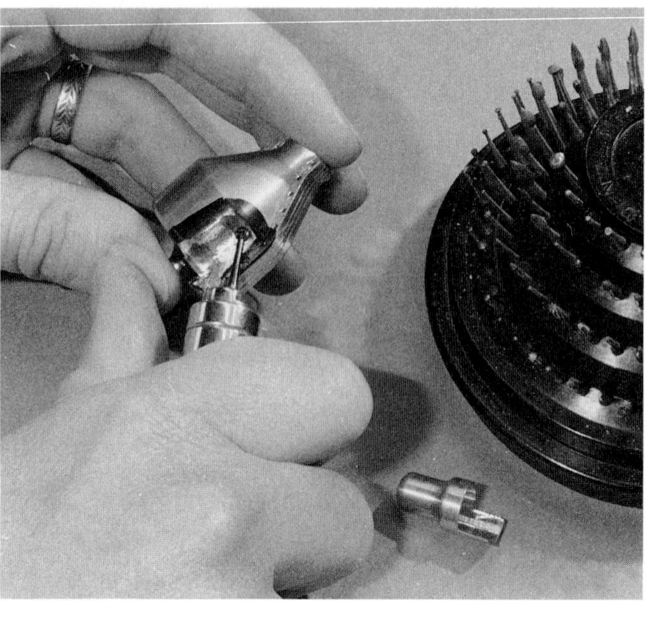

Plate 68

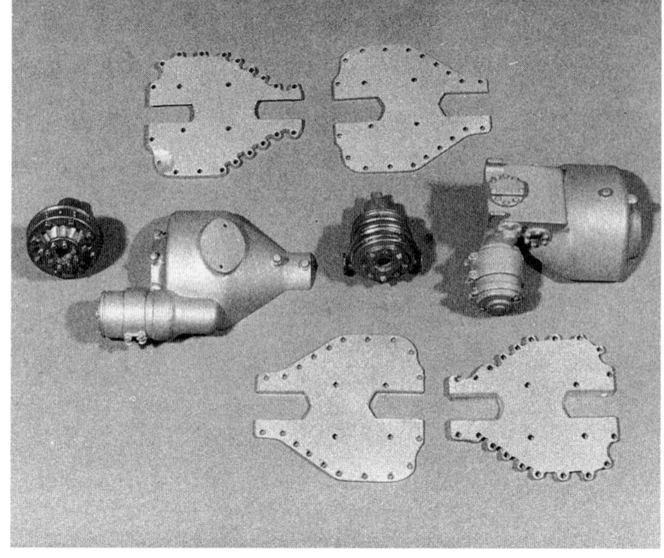

Plate 69

things down into workable pieces. If it is too complicated to make it as it is, then remove the complication and treat that as a separate part.

Plate 69 shows the top and bottom halves with most of these fittings silver soldered in place ready for the final assembly with the four centre plates. With the rear axle casing, both sides are almost identical, with a number of pieces made to pass right through from one side to the other, thus facilitating its assembly in one operation. With the clutch, the top and bottom halves have a number of detail fittings, but none are common to both, so I felt it was better to assemble the two halves separately with several dowel pins, to assure no movement when all the joints are reheated to melt temperature. It can be that in this situation, little new silver solder is needed to join all the parts together because when the assembly is fluxed and reheated, any surplus will tend to find its way to the new joint by capillary action.

The two dark items in the centre row (far left and centre), are the couplings that attach to each end of the clutch housing, made up from the row of parts at the bottom of Plate 67. The dark finish, as with that on the wheel rim bolts, is an electrolytic process that I will deal with when we discuss plating in the final stages of construction.

In Plate 70 the clutch inspection cover can be seen having the Bugatti name and monogram carved into it with a very fine dental burr; the plate has a boss formed on the reverse side so it can be held in a pin vice.

Plate 71 illustrates the completed rear and drive train including rear axle, clutch and the two large drilled plates from Plate 65 with the drive shaft between.

Plate 70

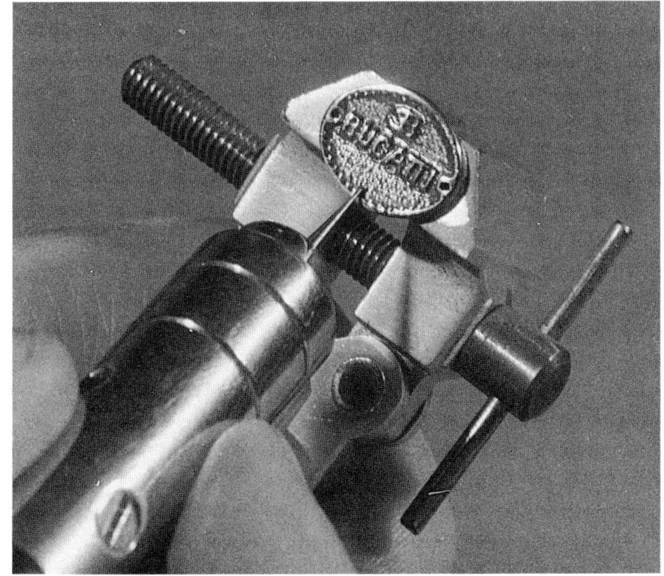

Plate 71

Plate 72

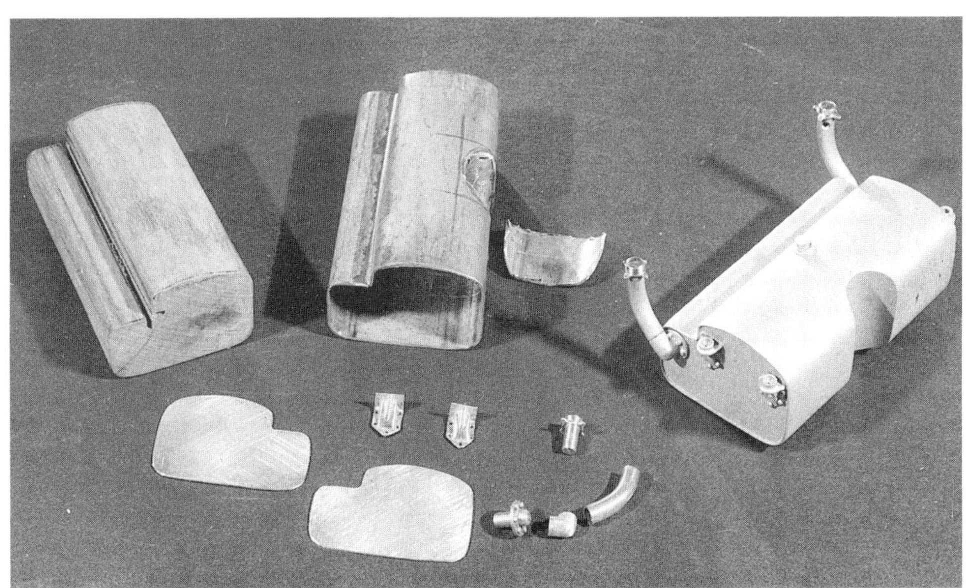

Now for something completely different. Plate 72 shows the individual parts that make up the fuel tank. We again make use of a pattern because it is much simpler to work a shape from a solid block to a given shape as a master, and form the pieces round this, rather than create the shape from a number of pieces using the plans directly. The material for the tank is 0.012 inches (0.30 mm) thick brass sheet, so allowance needs to be made for this when determining the dimensions of the hardwood master pattern, top left Plate 72. The pattern block is placed end on to a small rectangle of brass sheet and a line scribed around it. Two tank ends are marked out, thus, and cut to match exactly the end shape of the block. For the main part of the tank, a strip of suitable width and length is wrapped around the pattern block starting at the sharpest edge and trimmed to length so as to return exactly to the starting point. It will be found that the brass sheet will have a certain amount of spring in it and will not want to fit to the pattern shape. Remove it from the block and manipulate it with your fingers until it exactly conforms to the pattern shape, and the two edges will hold themselves together without assistance. Remove from the hardwood block, flux and silver solder these together, heating all of the brass sheet to anneal it at the same time. Now pickle this to remove the flux, clean up with abrasive paper and reshape to the pattern block.

It will be noted that there is a shaped section to the front of the tank that accommodates the rear of the axle casing with some clearance. This piece now needs to be removed. The operation can be done with the pattern block inside the tank shell, roughing out the unwanted metal with a small hacksaw or cutter disc and flexible drive. Remove the block and clean up with a suitable half-round file, then bend a strip of the same brass sheet to match the shape of the cut-out, and silver solder in place. If you use a small flame this time, and localise the heat to this side of the tank, you can silver solder this in place without disturbing the previous joint. Remember that it does take a slightly higher temperature to remelt the old solder than to melt a new one.

Again, clean up after pickling, then gently press in one of the end plates, flux and silver solder it in place, and then do the same for the other side. If you have made these exactly match the end profile of the pattern block, they should be a sufficiently tight fit in the tank itself to hold in place while the solder runs.

The remaining brackets and pipes, etc. are all attached with $\frac{1}{32}$ in (0.78 mm) rivets and held in place with soft solder, the heat being applied with the carbon rod or electric soldering iron.

Plate 73 shows some of the stages required to form the battery box. This was 'chemically milled', the new name for what used to be called etching. Since the introduction of the silicon chip and the PC board, this process has now become very specialised and precise. Most tool and parts catalogues catering for DIY electronics and the Hi-Fi market can be expected to list products that will assist a model maker to get involved in this most useful process. For those not familiar with its possibilities, the process enables a design drawn on paper to be directly transferred to sheet metal, either in relief, or as a pierced (cut through) design, without the use of conventional engineering-style cutting tools. It is one of those processes that is limited only by the imagination of the user.

In its most sophisticated form, one can produce a detailed plan view of the design required to be 'cut' in sheet metal, perhaps ten or one hundred times the finished size. This is then photographed with a special camera to produce a negative image on a transparent film at the exact size needed. Two identical negatives are produced and mounted in such a way that the image registers exactly one with the other when a sheet of metal is placed between them. The sheet of metal to receive the design is first treated with a special solution that is sensitive to ultraviolet light when dry. This is placed between the two films holding the image, and after a suitable exposure to a UV lamp, it is processed in a developing solution. This dissolves the sensitising medium on the surface that did not receive the UV light, so leaving a hardened image of the design on both sides of the sheet metal. The metal is now placed in an acid solution that will etch or dissolve the exposed metal from both sides until all that is left is the metal protected by the UV 'photo resist', as it is called. There are, of course endless variations of the process; one can etch a relief pattern on only one side, if need be, or combine the two, or etch, resensitise and etch again for stepped designs etc. There are companies available that will undertake this work for you at a price, to the design of your own artwork. As with most things, however, there is a short-cut DIY variation that can be made to work at a

Plate 73

fraction of the cost, given a little practice and perseverance. This involves a visit to your local photocopier, now located in increasing numbers in most small towns. Although these are known for copying the odd letter or receipt on to plain white paper, they do have a facility for copying a drawing on to a special heat-resistant clear acetate film. While the carbon deposit that forms the image with these machines is absorbed by the paper during the process, when applied to the clear acetate it stays as a hardened deposit on the surface. It will be found that with a little practise and the assistance of a quite hot domestic electric iron applied to the back of the acetate, the image can successfully be transferred to the cleaned surface of a sheet of brass or other metal. Such is the bond of the carbon image to the metal with this application of heat, that it will act in the same way as a photo-resist in the etching solution. Now with many of the newer photocopy machines that can enlarge, and of particular use here, reduce, the size of an image during copying, we have the makings of a very useful and inexpensive system.

In this process we are to produce the design as a positive image up to twice the finished size. The reason for working in the larger size and then reducing it is that it allows for much finer detailing. The image should be a dense black on white, filling in all the areas that you wish to retain, and leaving clear (white) those areas that you wish to be etched. In the case of the Bugatti battery box, the plan drawing was set out in the normal way, then the framework was blacked in, as was an area outside this, leaving a $\frac{1}{16}$ in (1.57 mm) clear border, broken only by several $\frac{1}{32}$ in (0.78 mm) wide strips. These little strips retain the piece within the sheet after etching which saves the problem of having lost pieces.

In the two film copies that were produced from the original box drawing, those lines around the centre bottom of the box were allowed to remain on only one, the other having been blacked over. Thus, while providing for the rectangles and triangles to be etched from both sides, these four lines would be etched only half-way through, from one side, greatly assisting in the folding of the finished box.

One other item that can usefully be obtained from the electronic tool and parts catalogue is a photo-resist pen. After the acetate film copies have been made at your local photocopier, and these have been transferred to the sheet brass with a hot iron, the photo-resist pen can be used to touch up any parts that show a need for it. Only etch those parts that you need to have removed or detailed; this will prolong the life of the etching solution.

For brass, the battery box is made from 0.012 in (0.30 mm) thick sheet, and the solution is made up of ferric chloride crystals and water; for details follow the manufacturer's instructions. This will also etch copper and nickel silver. The etch solution is best used in a plastic dish at a slightly warm temperature. Anyone selling photographic equipment can supply a range of sizes of suitable dishes at a modest price. Pick a size to suit your work and another half as big again. Place the etching solution in the small one and standing it in the larger one which is kept topped up with hot water. This will suffice to keep the etch solution at a reasonable temperature. Etching occurs more quickly in a warm solution, but will slow down noticeably as the solution becomes contaminated by the metal being etched.

If one is attempting to etch from both sides, then the correct register of the two master films is most important if the etching is to take place in exactly the same place on both sides. Make the acetate films as large as possible and tape them together on two edges with adhesive tape, one directly over the other, making sure the carbon image (the dull side) is on the inside of both sheets. Use a substantially larger piece of sheet metal than will be finally needed and place a narrow strip of double sided tape along one edge on both sides, well away from where the image is to be transferred. Insert the sheet metal between the two sheets of acetate and press firmly together so that all are bonded as one. A hot iron worked over this with great care will stick the film to the metal surface as it melts the carbon deposit of the image. After working over both sides thoroughly and with the assembly still warm, it will be found to be but a simple matter to peel off the film from each side leaving the carbon image deposited on the metal surface.

In Plate 73 we have at the top left a sheet of brass that has been almost completely etched through from both sides, and in which the holes are starting to appear in the corners. At the bottom right we see the framework being bent to shape, together with a block of hard wood equal to the inside dimensions of the box, used to facilitate the process. Top right shows the completed battery box that has now had all the joints silver soldered together.

Plate 74 illustrates a compromise solution to a very tricky problem. The brakes on the Bugatti Royale

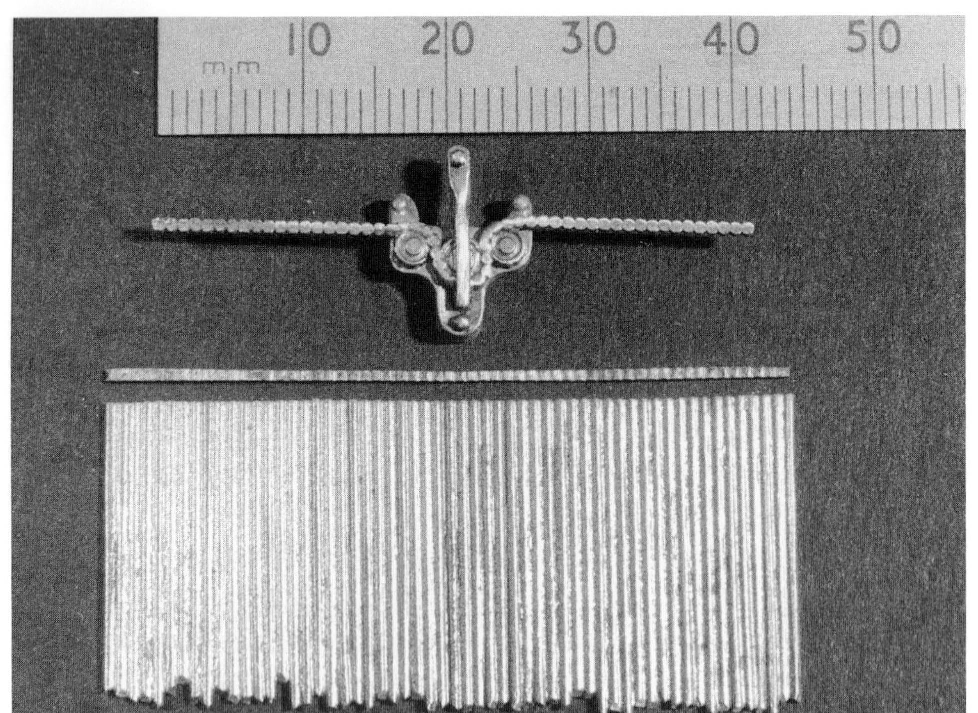

Plate 74

are cable operated, but where the cables change direction and one would expect to see grooved pullies, the Bugatti solution was to substitute short lengths of roller type chain and gear sprockets. As can be seen, in a scale of 1/15 these are very small indeed. If they were ignored altogether, however, the omission would be very noticeable. Rather than attempt to make the individual rollers and the necessary connecting links, I silver soldered together a number of lengths of nickel silver wire and then took a thin slice from the block so formed to simulate the side-on view of the chain. Geared sprockets were made on the lathe and mill; when assembled these then had the simulated chain wrapped around them and the whole assembly mounted on a fire brick specially carved out to take it. When fluxed and subjected to the flame sufficient to remelt the hard solder, the parts reformed as a single piece. On the full-size car a sprocket assembly fits on the inside of the chassis frame, there being one on each side. An arm from the foot brake attaches to the top of a post that is fitted in a slide mechanism and which carries a sprocket. As pressure is applied to the foot brake pedal, the centre sprocket is forced down so shortening the effective length of the chain and cables fore and aft, which in turn applies the brakes at the brake drums. The method is typical of Bugatti, being simple and efficient, applying the brakes and equalising the pressure to all four brake shoes without additional mechanism.

In Plate 75, we have a number of components combined to form a single piece for the convenience of building in miniature. This consists of a chassis cross-member that carries the gear change lever as well as brackets for the hand brake, foot brake and clutch linkage. The last two, with the pedal arms, are mounted on a countershaft held forward of the cross-member on two support brackets. It can be seen that because all these controls are clustered together and numerous linkages lead from this to other fittings, ie brakes, clutch and gearbox, there is a distinct advantage in having this as a complete and fixed assembly. Another advantage is that from the restoration photographs of the Binder Bugatti Royale chassis at the Harrah's Collection, taken when that car was in pieces, this whole assembly is shown as either chrome or nickel plated. I would doubt that the original was actually chrome plated, but nickel plating for most of these fittings originally could be a possibility. On this model the complete assembly

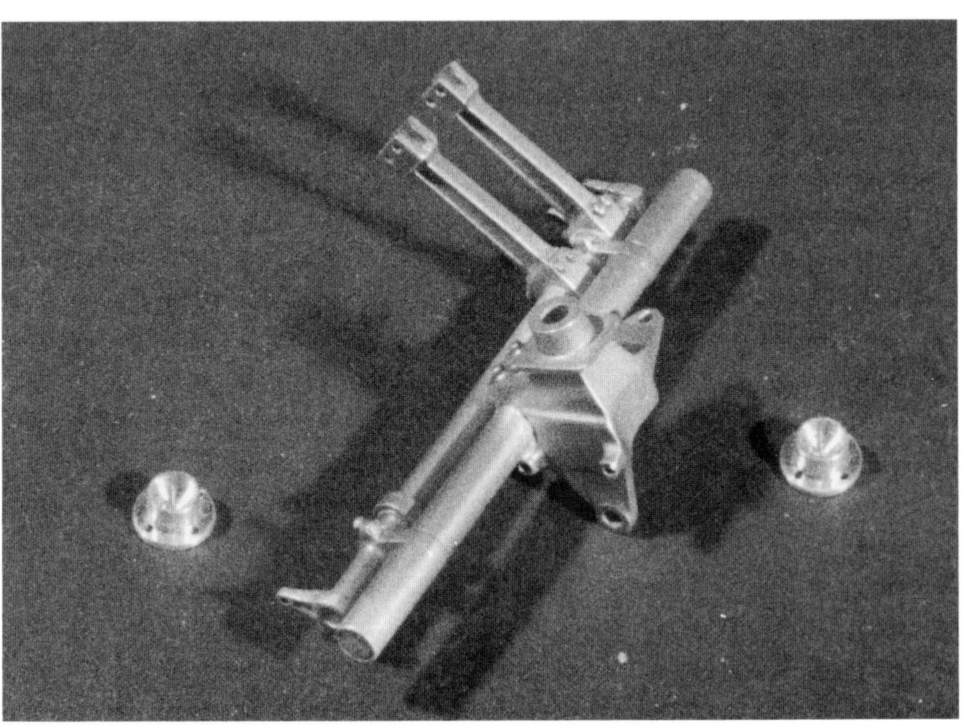
Plate 75

Plate 76

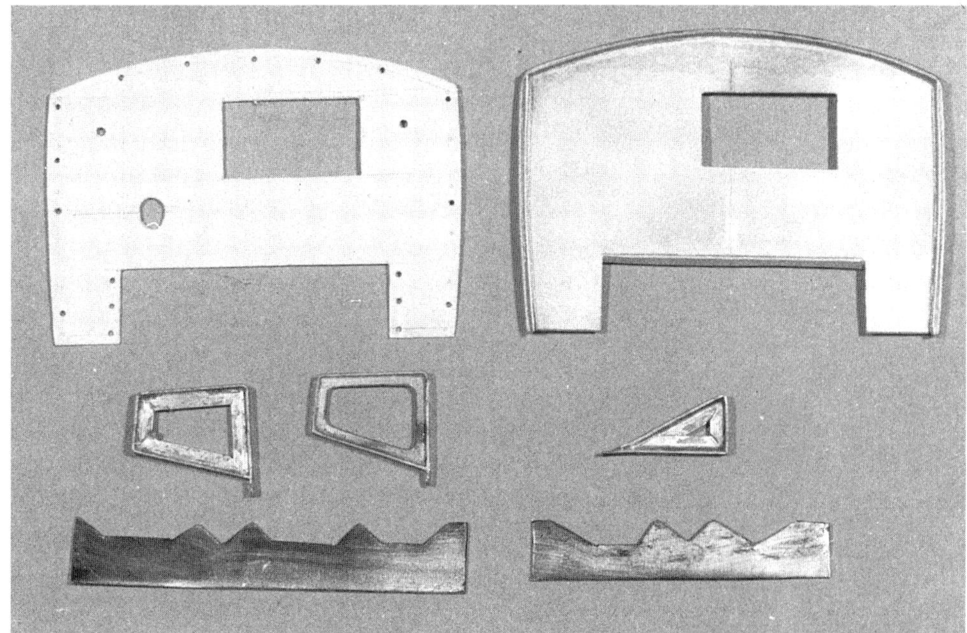

was bright nickel plated. The two pieces to the right and left of the main assembly are the flanged cups that attach the chassis cross-member to the inside frame. All the tubular cross-members are attached via these, which are fixed to the side frames with either four or six bolts or rivets depending on their size. Most are situated midway between the bottom and top flange of the chassis U-section, although these do have part of one edge removed so the cross-member can be mounted as high as possible. Similarly the cross-members that carry the clutch housing are set as low in the frame as possible.

Plate 76 illustrates the start of firewall fabrication. On the full-size car this is in part an aluminium casting with the greater part facing the engine, polished and provided with the traditional engine-turned finish. The method used to achieve this finish on the model is discussed at the beginning of the engine section. The outside beading, however, is chrome plated, a finish which is not possible, without a complicated process, to achieve on aluminium. Because the firewall requires fabrication using silver solder, it was made up from brass sheet and wire (on right) with a thin, 0.008 in (0.20 mm) sheet aluminium insert (on left) to give the required feel to the inside of the engine compartment. The two plates at the bottom are made up from scrap sheet and provide a guide to marking out and cutting the angles in the 'T'-section brass that was used to make up the dash board supports (centre left) and firewall-to-chassis frame bracket (centre right). The rectangle cut-out in the firewall accommodates a large oil tank that supplies the engine lubrication, the Royale having a dry sump engine. The actual tank sits between the firewall and the dash board and can be seen at the bottom right of Plate 77.

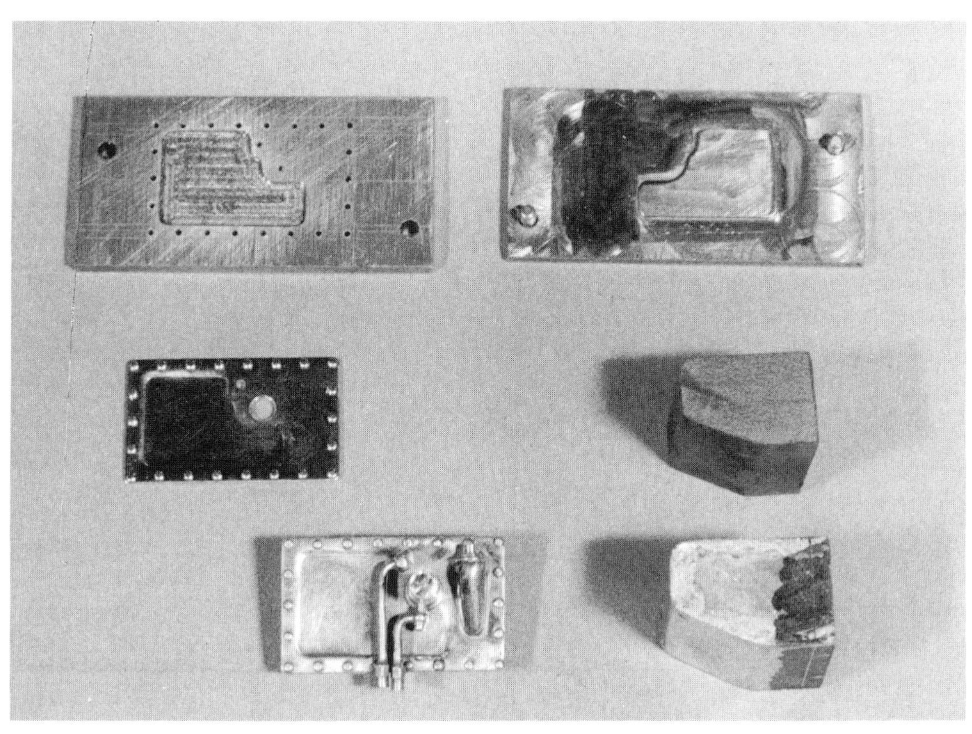

Plate 77

The front face of the oil tank is rectangular and provided with a series of bolts around its outside edge to attach it to the firewall. Inside this is a distinctively shaped recess. As this part is polished and chrome plated, we are restricted in the number of ways we can make this without creating for ourselves a considerable amount of work on its finishing. My answer was to make a pair of simple press tools or dies, shown at the top of Plate 77. I milled these from $\frac{1}{8}$ in (3.17 mm) thick steel plate, the depth of the recess being about 0.020 in (0.50 mm). Both were marked out from the plans, allowance being made for the thickness of the brass plate to be formed, and then milled with a small-diameter end-mill to provide a male and female die. Locating pins are fixed to one side that register in the holes in the other. The brass plate is placed between them and the assembly clamped tight together in a large vice to form the impression in the brass.

Another method of making this type of press tool is to mill, or otherwise machine, just one die. The one chosen would be the one producing the face of the pressed part that is most prominent, as it can be polished and provided with the most detail. A sheet of wax equal in thickness to the sheet metal to be worked is applied to its working surface. The wax sheeting can be obtained from engineering pattern makers' suppliers and some craft shops. Failing this, spray-paint a dozen or so layers of cellulose paint on to the pattern without a primer coat (so it can be chipped off later). A card box is now made that will fit the outside dimensions of the die exactly with the treated face of the die uppermost, with the box side wall extending perhaps about half an inch above this. This is now treated with a releasing agent and a casting resin is poured in to fill the box. The important requirement here is to provide sufficient thickness to the working area of the die, to give the necessary strength to prevent its cracking. Wire inserts can be incorporated in the resin die to assist in this.

I have used, quite successfully, ordinary polyester resin incorporating a large percentage of aluminium or other fine metal powder as a filler for a number of similar parts in the past. When the resin has cured fully the casting can be dismantled and the wax or paint layer removed leaving a male and a female die. The additional tank fittings, as with the steering box and arm parts to be seen in Plate 78, are all fabricated from brass stock and produced on the lathe and milling machine.

The item I wish to discuss in detail here is the steering wheel rim to be seen at the top left and centre. In the original specification for the Weinberger Bugatti Royale, this was said to have been made from ivory. It so happened that I did have in my store of odds and ends (never throw anything away, you never know when you might need it) a large victorian curtain pull (knob) made from ivory of suitable diameter. It was from this that these parts were made. A good substitute would have been a section of bone obtainable from your local butcher as the use of ivory is now undesirable for conservation reasons. It later transpired, however, that the original wheel rim was in fact made of wood, but we only learned this after two models had been produced with ivory steering wheels.

In the wood rim, eight pieces of fine-grained rosewood were cut and glued together to form a block equivalent to the ivory one shown here. The wood was cut in such a way that the four short internally projecting pieces directly in line with the spokes had the grain radiating from the centre out. For the four main sections, the wood grain followed the circumference of the wheel rim (Fig 7). Considerable time was given to ensure the accuracy of the lamination of the wood parts so that an exact centre could be determined, and so that the individual parts would be located in the correct place when the wheel rim was machined from the composite block.

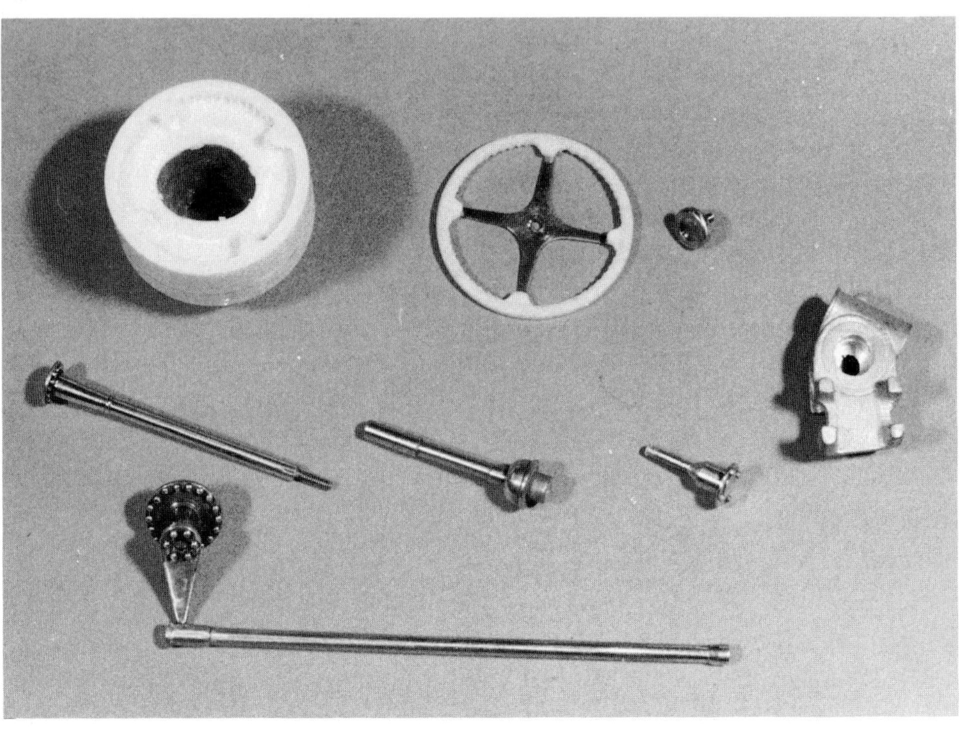

Plate 78

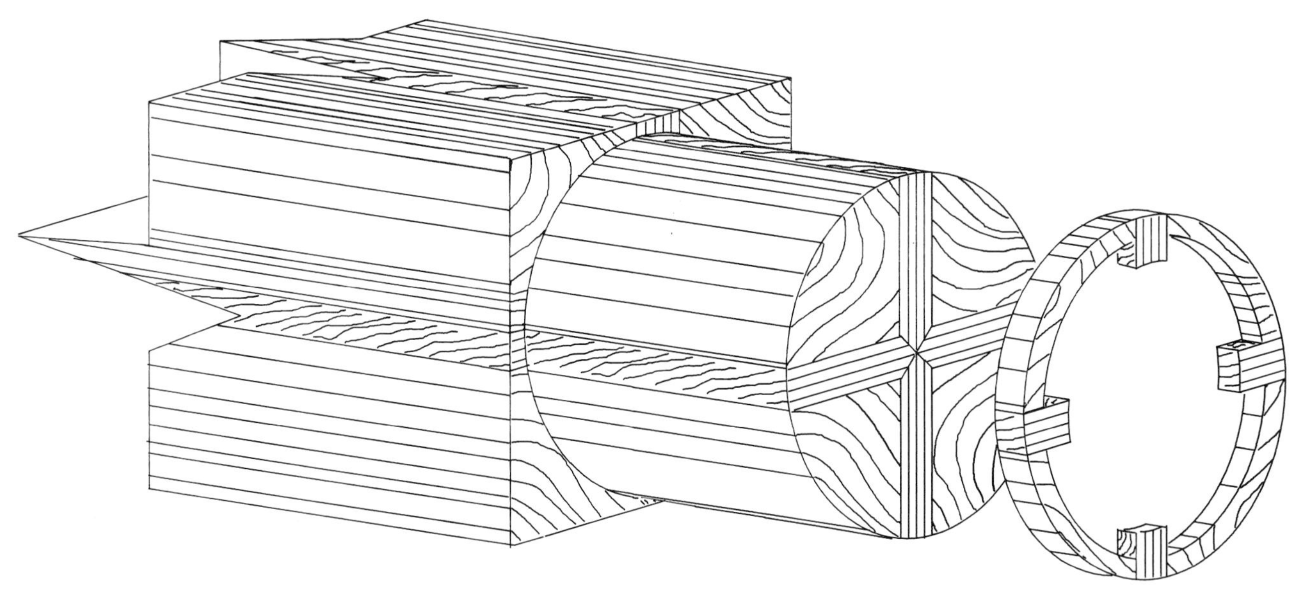

Fig. 7 A hard wood block fabricated from eight pieces resined together for turning the steering wheel rim.

The blocks, both ivory and wood, were mounted in the lathe and rough turned to almost the finished size with a smaller diameter stepped boss turned down at the rear for mounting in the chuck attached to the dividing head. The blocks were also rough bored out for the inside diameter at the same time. These were then mounted on the dividing head and milled as shown with four small lugs on the inside for fixing to the wheel spokes and the series of serrations around the inside of the wheel rim. The normal length of the small-diameter end-mill used for this is such as to allow for milling the width of two rims at one setting. Advantage should be taken of this because these items, whether in wood or ivory, are very fragile, and I broke several during the course of building the models. The spokes of the steering wheel are cut from 0.012 in (0.30 mm) brass sheet. These, after chrome plating, were glued with cyano-acrylate into a small slot cut into each of the internal lugs provided. The small abrasive slitting disc described in Part 1 and shown in Plate 26 proved ideal for this.

In Plates 79 and 80 we come to the radiator; the core in the first and the shell or casing in the second. The core of a Bugatti Type 41 radiator is made up of square tubes. This is unusual, most radiator cores being made with hexagonal cross-tubes, as is the restored one now fitted in this Royale. Starting with the core first, a piece of brass plate was selected that was slightly larger than the frontal area of the finished radiator and of $\frac{1}{8}$ in (3.175 mm) thickness. This was placed in a vice mounted on the milling table and received a number of slots across its surface, both north-south and east-west, sufficient to leave standing proud a series of squared pins equal in number to the square tubes in the radiator core, Plate 79 top left. This was accomplished with the aid of a disc-shaped milling cutter called a slotting saw that has cutting teeth around its outer edge only. Its width was originally 0.020 in (0.50 mm), but with the aid of a sharpening stone, I was able to reduce the width of each cutting tooth by half. This produced a tapered groove approximately 0.035 in (0.88 mm) deep by 0.010 in (0.25 mm) at the bottom and 0.020 in (0.50 mm) at the top. A similar pattern block can be made by hand with the aid of the groove-making sheet-metal cutting tool shown at bottom left in Plate 27.

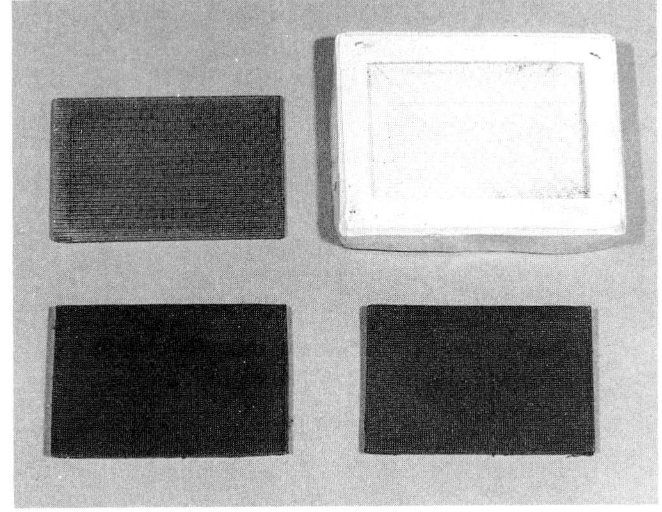

Plate 79

An epoxy resin putty type material was then used to make a mould of this by pressing it on to the machined surface, which when set, produced a most realistic pattern of minute square holes. The epoxy putty is another most useful new product readily obtainable from car repair shops and DIY suppliers. It is sold as a two colour ribbon of stiff but pliable plastic. One colour is the resin while the second is the hardener (catalyst). When twisted and kneaded together until only a single colour remains, it becomes activated and will soon 'go off'. This material will be found to have many uses in model work.

To prevent the epoxy putty from sticking to the brass pattern, I first applied a liberal coating of

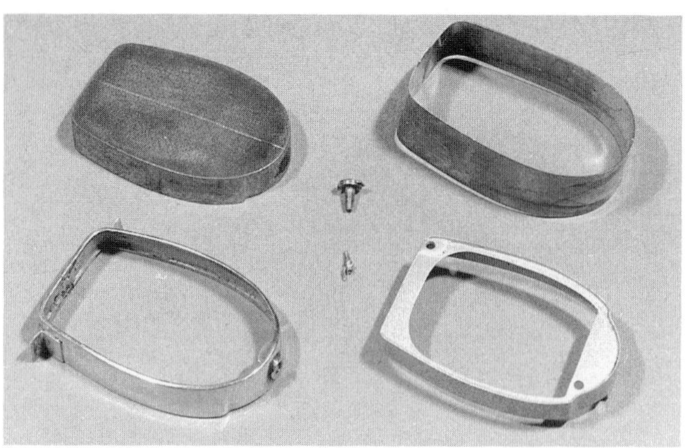

Plate 80

petroleum jelly to it before pressing the pad of epoxy into place. Two pads made from this pattern will provide the complete radiator core. If you can obtain the epoxy in black for a job of this sort, so much the better, because the final colour needs to be black. Unfortunately, I could only obtain it as a yellow and blue tape which, when mixed together, produced a bright green putty. To paint this black would only obliterate the fine detail so painstakingly achieved, so moulding it in a black material is the only answer. Polyester resin which is clear can take a dense black pigment, but it does have the tendency to stick to almost everything it comes into contact with, without the barrier of a release agent. As painting a release agent on to the pattern would again obscure the detail, I turned again to the one material that epoxy resin will not stick to, which is silicone rubber. The epoxy pad taken from the brass pattern was used to produce a silicone rubber mould, Plate 79 top right, which makes it an exact copy of the original brass master. Into this was poured a black pigmented polyester resin and catalyst mix which, when set, produced one half of the radiator core for use in the model. Because polyester resin on its own is very brittle, two layers were applied to each piece of the core while in the mould. The first application contained the black pigment, while the second, applied just as the first had started to set, contained a layer of fibreglass strands normally obtainable from the same supplier as the polyester resin. The two sides of the radiator core made in this way can be seen at the bottom of Plate 79.

The radiator shell, because it is a simple shape in this case, is made from 0.012 in, (0.30 mm) thick brass sheet. If it were more complicated than this – a Bentley or Duesenberg, for example – then copper would be used in place of brass, but the procedure would be the same. A master pattern is made from a solid block of metal. Cast iron was used here, but steel and brass would also have served. This is filed or machined to the shape and size of the radiator, less the thickness of the metal to be used (top left Plate 80). A strip of brass of ample width but of a length just sufficient to pass around the sides of the master pattern, now has its two ends silver soldered together. While being heated, care is taken to apply sufficient heat over its whole area so that it will be in an annealed state when it emerges from the pickle bath. The brass ring so formed is placed over the pattern block, and with the aid of a small hammer, (centre Plate 28) the edge that is to be the front face is forced over on to the top surface all the way round. The sides are also worked with the hammer to make them tight and true to pattern.

Because the pattern block has been made to the correct depth, this can now be used as a guide to scribe with a pointed tool around the inside of the radiator shell at the back, so that all waste can be removed with the snips. Mark out directly from the detail plans, the front face of the radiator shell to indicate the width of the flange, which in this case includes a small area at the top centre for the radiator badge. With the aid of files, the waste can be removed from this. I always soft solder a 0.020 in (0.50 mm) thick strip of brass along the inside back edge of the radiator shell, so that when the completed radiator is assembled with the bonnet, there is ample material to allow the bonnet to fit flush with the shape of the outside of the radiator. Two brackets and fittings for the radiator cap are also soft soldered in place now, as can be seen in Plate 80, bottom left. At the bottom right is the completed back of the radiator. This is made from the same brass sheet, bent and manipulated to fit exactly inside the outer shell, with a section of sheet brass cut as indicated and soft soldered just inside the outer face of this. A small 0.040 in (0.10 mm) thick strip of brass is soft soldered to the inside of the top and bottom of the rear section, so that when the two parts are put one inside the other, a hole can be drilled and tapped to take the radiator cap at the top, and a second one at the bottom can be provided for the tiny drain cock. These two items can be seen in the centre of Plate 80. With the two parts of the radiator core cut to shape and fitted inside, the radiator cap and drain cock secure the assembly together. The two external brackets are later drilled to take four small bolts, when the completed radiator is fitted to the chassis frame.

In discussing the chassis parts, I have endeavoured to pick out those items that best illustrate how the total assembly was made, because of the materials or techniques used to produce them. Although dimensioned sketches are made for all of the parts that need to be turned on the lathe, items made from sheet material can, in general, be made directly from the information in the scale plans and photographs. The one principle, though, of all this work, is that if for any reason a component is too complicated to make as you see it, then break it down into as many parts as is necessary to remove the difficulties.

PART THREE
The Engine

Shown in Fig 8 are my rough drawings for the engine blocks. The basic outside dimensions were taken directly from the scale plans with the remaining sizes being deduced. Plates 81 to 84 show the machining (milling) of the main block which I decided to split into two parts. The engine sump and crankcase of the full-size engine are also in two parts, though they are one inside the other. Like the Bugatti wheel, to manufacture the miniature in the same way as the original would require a great deal more work than is necessary, and would give no advantage in the visual aspect of the finished item.

The reason for wanting the engine to be in two pieces was so that most of the external blocks and fittings could be attached with small bolts from the inside, which could thus be hidden in the final assembly. The line of the break is where, on the full size engine, an angled bracket is attached to the side of the sump. This bracket follows the line of the underside of the chassis frame and, as we will see later, two louvred panels are attached, one on each side, between the sump and the chassis frame. When the finished engine is fitted into the completed chassis, this break is not visible. The simplest way to machine two pieces such as this, that are required to fit perfectly together on an angle, is to first mark out a

Plate 82

Plate 81

Plate 83

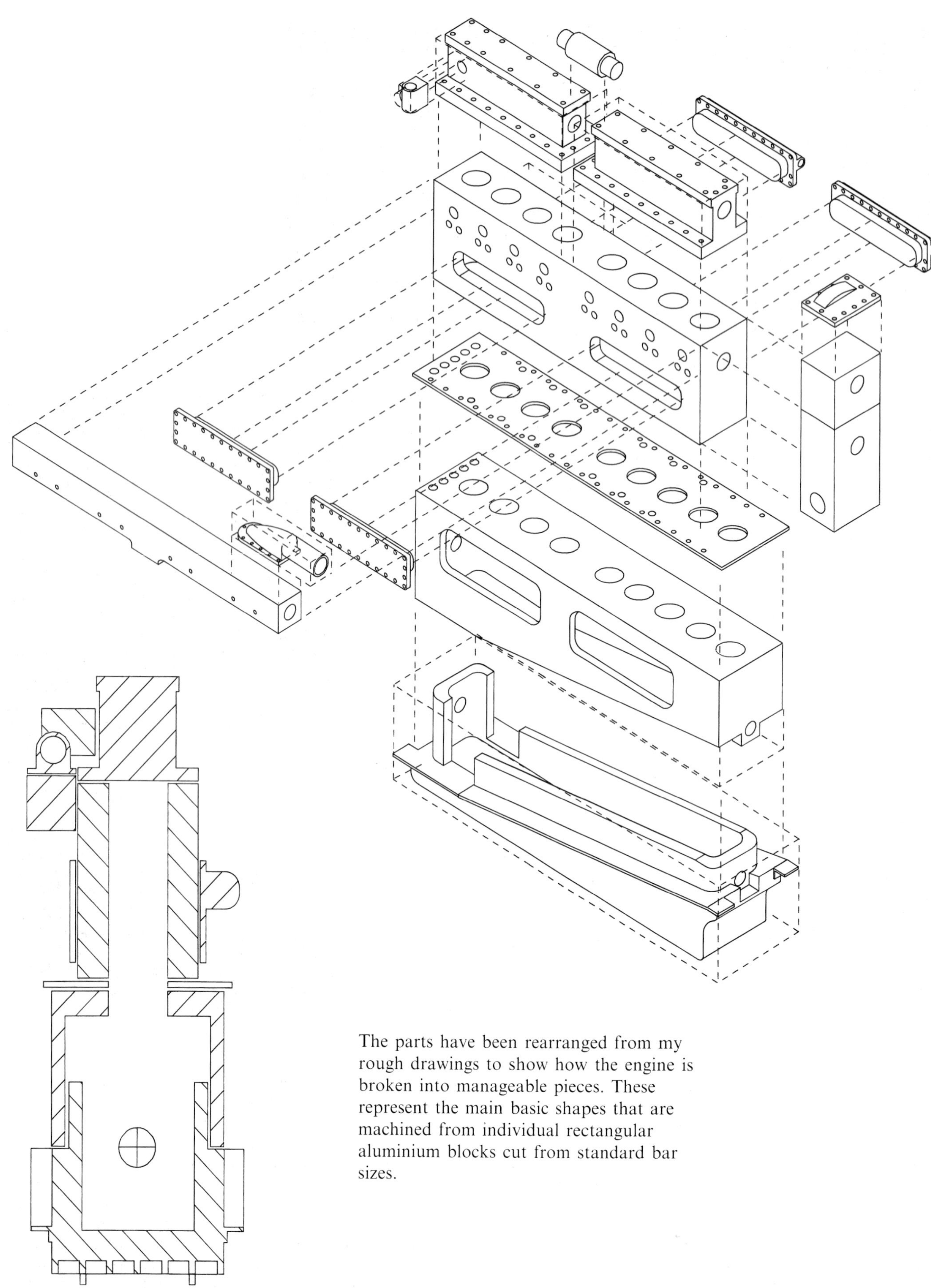

The parts have been rearranged from my rough drawings to show how the engine is broken into manageable pieces. These represent the main basic shapes that are machined from individual rectangular aluminium blocks cut from standard bar sizes.

Fig. 8 Sketches for the Type 41 Bugatti engine, with the dimensions removed so that the parts can be seen more clearly (not to scale).

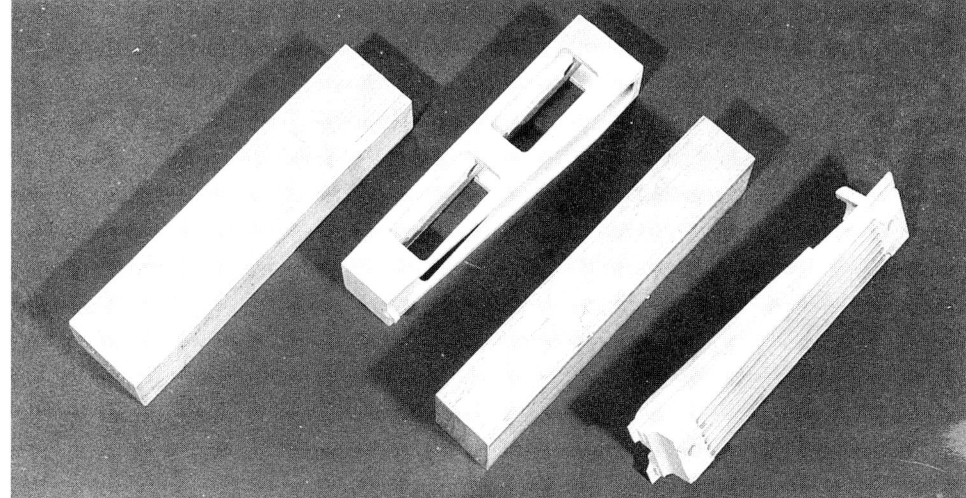

Plate 84

Plate 85

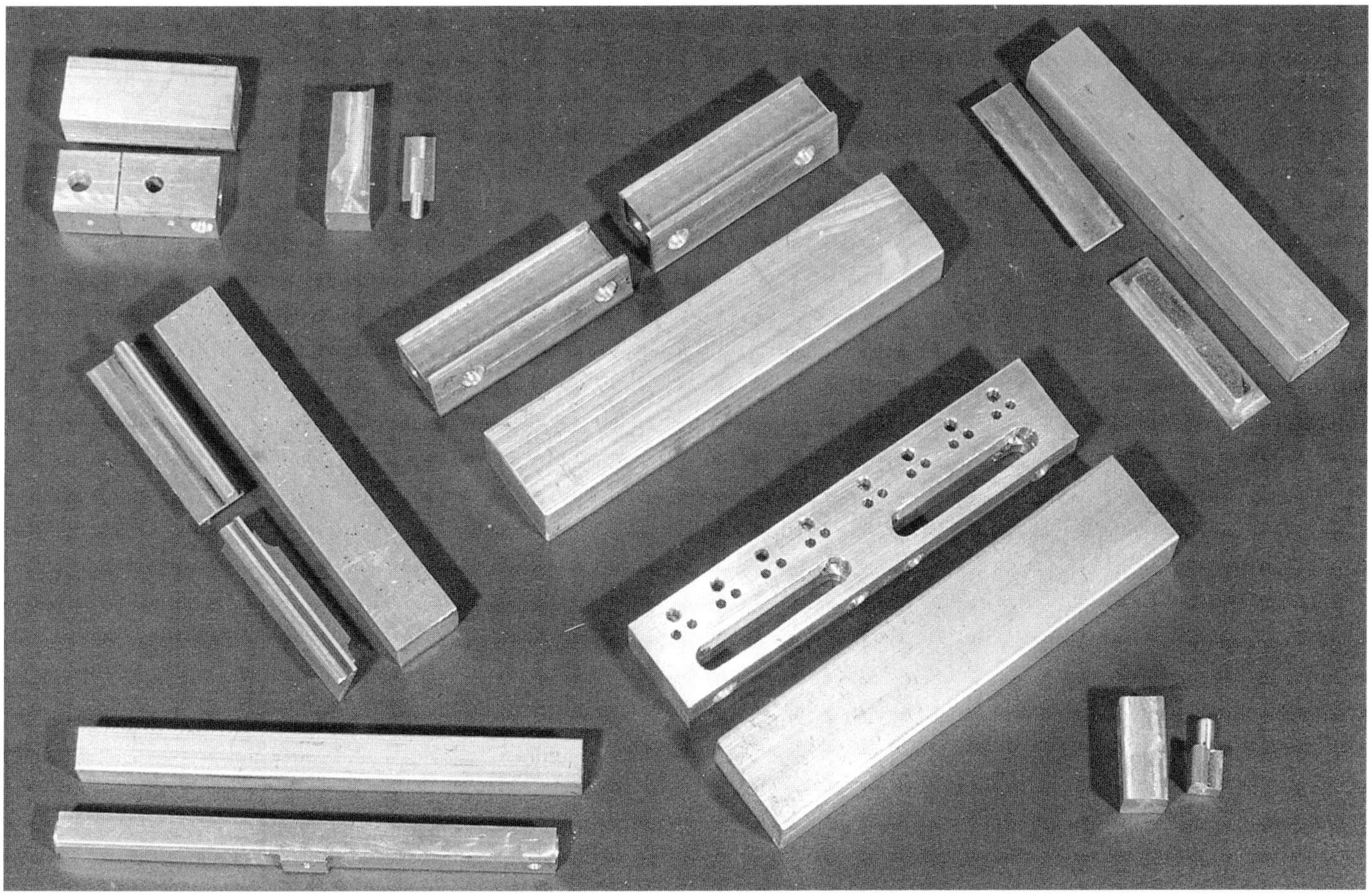

guide plate and machine the angle on this. The guide plate used here can be seen at the bottom of Plate 83. In use, it is placed under the block being machined (as in Plates 81 and 82) when work is in progress on that particular face. In Plate 84 we see the two basic aluminium blocks cut from a machining-quality rectangular bar, together with the machined sump and crankcase made from a second pair of blocks. Note in Plate 83 that a generous amount of metal is provided for the inner wall on top of the bottom part, to facilitate its location into the upper part. When complete, threaded holes are positioned at the front and rear of the crankcase/sump assembly on the centre line of the crankcase bearings. Into these are threaded the drive coupling to the clutch housing at the rear, (similar to the one shown on the far left of Plate 69) and the pulley for the fan belt at the front. These then lock the assembly together in a similar way to that accomplished by the various radiator parts.

Plate 85 shows most of the remaining aluminium engine components made on the milling machine; each component is shown together with a block similar to the one from which it was machined. In Plate 86 we see the tooling for the four inspection panels that are a feature of the Type 41 Bugatti engine. They were pressed out of sheet brass with the aid of the two steel press tools to be seen on the left, these being made in the same way as those shown in Plate 77. The Bugatti nameplate was etched in brass as described earlier and soft soldered in the centre of each inspection cover

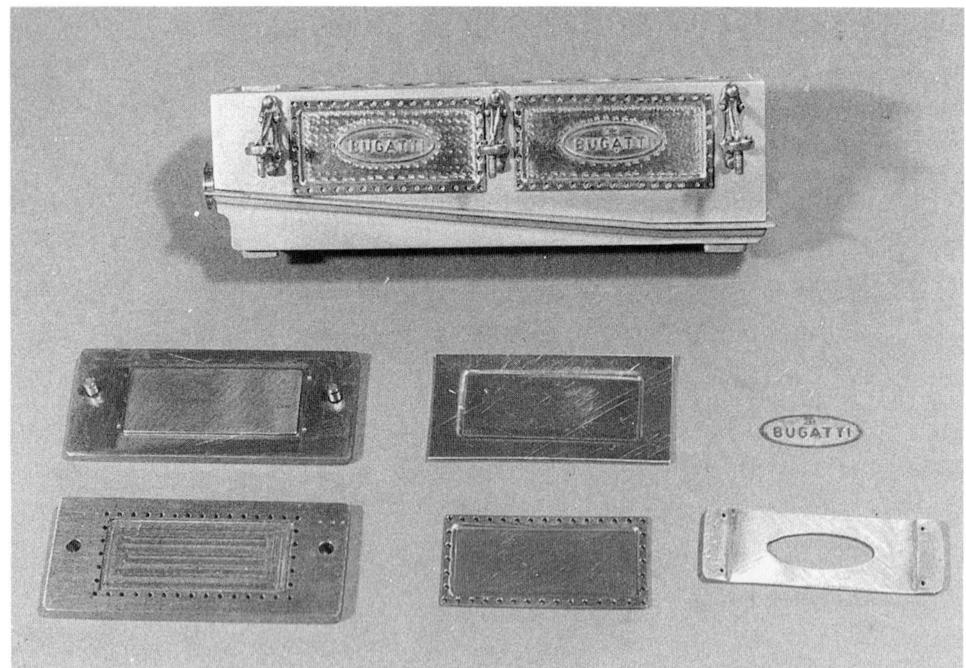

Plate 86

with the aid of the locating jig shown at the bottom right of Plate 86. This is made from a thin sheet of aluminium that has been drilled with four locating holes that match the four corners of the cover. The centre has been very carefully marked out and provided with an oval aperture that exactly matches the Bugatti nameplate. If the latter is 'silvered', ie has soft solder applied to its rear surface, and is placed inside the aperture of the locating jig attached to the inspection cover, then an application of heat under this will melt the solder and fix the nameplate in the desired position without having to scratch mark the cover. Because the cover is polished and chrome plated when finished, to avoid marking the surface is to be recommended.

It will be noted that these panels are provided with what is called an engine-turned finish, that is, the surface is covered by small circular markings. This is a typical finish for the larger engineered automobile parts of this period. To recreate this in miniature, the most useful tool that I have found is that shown at the top right in Plate 26, an impregnated rubber 'point', as it is called, from the dental trade suppliers.

The smallest one obtainable is mounted in a flexible drive and run at high speed. To make the marks, just lightly touch the surface with the revolving point, moving along in regular rows. In Plate 87, we see a similar tool being used to apply another finish, one that is peculiar to the Bugatti Type 41 engine. In full-size practice, this is applied in the final stages of assembly with a hand scraper, the entire area of the part being subjected to the random application of this tool, resulting in a most attractive mottled finish, as can be clearly seen in the photographs of the finished engine Plates 96 to 99.

I have been told by someone who witnessed the restoration of one of the Bugatti Royale engines, that it can take well over a month for one man to apply this finish to all of the individual parts. Here we see a less laborious approach that uses a 'cup' instead of a 'point' to work up a similar finish. This is made from

Plate 87

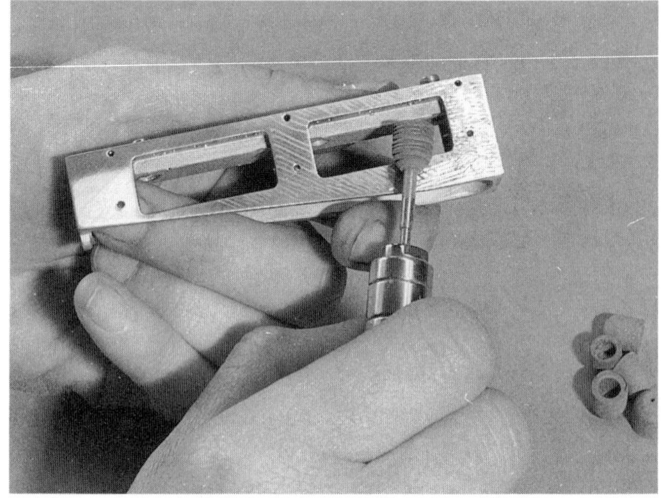

the same abrasive impregnated rubber material and has a small screw hole in the centre for mounting on a short stem or mandrel. Several can be seen at the bottom right of Plate 87. The mandrel and cup are powered by the flexible drive and first rotated against a thin piece of hard steel, such as an old hacksaw blade, to acquire a series of grooves. Before applying the mottled finish, the part to receive it should first be made smooth and then given a high polish. The grooved cup, running at high speed, is gently brushed over the surface to leave short stroke marks. These can be taken diagonally first from one corner, then the other, then vertically and horizontally, in short strokes at random all over the surface. The final application should be of short but slightly curved dabs with the tool from all directions, until the entire part takes on the desired mottled finish.

The actual cylinder block is painted black which should be done with the rest of the painting in the final stages. However, Plate 88 does show this piece already painted with two panels and water pipe attached. Below this is a strip of steel used as a drill jig to drill the holes in the panels. It takes less time

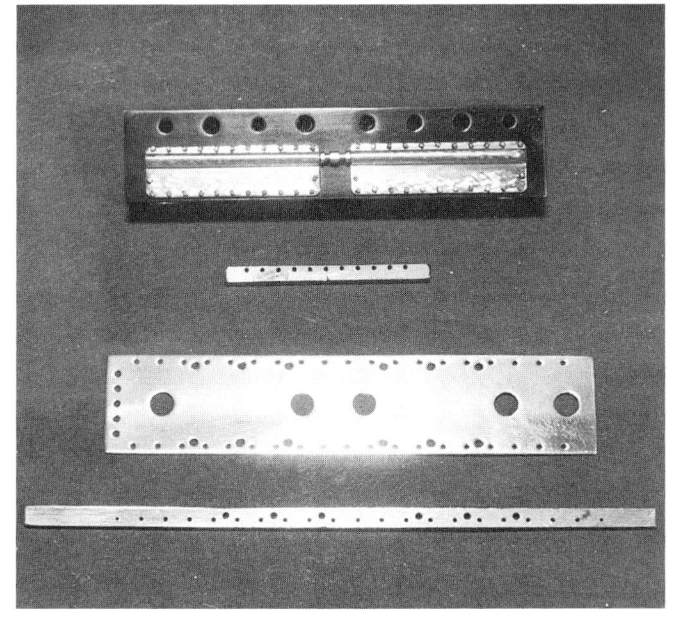

Plate 88

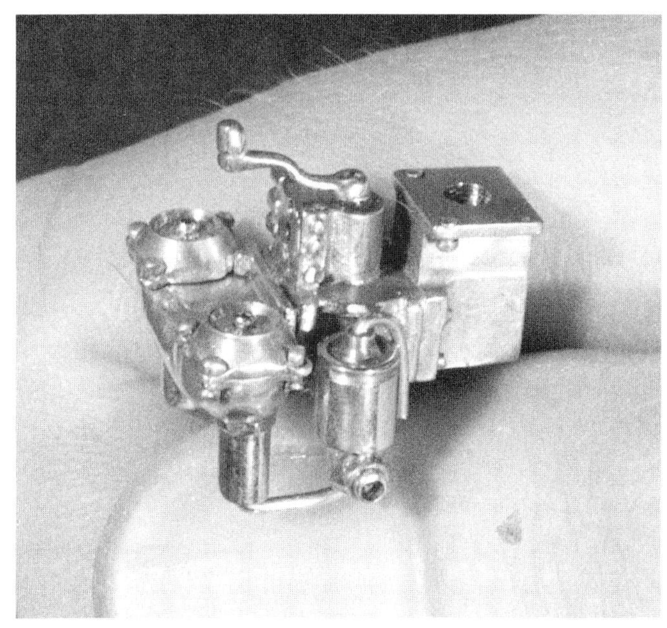

Plate 90

and assures improved accuracy to mark out and drill a single piece of metal with a series of holes, and use this as a drilling jig where the same pattern of holes is to be repeated several times, than to mark out and drill every hole separately. The plate in the centre is cut from 0.030 in (0.76 mm) aluminium and fits between the crankcase and the cylinder block. It carries a series of bolts and fittings that need to be precisely placed, so again a drill jig (at bottom) was employed.

We now consider some of the engine fittings, all of which were made via the process of fabrication, but these are of particular interest for the special problems they presented and the solutions found. The first is the carburettor (Plates 89 and 90), which is invariably one of the smallest and most complicated parts of the engine to make. In Fig 9 we have the rough drawings that were made to establish how the item could be broken down and the various sizes of the individual

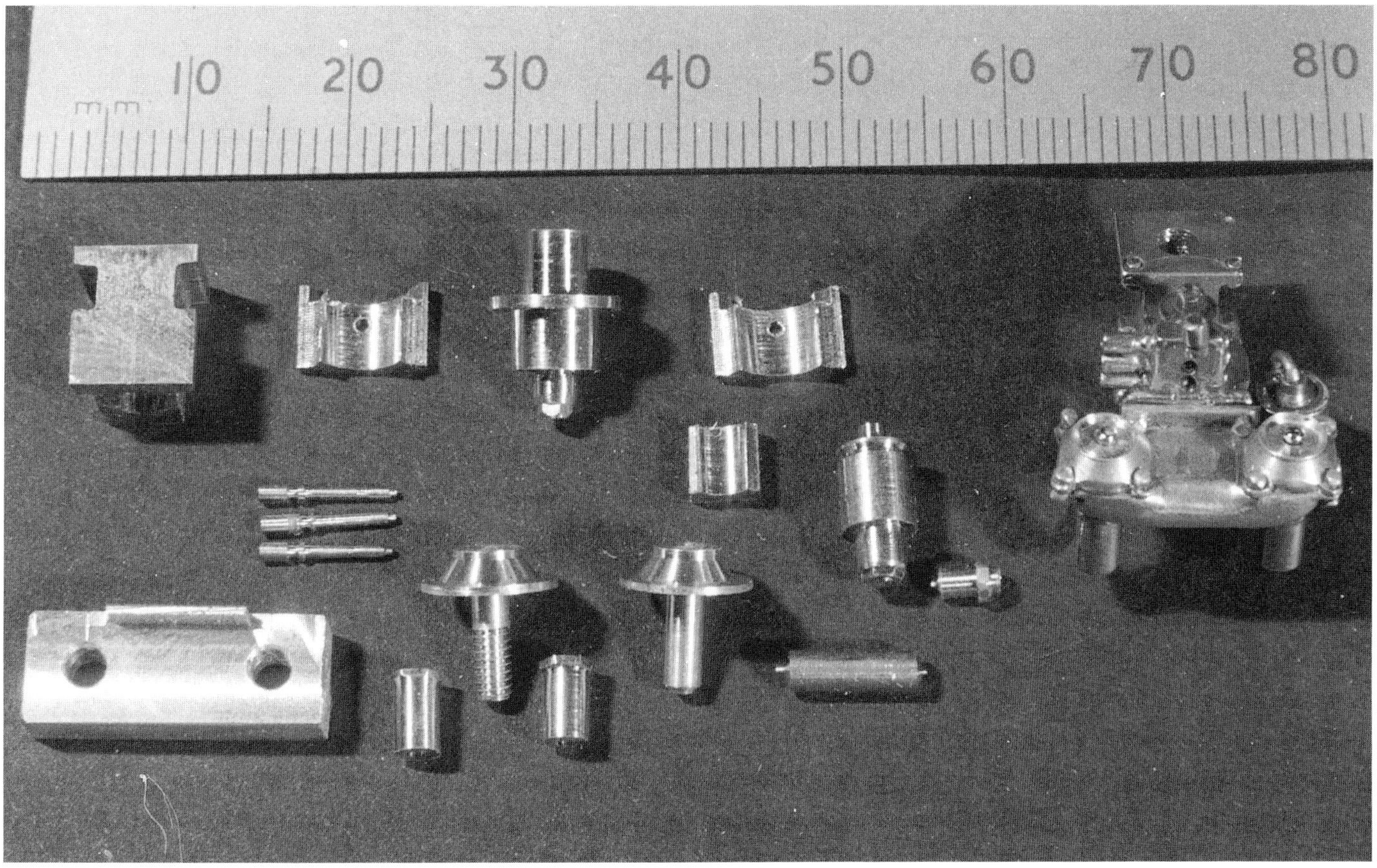

Plate 89

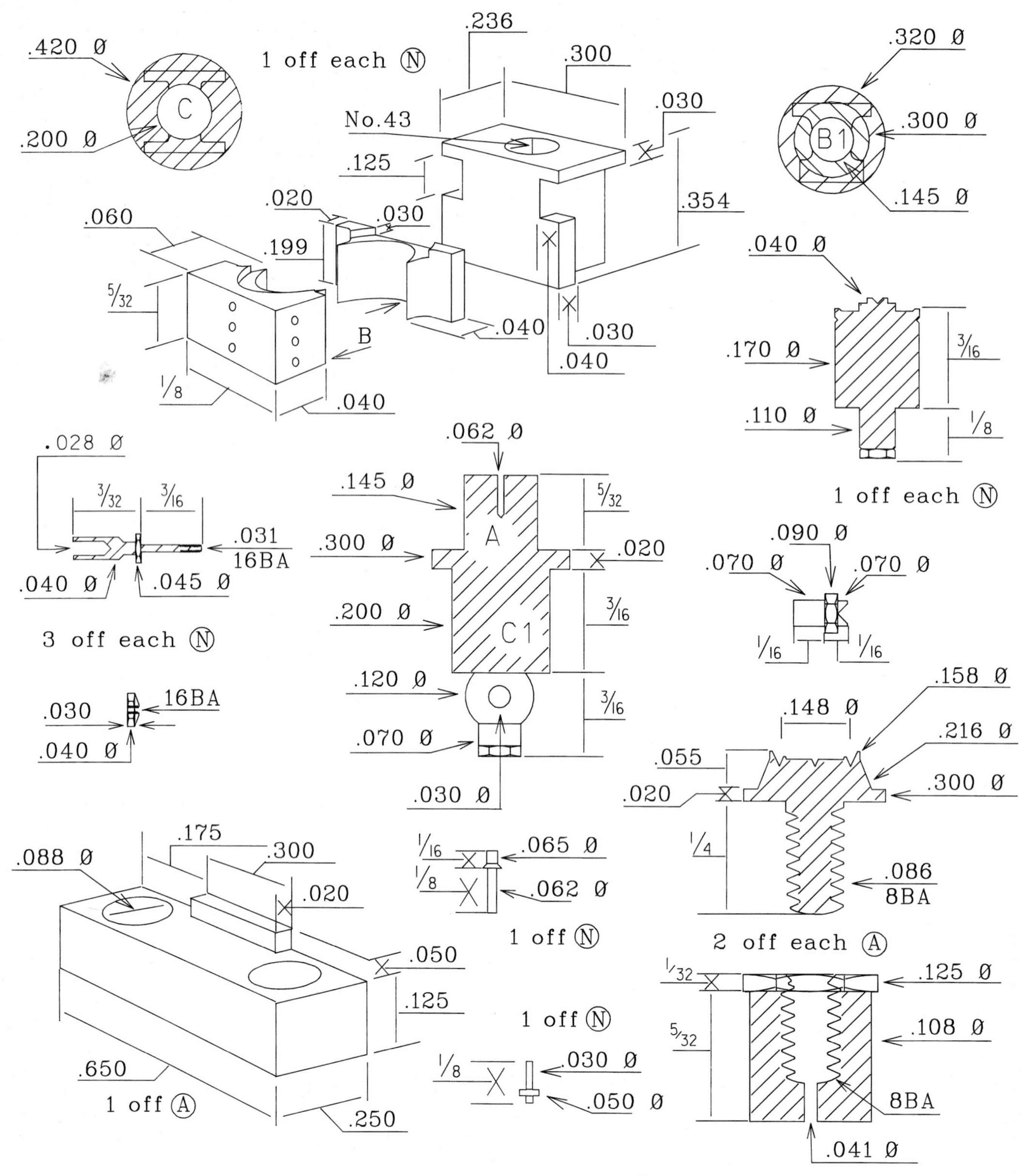

Fig. 9 Rough sketches for the carburettor parts in nickel silver and aluminium.

parts decided upon. Note that some parts are machined from aluminium 'A' while others call for nickel silver 'N', so matching the external finish of the full-size example. One piece of note is the central barrel with the control lever on top. This is made up from pieces A, B and C. Pieces B and C, being so small, would be almost impossible to make individually, so they were machined in pairs on the end of a length of nickel silver bar material. This was first mounted on the lathe to receive the centre hole and have the outside diameter turned down to size, after which it was transferred to the milling machine to receive the flats. After milling was completed, the piece was returned to the lathe to be separated from the main bar with a parting tool. The same sequence was also used to produce the two parts at 'C' which match

Plate 91

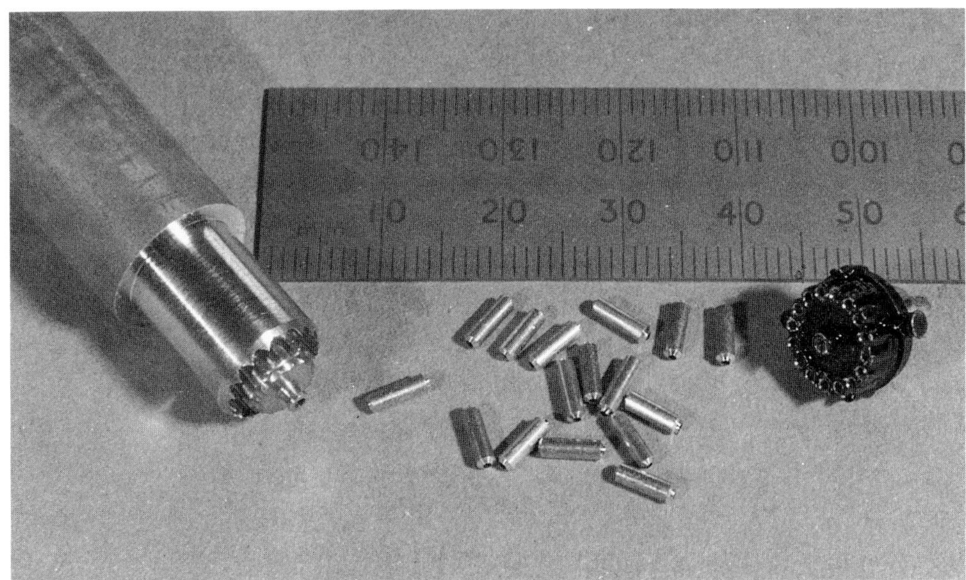

the diameter at CC_1.

All of the nickel silver parts were assembled with 1/32 in (0.78 mm) brass pins, drilled and attached where they could not be seen, and then silver soldered. The aluminium parts were attached to the main body by small screws from the back which allowed them to be hidden when the carburettor was fitted to the engine.

Plate 91 illustrates the not uncommon problem of how to drill half a hole; in this case sixteen half holes. This occurs here in fabricating the distributor that supplies power to the sixteen spark plugs on the Bugatti Royale engine, there being two plugs per cylinder. Because the distributor top has a very complex shape it could obviously not be turned on the lathe or milled without a very special cutter. Essentially the outer wall of the distributor is formed from the sixteen individual turrets that take the individual plug leads. The answer was to treat each of those 'turrets' as a small tube and drill a solid piece of brass bar to take each of the sixteen tubes. After drilling the holes with the aid of the dividing head, the piece was returned to the lathe to have the outer portion of the ring of holes removed. The incomplete part is shown at this stage on the left of Plate 91. The next stage was to flux each of the sixteen tubes before assembling them into their respective (half) holes and run silver solder around the assembly. This was then returned to the lathe to have the remaining diameters turned to size and finally to be parted from the bar.

In Plate 92, we find another recurring problem when making parts for automobiles of this period. This concerns the centrifugal water pump, for they invariably have an outside diameter that is not concentric with the main body of the pump. This is because the rim of the outer casing increases in size as it passes round the circumference of the pump body, until it extends to form the main outlet pipe of the water pump. The pump seen here made things even more difficult, because the inlet pipe was situated in the centre of the front face, as can be seen by the finished one on the right of this Plate. The answer is to turn the main body of the pump as shown, by the piece at the top centre. A length of brass rod of a size to match the outlet pipe and centre groove of the pump body, is now formed into a hook shape (far left Plate 92). This can be assisted using heat from a gas flame, bending the pipe while near red hot, rather than attempting to anneal it, as we are using turning quality brass. When the curve comes near to fitting the pump body, allow it to cool. With the aid of a file, the end of the hook is now reduced progressively along its length to about two-thirds of the length of the curved part. This is now taken down to a point, but rather flattened on the outer surface so that the full width of the metal is maintained. Finally, the top surface of the tip is given an offset groove with a

Plate 92

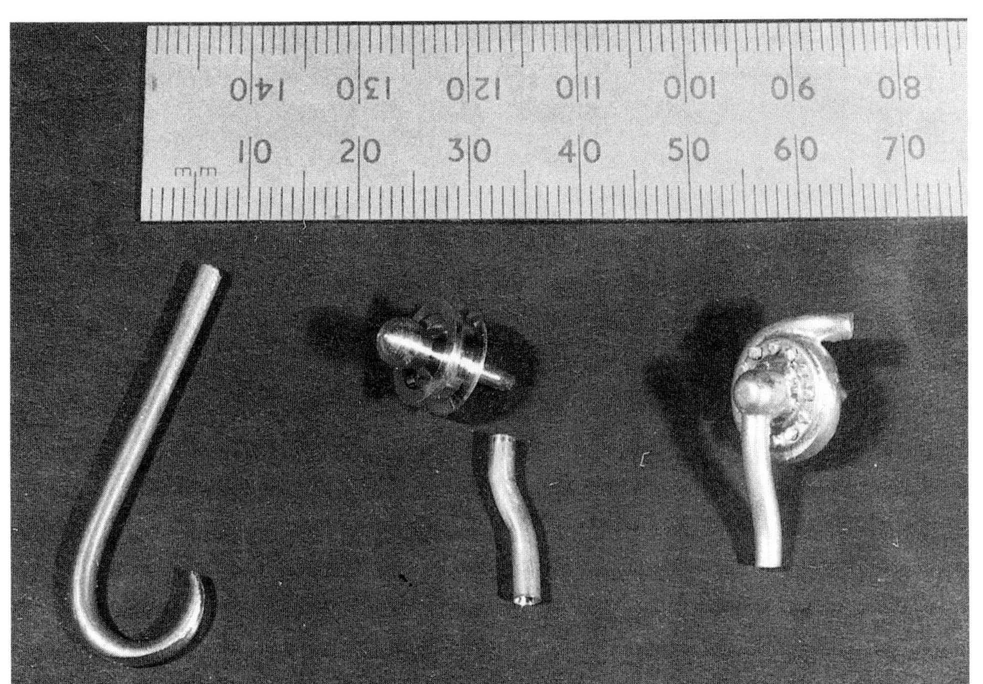

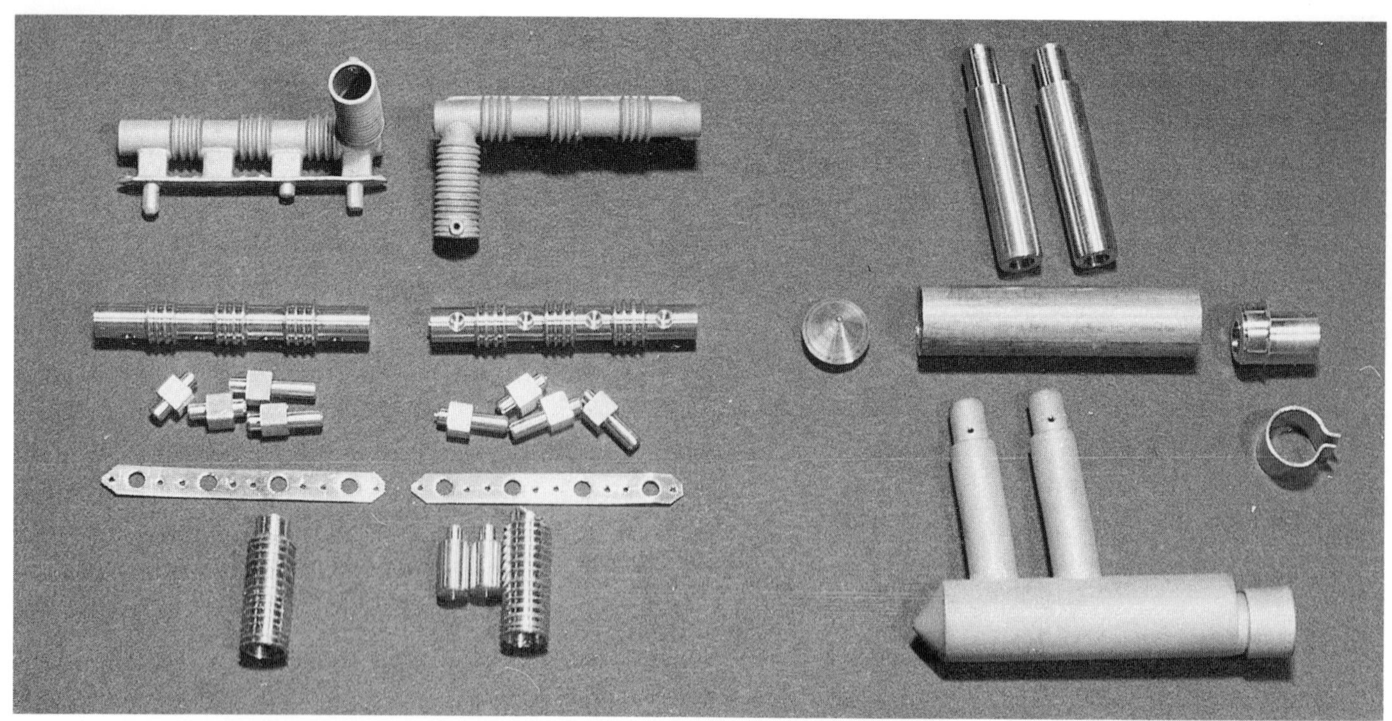

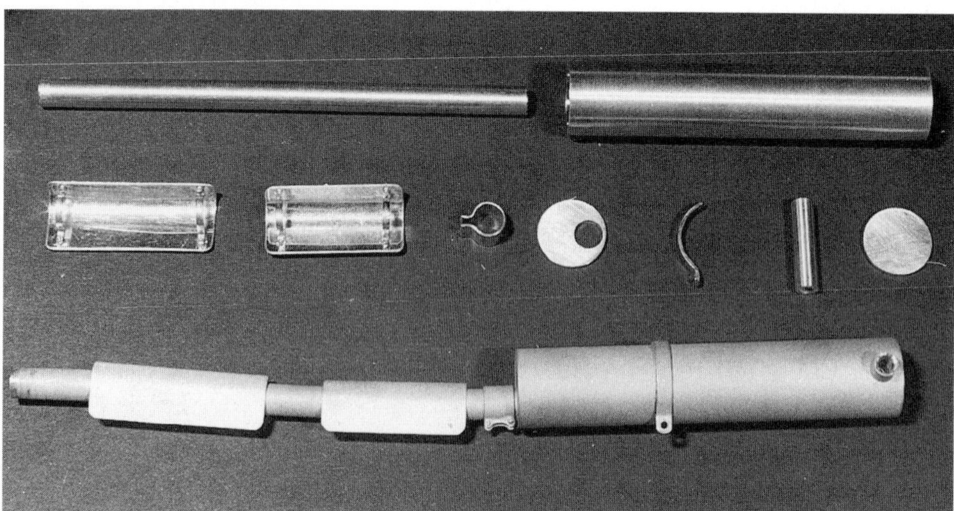

Plate 93

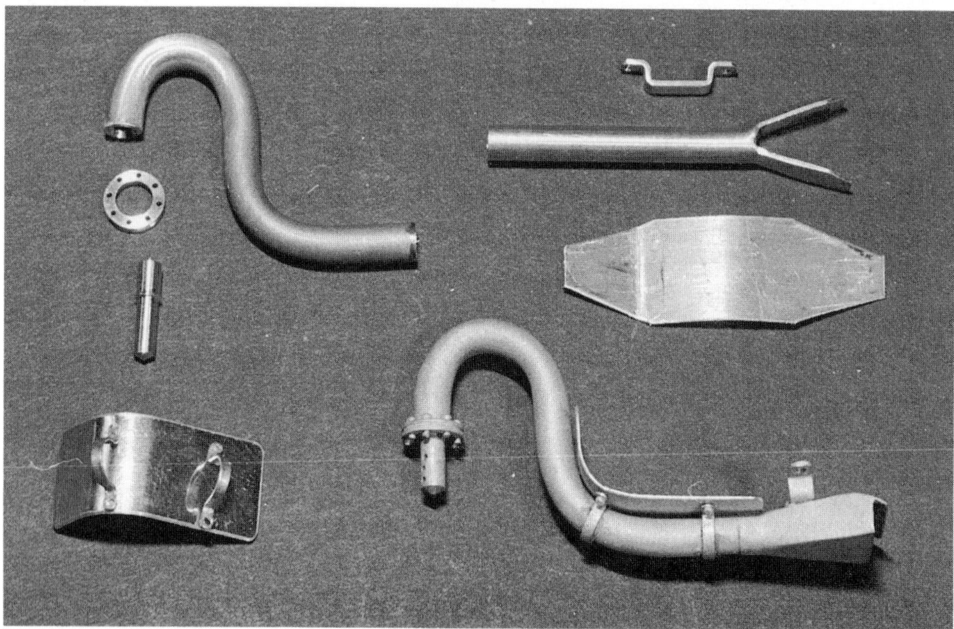

Plate 94

Plate 95

small round file to take the end of the outlet pipe as it bends off from the outer diameter. The length of the bar is again heated so that it can be bent fully round the centre part, and with the aid of a large pair of pliers, made to fit tightly into the groove. It is then permanently fixed in place with silver solder. The next operation is to drill for, and fit the ring of bolts, these being held in place by fluxing the assembly and reheating to silver soldering temperature to allow that solder used for holding the previous part, to flow around the additional pieces. With this done, the last item to be fitted is the inlet pipe to the centre boss, with the aid of a locating pin in the centre and hard solder.

Plates 93 to 96 illustrate the parts that make up the complete exhaust system. Each photo illustrates both the component parts and a fully assembled piece of this pipe work.

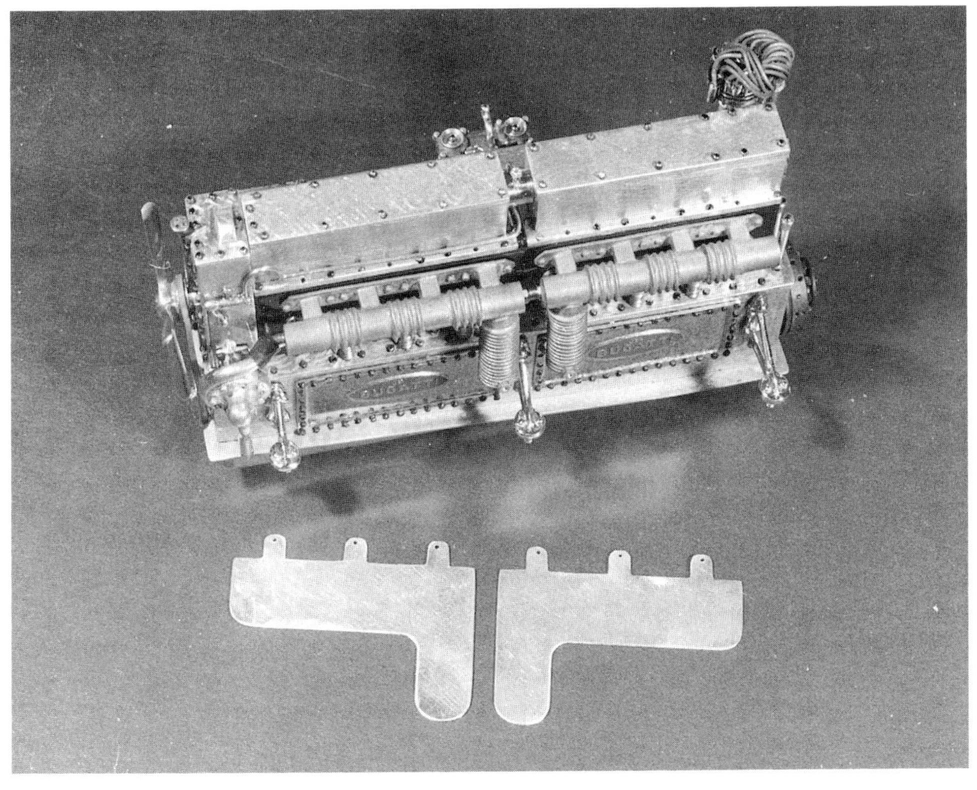

Plate 96

The material used is brass throughout except for the heat shields, which are formed from very thin – 0.008 in (0.20 mm) sheet aluminium. The finish that I aim for on items such as this is the dull grey old-used look of iron or steel, maybe a little burnt but not yet rusty. To get this the parts are painted all over with soft solder paint, then heated with a flame until it melts. With the solder still in a molten state, a piece of linen cloth is used to wipe off any excess, so leaving a smooth finish. It may take several applications of the flame and cloth, (not of course together), to achieve this over the length of larger items.

These particular parts were then sand-blasted at quite a low pressure so as to give the dull finish, and then placed in a weak pickle bath. The acid will change the colour of the tinned area to a dark grey, although if the pickle solution has been used previously for cleaning brass and copper, then a reddish copper deposit will be seen with the dark grey as well. Some of this will wipe off when you have rinsed the pieces in clean water and dried them, but I think the 'used' finish obtained by this method helps to add character to the model.

In Plate 97 we see the inlet side of the finished engine, and in Plates 98 and 99, the fully assembled chassis and engine. At this stage all the parts are held in place either with small bolts or dowel pins or both so that various components or assemblies can be removed as necessary for the next part of the build-up, fitting the wings and body. Also, when everything is complete, it will be taken apart to separate those pieces needing a paint finish and those requiring chrome or nickel plating from those needing no further attention.

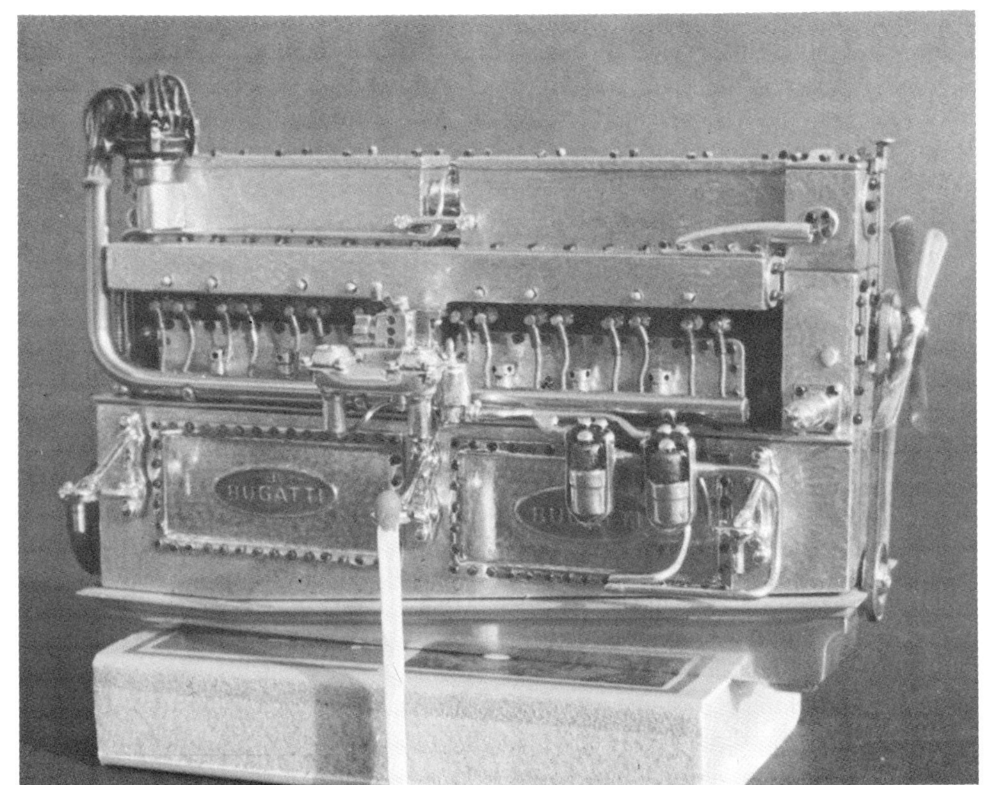

Plate 97

Plate 98

Plate 99

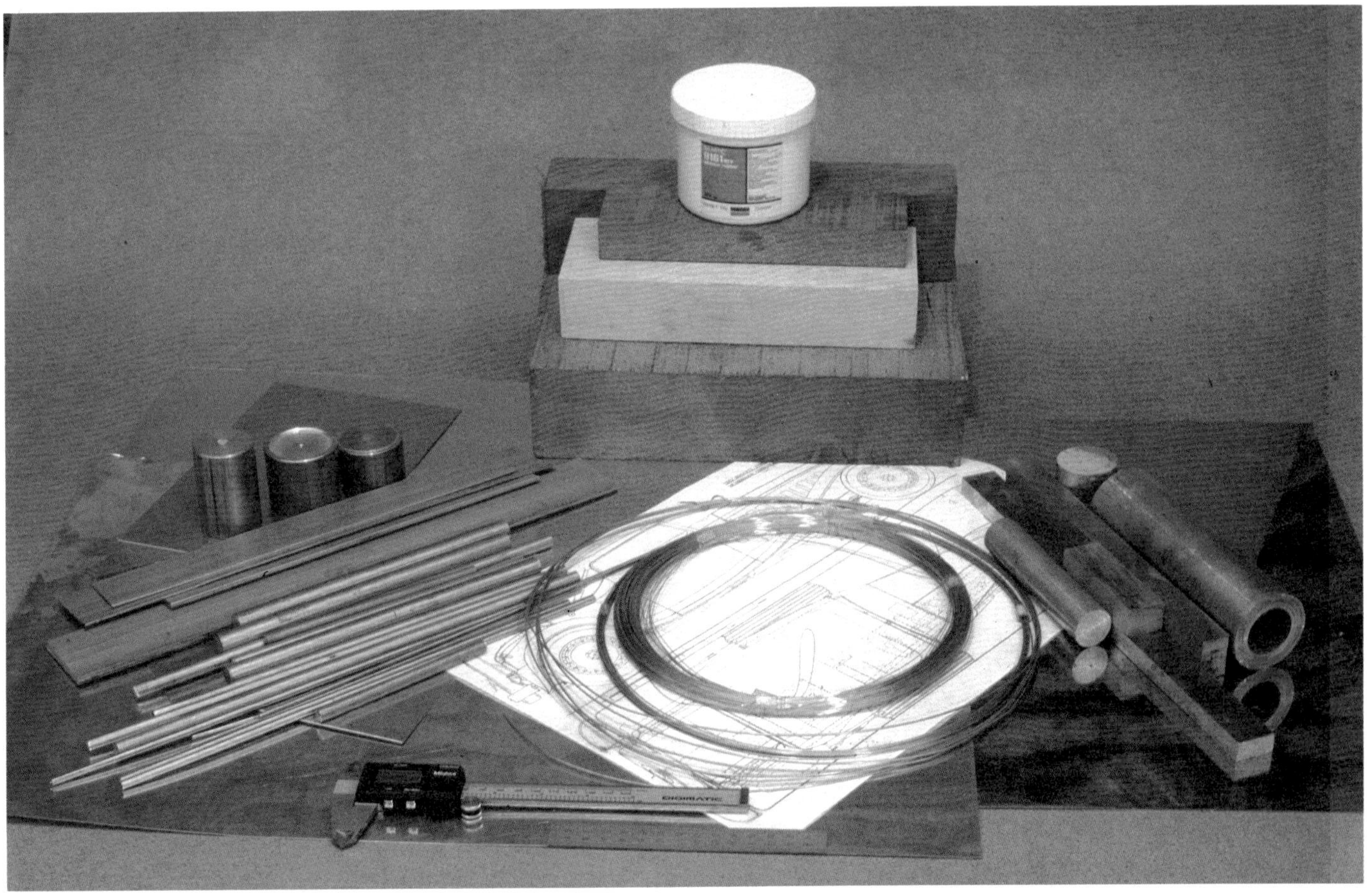

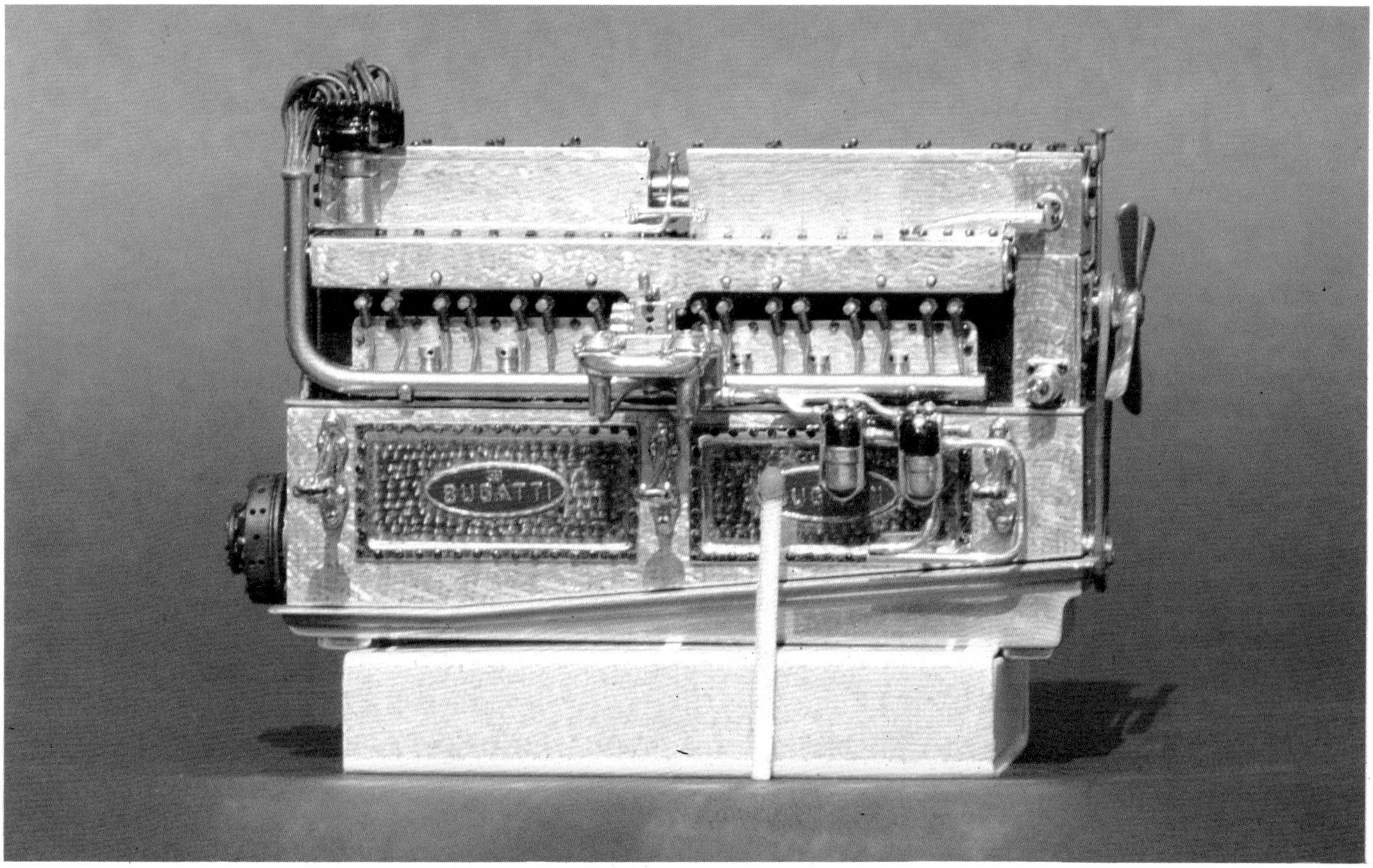

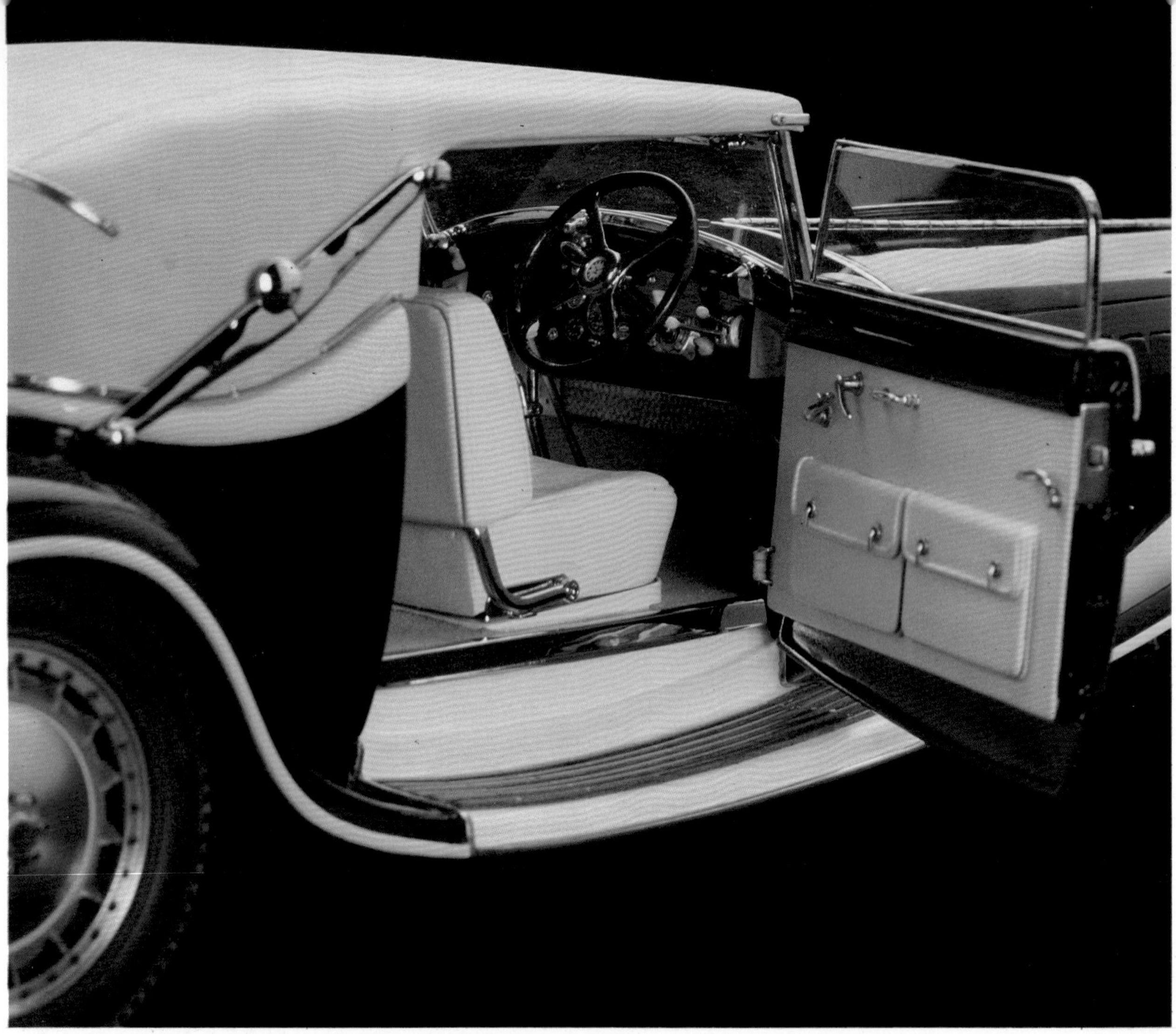

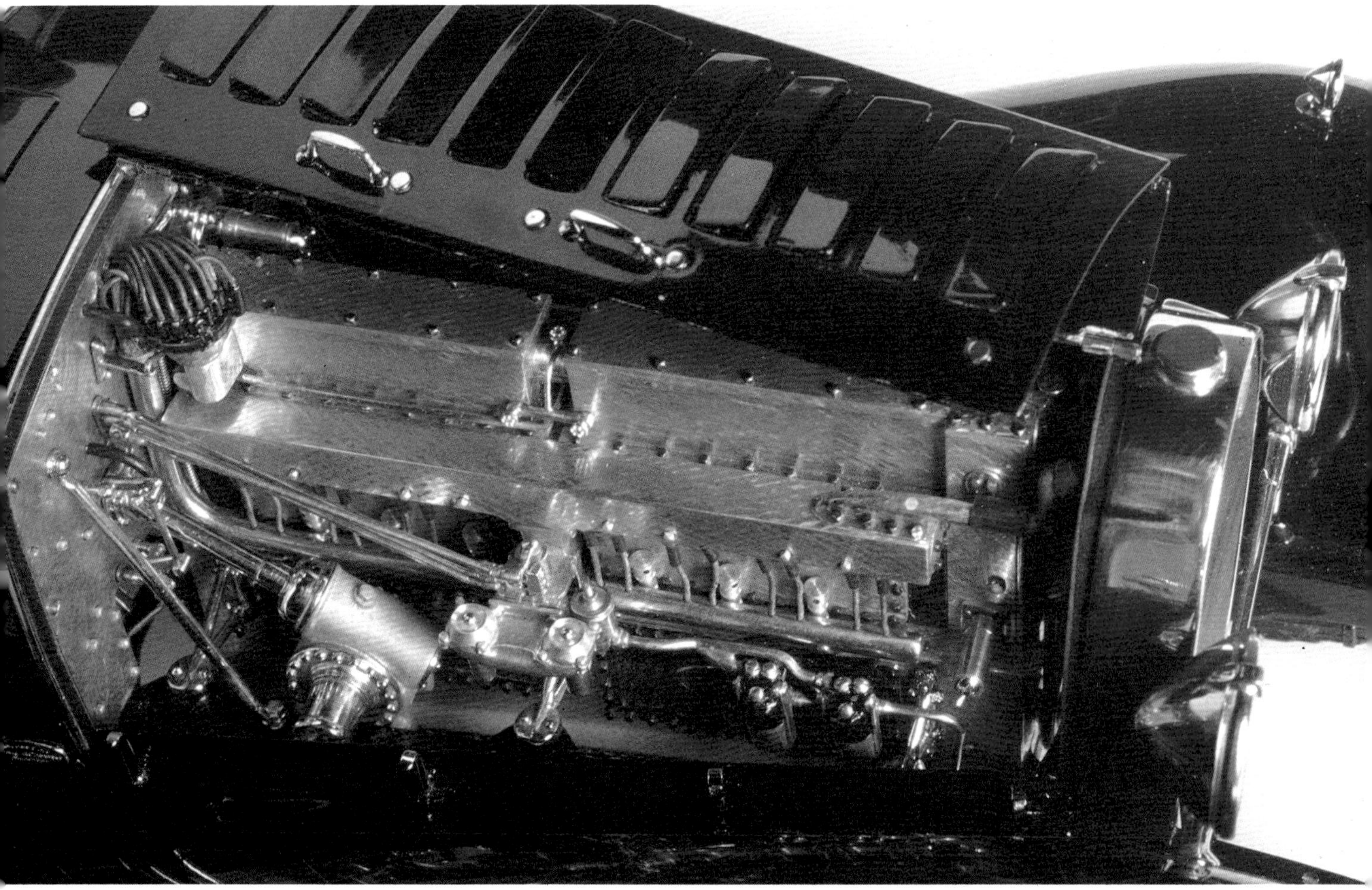

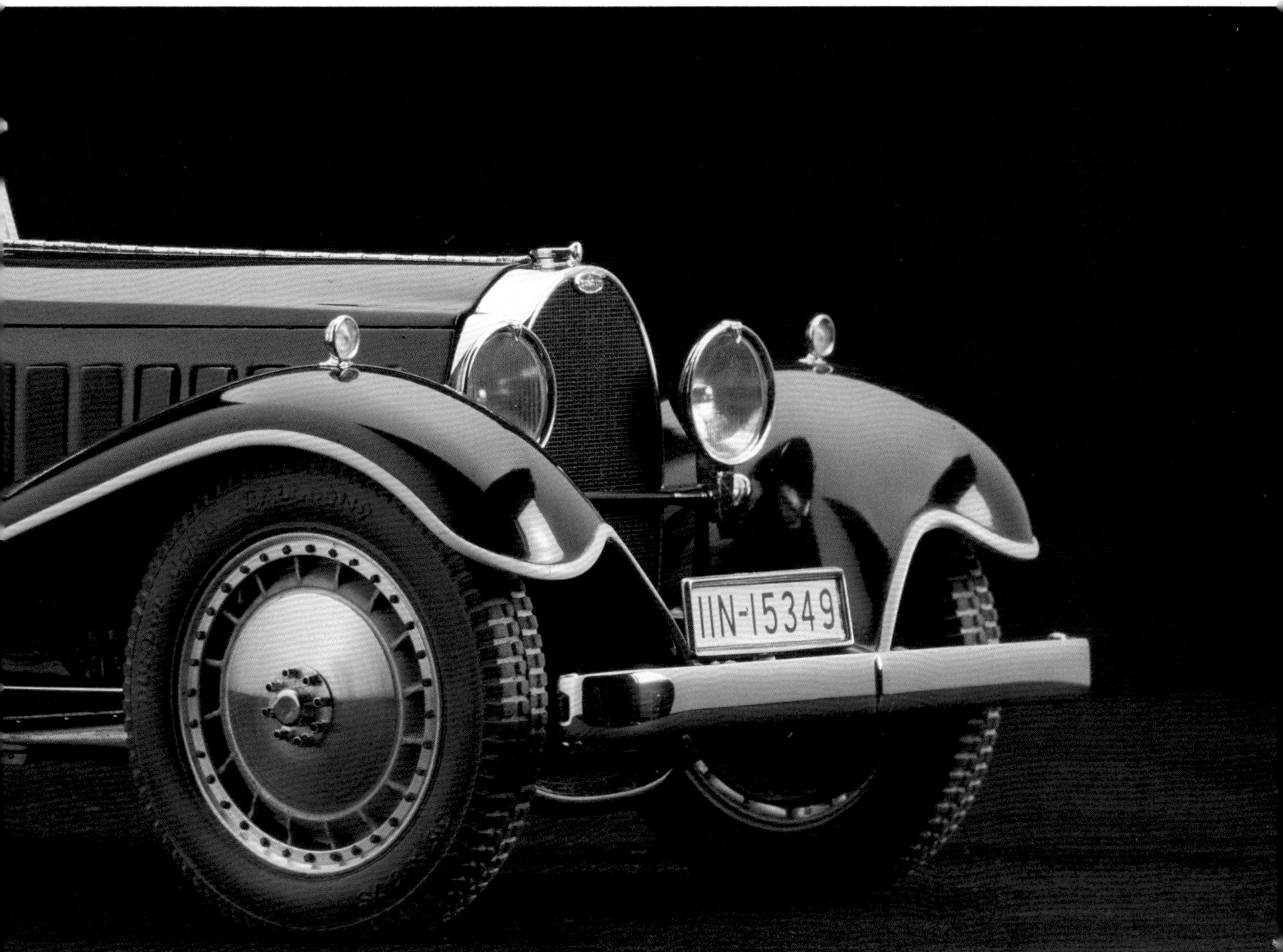

IIN-15349

PART FOUR
The Bodywork

ONE OF THE great joys of scratch building models, and of automobile modelling in particular, is the diversity of the materials used and, in consequence, the tools and techniques to work them. It is a long-held opinion of mine that if the skills and techniques of model making formed a subject taught and encouraged in schools, then the general awareness of all aspects of design, materials, tools and the skills necessary to manipulate them would bring about a much more healthy respect for all that is about us.

So to the bodywork, the first stage of which is to make a series of wooden pattern blocks around which the sheet-metal body and panels can be made. This is necessary, for although we will not actually use these to hammer the metal shape on, they are our guide to what the various shapes should be. The material can be any hard wood that is available. By hard wood, I do mean wood that is 'hard' in itself. Hardwood is a term used in the timber trade to describe in general timber from deciduous trees, while softwood denotes timber from pines and similar evergreen trees used principally for the building trade. In general, hardwoods are close grained and softwoods are coarse grained, but there are exceptions to all of these, and one can find 'soft' hardwoods, and 'hard' softwoods. If a particular piece of wood is close grained and tough to the tool (hammer and chisel), and properly dried, then it will be suitable for the job. The timber used here is Afromosa for the wing patterns, and beech for the body and hood, but only because I happened to have to hand some of a suitable size. The Afromosa is not an ideal wood because it has a tendency to change its shape due to internal stresses being released as one works it. Afromosa is a typical 'furniture' timber and not normally used in pattern-making. On the other hand beech, although it, too, is also a furniture timber, is ideal because it is hard, dense, heavy and very stable.

The pattern blocks are all marked out directly from the body and wing shapes indicated on the scale plans. This is undertaken via a series of card templates having the necessary detail and shapes traced on them, with the aid of carbon paper, from the plans. The wooden patterns have a dual role, for they are made in such a way that they can be used as a cutting guide for joining several panels together, as well as being a true three-dimensional shape of the piece being made.

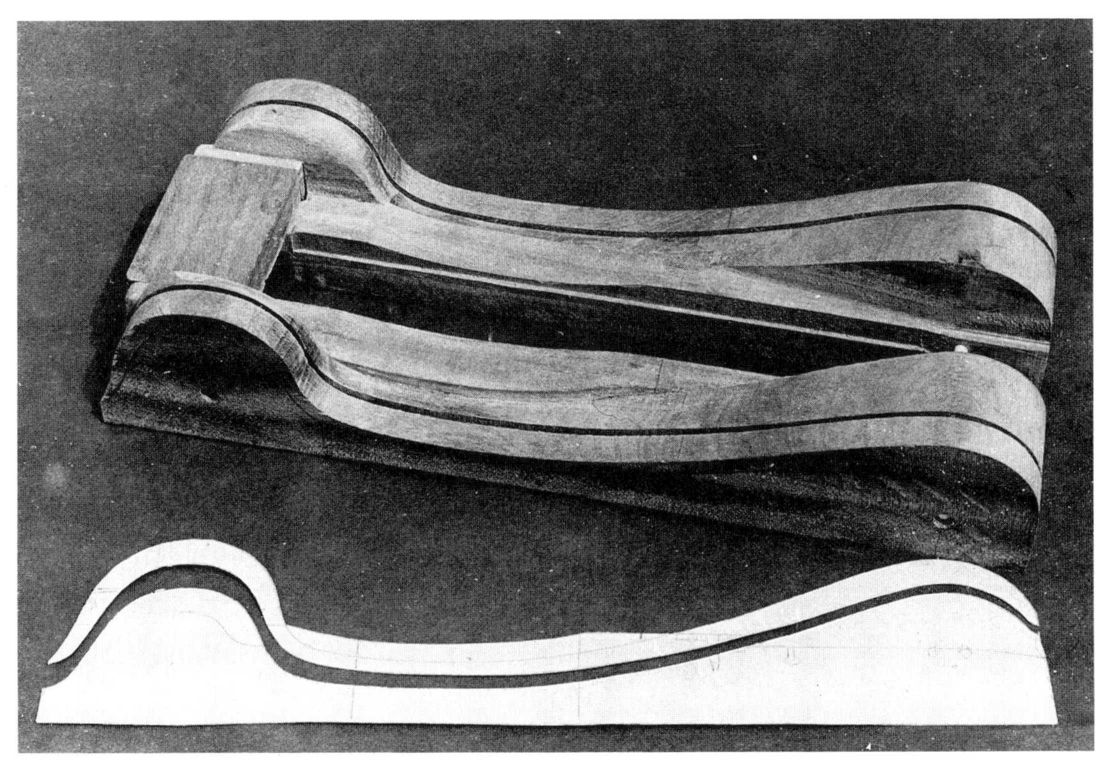

Plate 100

Starting with Plate 100, we see at the bottom the card template being used to mark out the main timbering for the wing patterns. Two things to note here are that two pieces of wood have been used for each side and that the shaping is in profile (side view) only, or nearly so. The reason for splitting each side into two pieces will become apparent later, but it does have the advantage that

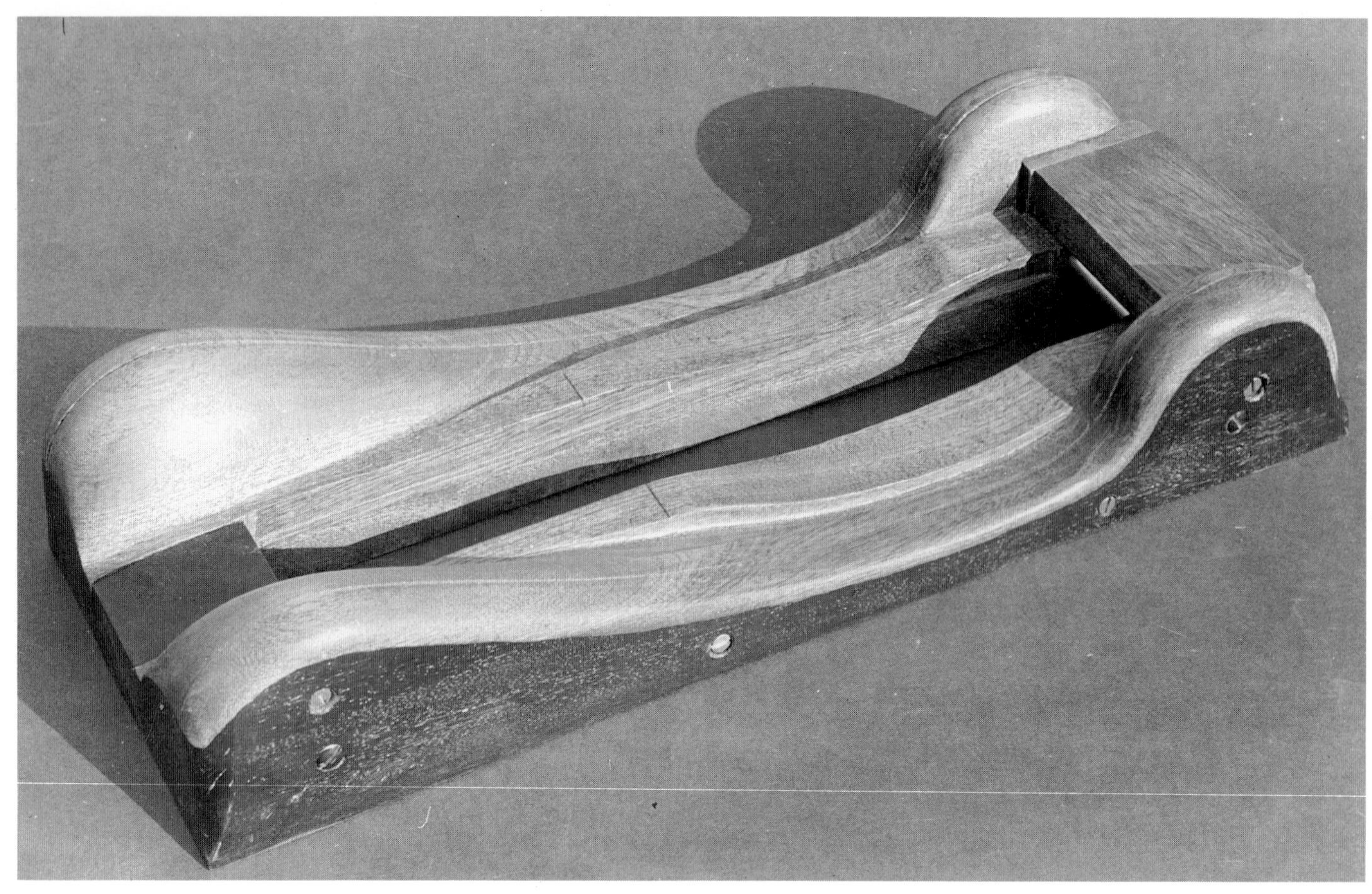

Plate 101

the two outside pieces can be dowelled together, marked out and shaped according to the pattern first, then used as a guide to cover the inner pieces to match exactly. The dowel holes, front and rear, are located at the positions of the two axles and are taken through all four pieces of wood. The filler pieces, front and back, are also held in place with wooden dowel pins, the front one acting simply as a filler piece to keep the front wings apart by the correct amount, while the rear block will be used later as a pattern for the sheet metal that joins the rear wings together. With the filler pieces removed and the axle dowel pins passing through all four side patterns, any combination of these four parts can be assembled to assist and double check with the shaping of the wing line. Were we to be working on a single block of wood, then some difficulty would be experienced in maintaining the precise shaping and flow of line, one side with the other. For this first stage of shaping, all the work should be kept square with the sides, and only after you are completely satisfied that it matches the profile on the plans exactly, should you move to the second stage. This is to look at the pattern from the front, rear, and above. Mark out all shapes and steps etc. required to carve these, but again maintaining the squared sides to the maximum dimensions. This is the stage to which the patterns have been taken in Plate 100.

Only when the basic profiles have been found should the radii and angles be added to give the true rounded form of the final shape, as shown in Plate 101. This approach allows us to deal with the many problems one at a time, without removing the evidence of where we are aiming for before we actually get there. Note that all that remains of the original side view profile, that in the previous photograph extended to the full width of each fender, is the centreline represented by the join of the two halves on each side. By making the pattern in this way we can be certain that it is correct and is an exact copy of the one on the opposite side.

In Plate 102 are the body and bonnet patterns, which, although somewhat more complicated, were tackled in exactly the same way. In this case, the body pattern was made up from three blocks of wood assembled with concealed dowels. The centre piece, flat topped and raised above the two side pieces, is drilled first and then used as a guide to drill each of the side pieces. It will be seen again here that it would be much more difficult to carve the top shape on both sides to match exactly, with the centre block in place. With it removed, one is dealing with a narrower piece of wood, and one can carve the shape directly from one side to the other. This applies to the shaping of the sides, and the front and rear. Having the two side pieces only loosely dowelled each side of the centre piece throughout all the carving operations, allowed them to be taken apart from time to time, to double-check them one with the other on each of the plans being worked. Only when I was satisfied that all was correct with the plans, and that the image was mirrored one side with the other, did I glue all three parts together.

The principal reason for leaving the centre section as a raised block was to locate the pattern for the folding top, Plate 103. As with the previous examples,

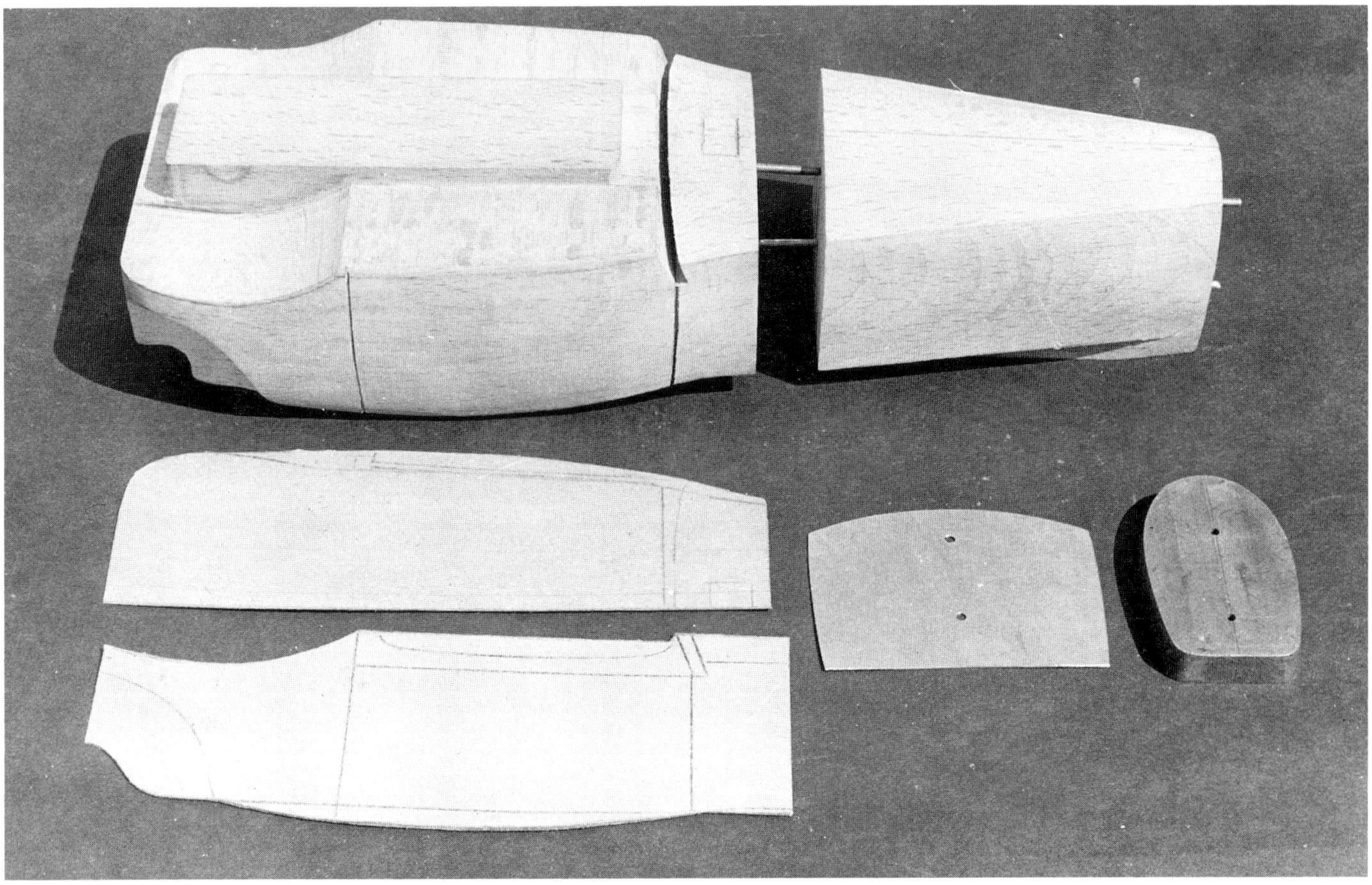

Plate 102

Plate 103

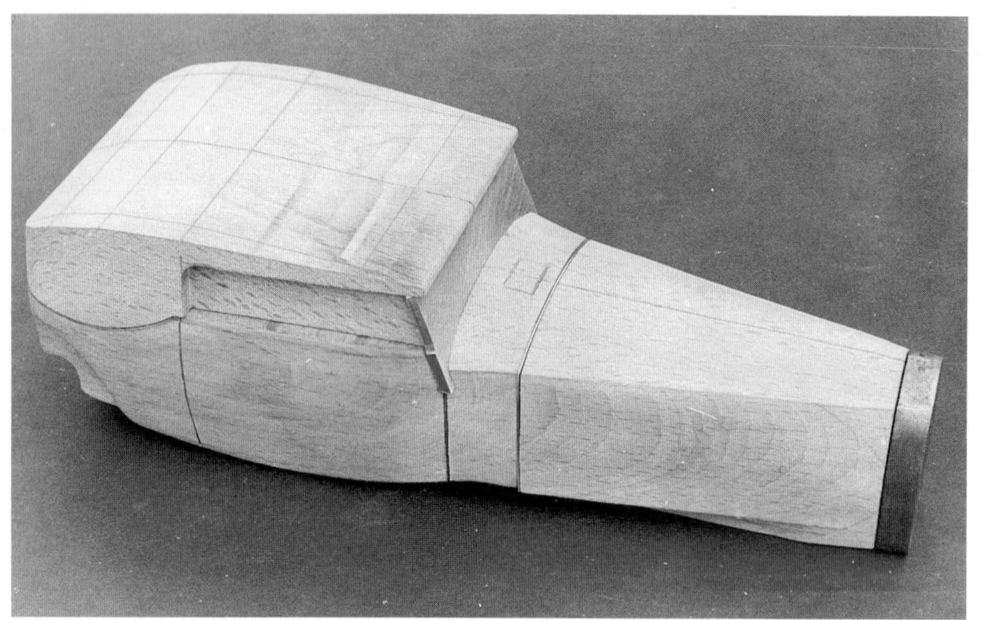

Plate 104

the card templates containing relevant shaping and detailing are to be seen in the foreground of each photograph. Note that where the plan view necessitates a separate template because of detail shaping, only a half template is actually used. In this way we can be certain that, by marking out from this on each side of an indicated centre line, we can have an identical guide line for the intended shape on each side of the pattern block.

In Plate 104, we see the complete body, top and hood patterns. The radiator and firewall patterns, used to make their particular parts earlier, are used here again as a guide for the front and rear shaping of the hood block and cowl section of the body. Plate 105 shows the complete and assembled patterns standing with the Bugatti Royale chassis.

The following sequence (Plates 106 to 117) of photographs fully illustrates the methods that I employ to produce all of the sheet-metal parts for this model, including those for the body and the top. We start with a paper pattern (Plate 106). Note that because of the complicated and closely contoured shape, particularly of the front wings, each wing is made in two sections. A separate paper pattern is required for each piece, so five are required in all, including one

Plate 105

Plate 106

Plate 107

for the centre running board section. Each pattern should be laid on its wooden master and marked around the edge approximately to match where the intended panel is to fit. The amount of folding and creasing of the paper to accommodate the multiple curves will give an indication of the contortion you will be inflicting on the sheet metal to make it conform to this.

Sheet copper, of 0.012 in (0.30 mm) thickness was used in this example and is cut to match each of the paper patterns, making an allowance of about $\frac{1}{4}$ in (6.35 mm) all round to take care of the changes in shape we are about to make. Two copper pieces

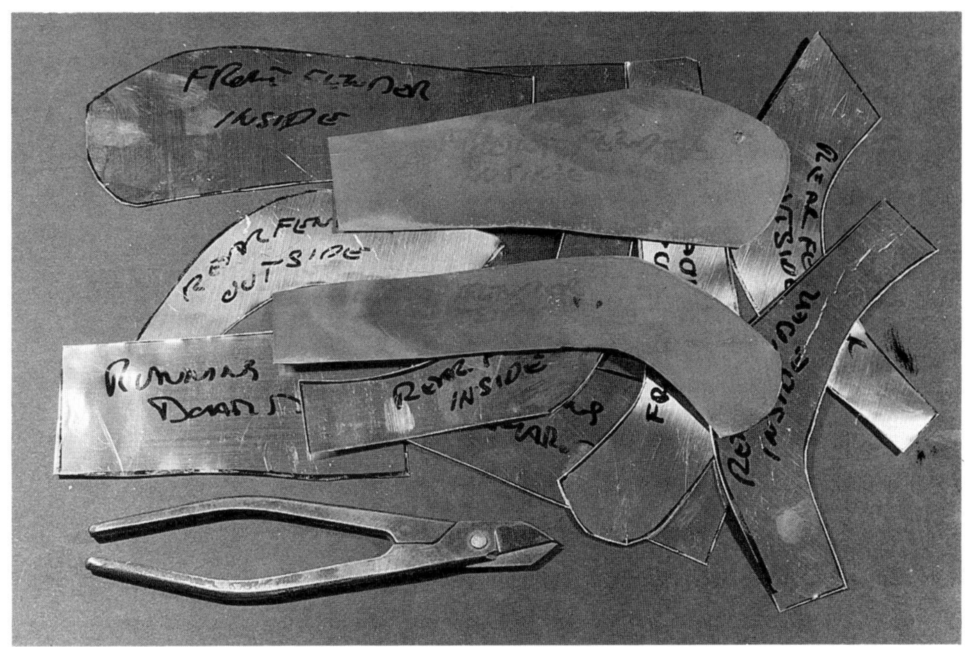

are required for each of the paper patterns (Plate 107) which are then annealed to bring them to a soft state. The next task (Plate 108) is to crimp the edge of the first piece at the places of maximum contortion until it roughly conforms to the shape required (Plate 109). The pliers used for this are called round-nose pliers, and as can be seen, only the smallest size need be procured.

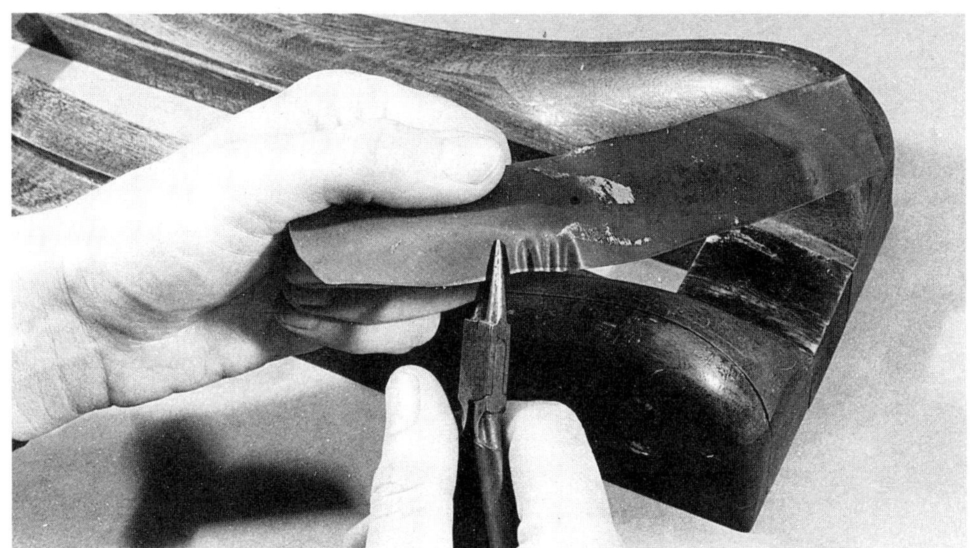

Plate 108

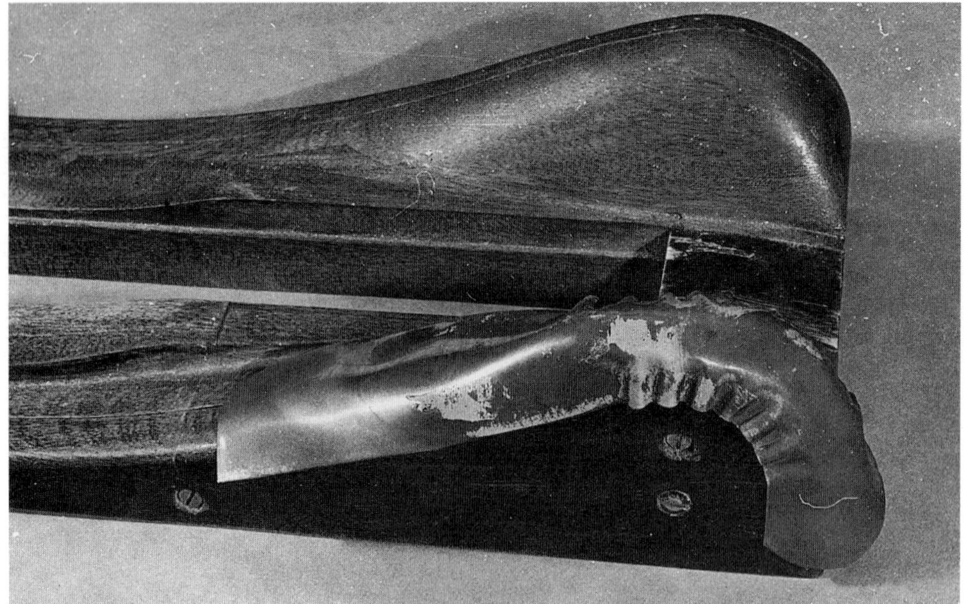

Plate 109

Plate 110

In Plate 110, can be seen the 'ball' of the repousé hammer being used to flatten each of the crimps just made. The art here is to aim for and flatten first the outermost edge of the crimp. Bear in mind that the copper is in a very soft malleable state and that as soon as you work it with the hammer, it starts to harden. The process that we are undertaking is to force the molecules of copper back onto themselves, so that we actually thicken the edge and shorten it. Were we to aim the hammer at the centre of each crimp, we would just spread it out whence it came. By aiming for the edge, we can harden it to prevent this happening, so the 'hump' of crimp has nowhere to go other than into itself. Note that we are not attempting to 'work' the metal over the hardwood pattern; if we did at this stage, we would end up with a badly beaten and bruised pattern that would be useless for the purpose for which it was intended. As much work as possible is undertaken on a large block of metal, in my case the large, heavy lump of cast iron obtained from a local scrap yard.

At first the beaten copper wing part will look very rough and nothing like you intended. After annealing, crimping and beating a second, third and maybe a fourth time, however, the parts will start to look like those in Plate 111. At this stage after the next annealing, the sheet copper can be gently worked by tapping with the flat of the hammer over the wooden pattern block. By this time it may well be found that the curves and rounding out has gone further

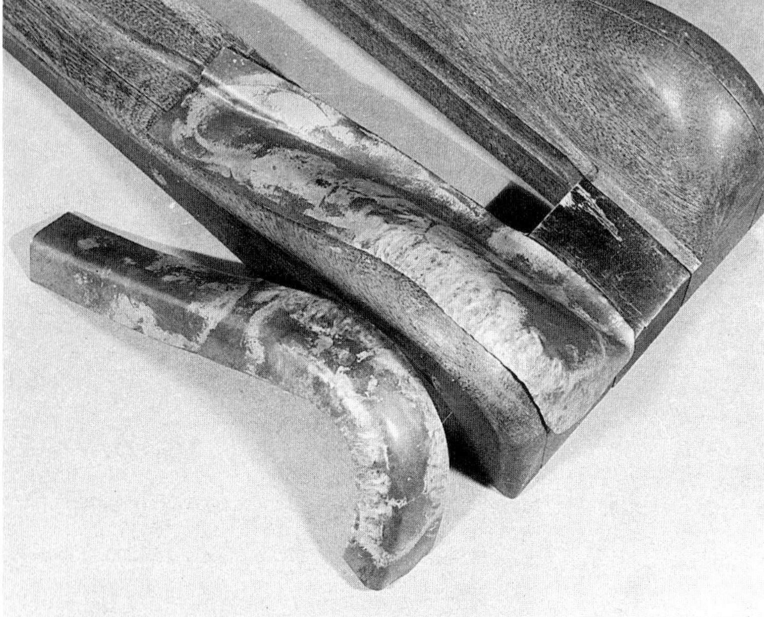

Plate 111

Plate 112

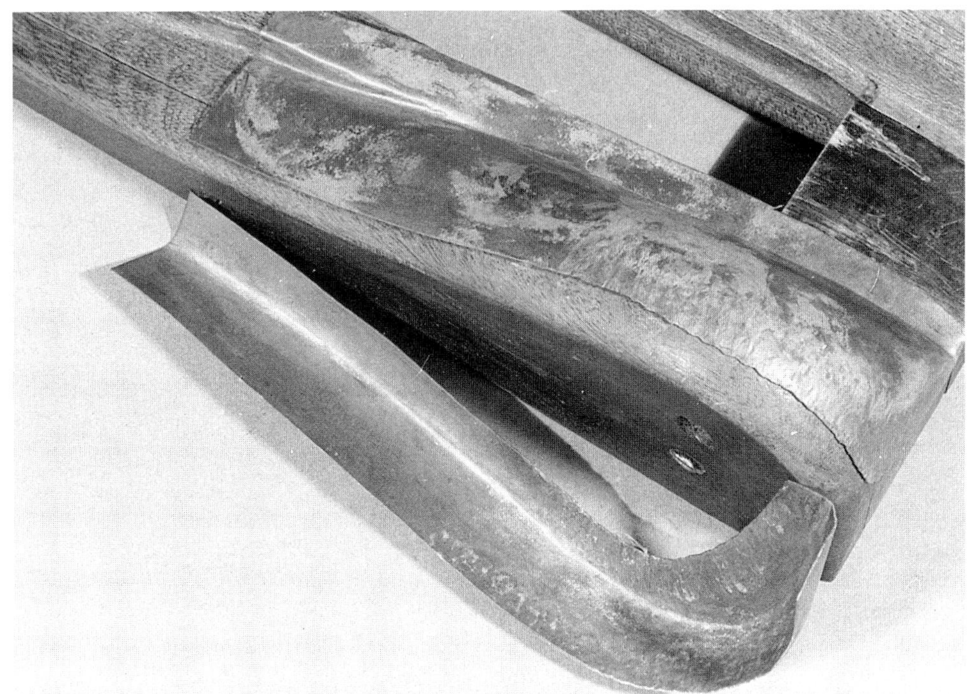

than you intended. This is good, for the wood patterns are ideally used for stretching the soft metal plates tightly over their contours.

Plate 112 illustrates this stage for the two halves of the front right wing. As we have seen, the patterns were made in two parts each. The reason now becomes apparent, because we can open the join and use the line so made on each half as a guide to scribe a cutting mark on each of the pieces. When the pieces have been cut to this line (Plate 113), and have received the attentions of a flat file to true up the edge if need be, the two pieces are held together with some scrap strips of copper (Plate 114) and silver solder is run around the joint, removing the retaining strips with tweezers as one goes. After the heating from this operation, the now complete wing will again be soft and malleable, which is ideal for working it to fit the master pattern exactly.

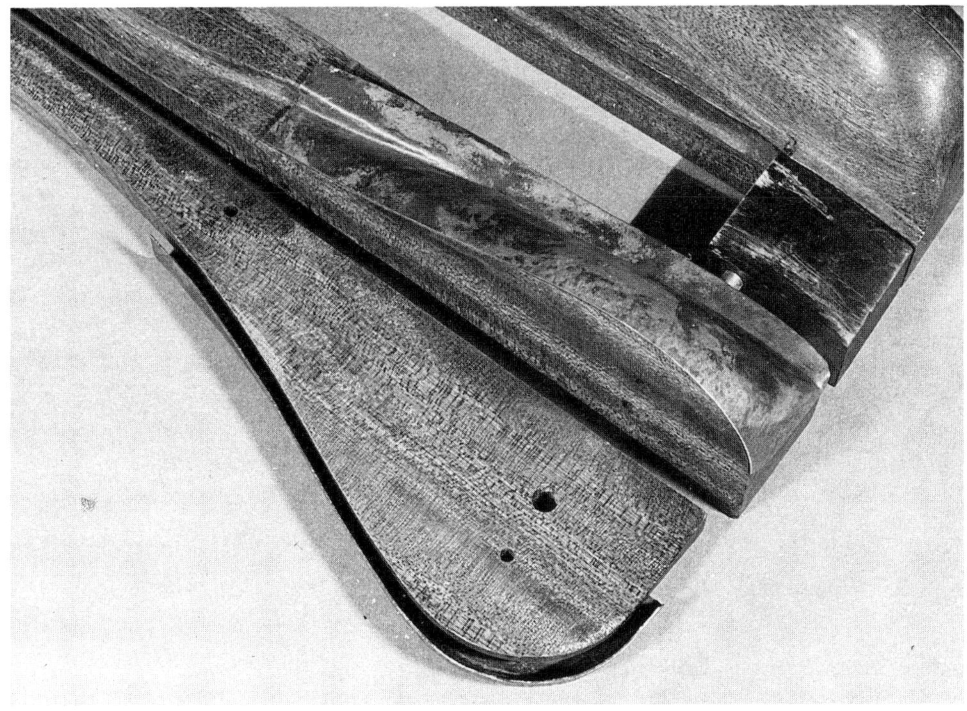

Plate 113

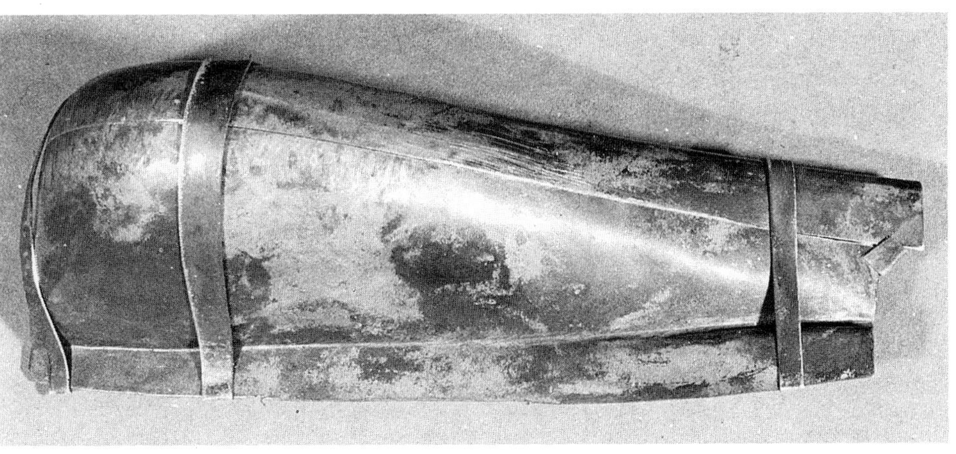

Plate 114

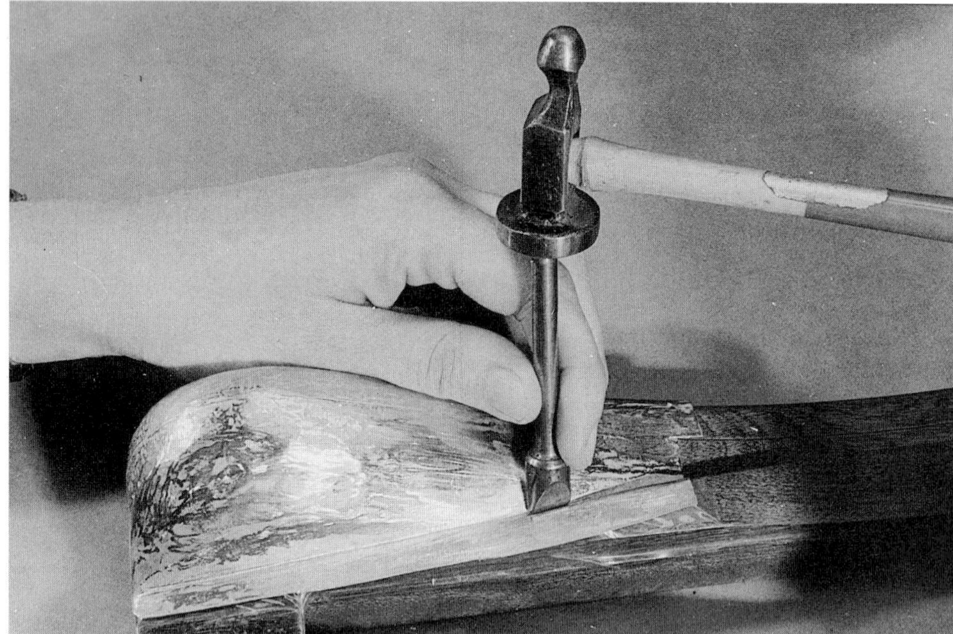

Plate 115

Plate 116

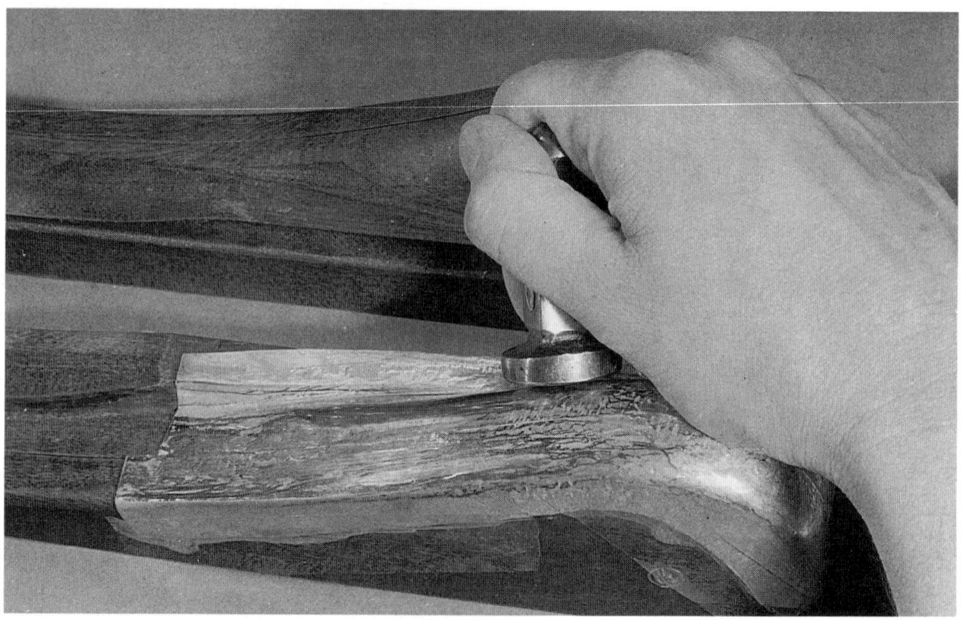

It will be seen in Plates 115 and 116 that Sellotape is used to hold the fender in place for the final working. This will be found most useful in any work of this sort. When all is tightly fitted in its appointed place, the surface should be rubbed vigorously all over with the flat face of the hammer (Plate 116). This will smooth out any dents or wrinkles and will work-harden the surface.

After the Royale wings were made in this way a single piece of sheet copper was worked over the centre section, incorporating the running board, one for each side. With the wings in place on the wood pattern, the last two sections were placed over these to make the cutting lines both front and back. When these were trimmed back to match exactly, the assemblies were silver soldered together to form the two complete wing sections shown in Plate 117. After a good going-over with the flat face of the hammer, they were cleaned up with a medium grit abrasive paper on a cork block. As can be seen, the sides have yet to be trimmed back to shape. The bottom half of the original card pattern, shown at the bottom of Plate 100, was used as a guide to mark out the wheel arches and remaining

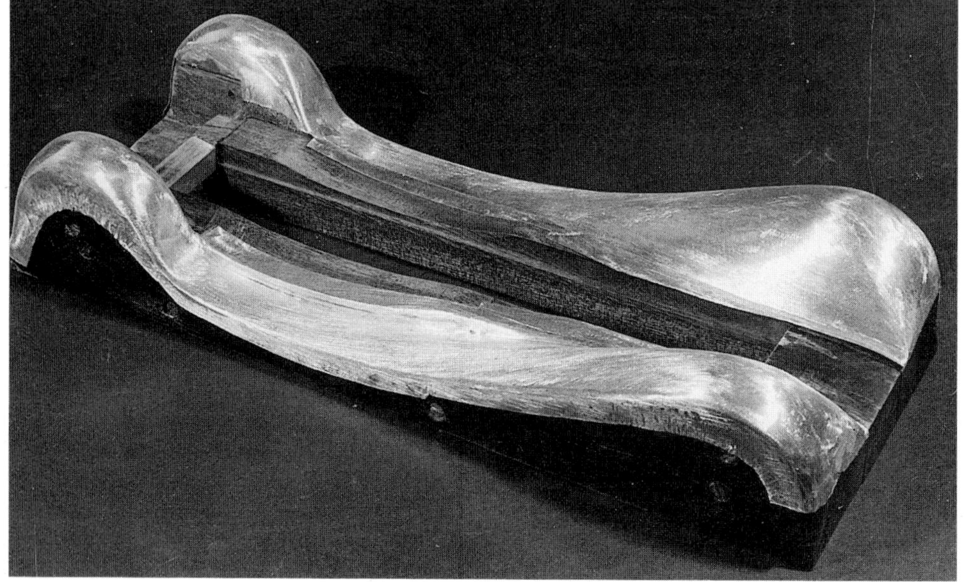

Plate 117

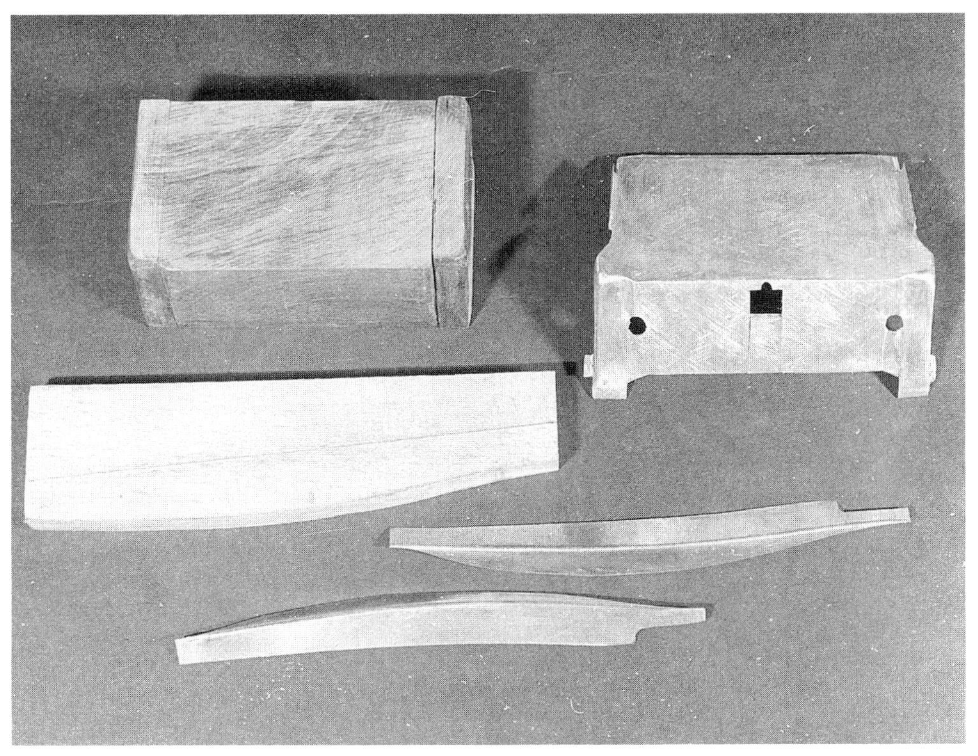

Plate 118

detail for trimming. In Plate 118, can be seen the rear 'filler' hard wood pattern (top left), and (to the right) the sheet metal panel made over it. The cut-out in the centre is to take the spare wheel bracket, the panel below the opening being fitted with two runners on the inside, so that it can be slid out for fitting over the chassis. The panel and its runners can be seen more clearly in Plate 172 which shows the underside of the rear chassis. Also shown in Plate 118 is a small hard wood pattern to provide the shaping for two sheet metal filler pieces, one of which can be seen being fitted in Plate 119.

Note in Plate 119 the wooden jig used to assist

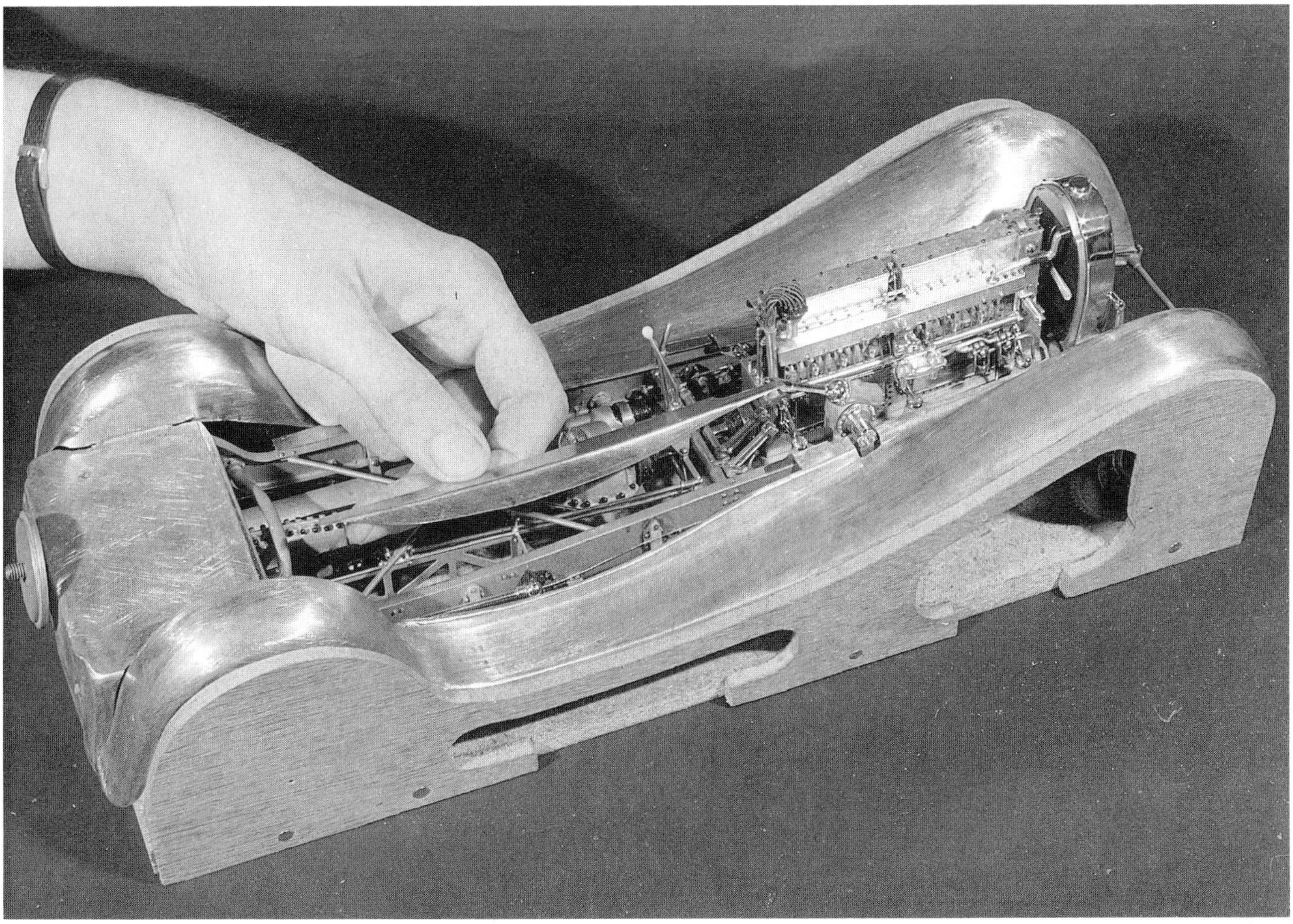

Plate 119

Plate 120

with the assembly of the wings to the chassis.

It will be found that even large pieces do not necessarily fit where you expect them to, and it can be most difficult to change some of them at a later date when the mistake may become apparent. To overcome this I always spend a little time making up one of these jig boxes. The base is the exact width of the outside dimensions across the wings, while the sides, which are cut and shaped together, match that of the wing horizontal line. Cut-outs are provided to facilitate access to the underside of the wings and wing stays. With the completed chassis standing in the centre of this, held in place with small blocks on each side of the wheels if necessary, the wings and their various fittings can be trimmed and otherwise manipulated until they make a perfect fit to all the required contact points. Holes provided for the fittings such as those shown here, as well as the rear cross panel just dealt with, can now be soldered in place. This last piece is so fitted as to look as though it is part of the rear wings, and in fact it joins the rear wings together without any beading, which is most unusual but looks rather splendid. It can be more clearly seen in Plates 133 and 134. The rounded fillet blending the three parts into one is built up of soft solder.

Returning to our next stage, Plate 120, we see the start of the engine bay. The engine has been removed, and the firewall and radiator fitted, so that an angled filler piece can be soft soldered to the wing sections between them. A second pair of parts can be seen at bottom left. To the right of this is a pair of press tools made up from scraps of brass, to form a small box-like fitting that covers an opening into which the end of the steering arm protrudes. It might at first seem to be a long answer to a short problem, to go to all the trouble of making a two-part press tool for such a simple item. The rounded nature of this piece could, however, have taken almost as long to make, but would still not have looked as authentic as this. It is the attention to detail of the small things that will make the big ones look correct.

With the engine bay boundaries all set, we are now ready to start the cover for it, ie the hood or bonnet depending which side of the Atlantic you come from. It was for this, and in particular the shaping of the top panels, that the hardwood pattern was made, which can be seen on the left of Plate 121. The sheet material used here is 0.012 in (0.30 mm) thick cold-working brass, the reason being that the comparatively straight sides and top, no double curves, will benefit from the slightly stiffer material. The pattern block is provided with the necessary guide lines to indicate to where the individual panels need to be trimmed back, which after the shapes have been established, is the next operation.

The making of hinges for the bonnet is covered in detail in *The Complete Car Modeller,* so I propose to cover it only briefly here. It is possible now to obtain a stainless steel tube with a hole through the centre of 0.010 in (0.25 mm) diameter or less, and it is

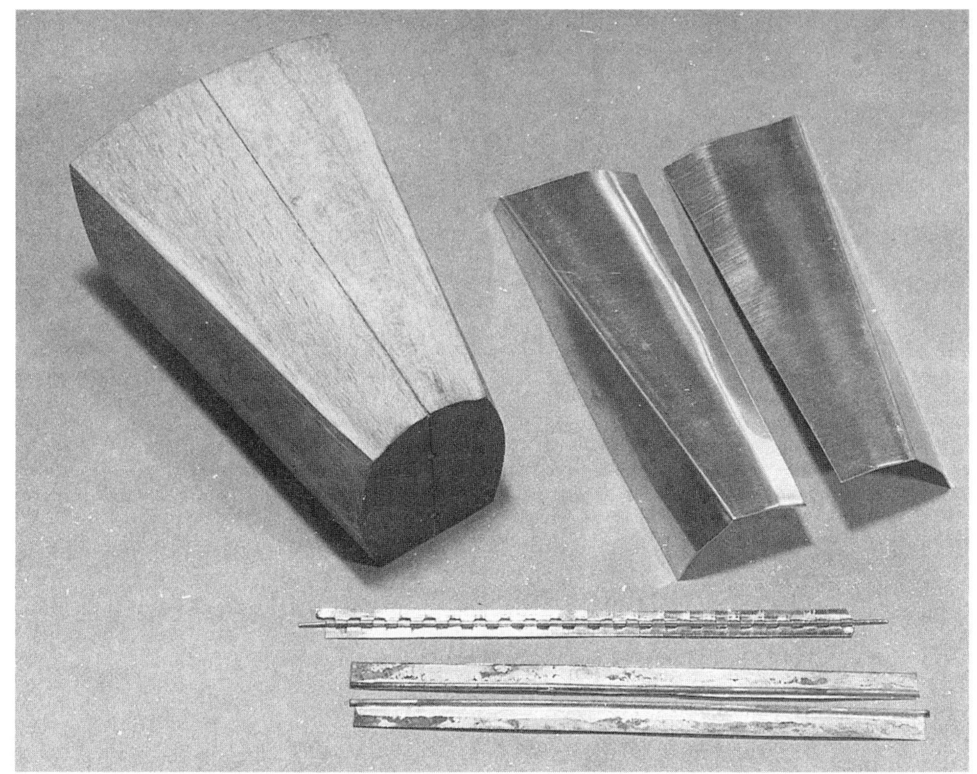

Plate 121

obtainable in lengths of 1 metre (3 feet). The problem is to find the supplier; however, with luck the trade directory in your local library will have the name of a manufacturer of hypodermic needles and a word with them could lead you to a number of very useful sizes of this most useful material. The reason for using stainless steel, of course, is that one avoids the problem of chrome plating.

Six strips of brass are selected of 0.010 in (0.25 mm) thickness by $\frac{1}{2}$ in (12.7 mm) wide and $\frac{1}{2}$ in longer than the length of the bonnet. Silver soldered to each of these is an equal length of stainless steel tube, two of which will have a bore of 0.031 in (0.78 mm) diameter for the top of the bonnet, while the other four will have a bore of 0.010 in (0.25 mm) for the bonnet side hinges. Each of these pieces, brass strip with the tube attached, is mounted in a vice on the milling machine and presented to a $\frac{1}{8}$ in (0.31 mm) diameter end mill in such a way that it will place a slot of equal width across the top edge of the strip and tube. This is then repeated for the full length at $\frac{1}{4}$ in (6.35 mm) intervals, so that it takes on a castellated appearance. The depth of cut should be equal to the diameter of the tube. Two pieces are made and fitted together and a wire of suitable thickness is passed down the centre of the tubes. Thus we have a hinge similar to the one shown in Plate 121. The width of brass strip is cut back to about $\frac{1}{8}$ in (3.17 mm) or less and tinned ready for fitting to the hood panels. The two parts at the bottom of this Plate are a pair of brass strips with tubes attached ready for milling the slots.

The sides of the Bugatti Royale bonnet are adorned with an array of eleven opening louvre doors. There are several ways of making these, my own solution (Plate 122) possibly being the most accurate one. For the average model maker, however, this solution is, perhaps, the most complicated one. The pieces were made using my own louvre press modified to take a special-purpose press tool made from gauge plate, which is readily obtainable soft, but very tough, tool steel. Most tool shops stock this in metre (yard) lengths of various widths and thicknesses. It is an extremely useful material from which to make all form of tools. The press tool has been designed so that after the first hole has been cut out, the workpiece can be moved through the

Plate 122

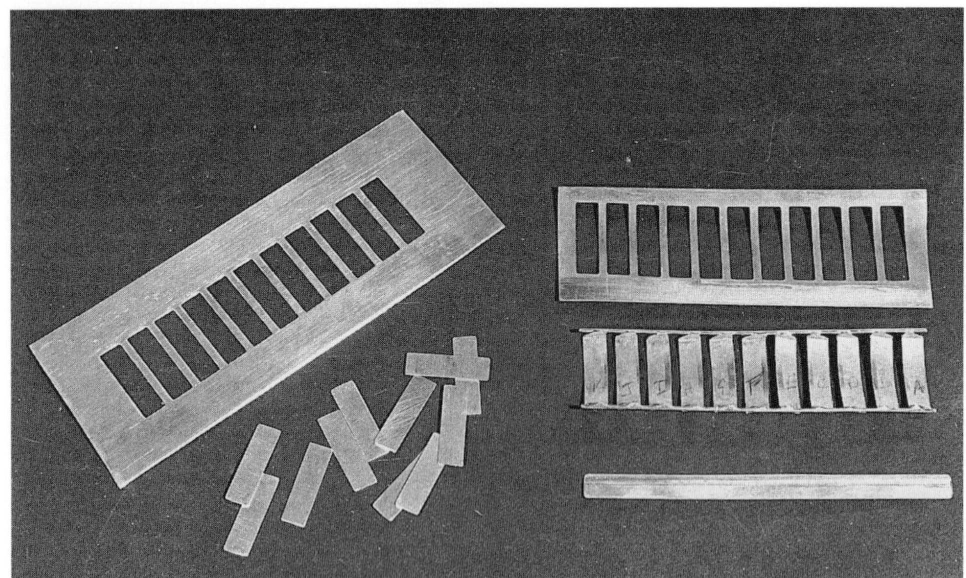

Plate 123

bottom part (the anvil). A plunger, to the left of the press cutter, is then depressed locating the brass strip in the correct place for the next hole to be cut. In this way, all twenty-two holes can be cut without any marking out at all, and the pieces removed by the press cutter can be reassembled to form the actual doors.

The other way of cutting these holes is to mark out the sides and drill $\frac{1}{16}$ in (1.57 mm) holes in the corners of each rectangle. Then with the aid of the flexible drive and disc cutter, very carefully remove each small panel. One would then need to cut out the actual doors from more brass sheet, but that is the least of the work. In Plate 123 at the top right, we have a bonnet side panel trimmed down to size and shaped ready to assemble on the model. The side is gently curved for all of its length, more so at the front where it fits the radiator, but also slightly at the rear where it meets the scuttle side wall. It is important at this stage to achieve this shaping, for each of the doors has also to match the curve, each one, therefore, being slightly different. The easiest way to do this is to fit each door into its respective opening and pass Sellotape along both sides to hold them in place. Now bend the complete assembly until it conforms exactly to the desired shape. Remove the tape and mark each door with its place of origin. The doors all now require a small triangular tab silver soldered to their top and bottom edges. When this is complete and the parts cleaned up, they are ready for fitting.

To do this, a wide strip of Sellotape is placed over the inside of the bonnet side and a sharp knife run down both sides of each opening. A small cut is now made across the centre of each and the flaps of tape so made folded through and stuck down on the outside. Two lengths of nickel silver wire are then cut, equal to the length of the bonnet, and Sellotaped at the top and bottom of the row of openings. The tape holding these wires in place is placed at the extreme ends of the bonnet away from the openings. The doors are then lined up in the correct order, each being passed through the opening from the outside and soft soldered by its tabs, top and bottom, to the two wires on the inside, the Sellotape preventing the solder getting on to the bonnet side. Each of the doors is soldered to the two wires in turn, noting that the first five back from the radiator open forward, with the remaining six opening to the rear. When complete the assembly can be taken out and the Sellotape removed. My reason for separating the doors from the bonnet sides in this way is that they should look as though they are each hinged from the inside, which in full-size they are. Were they to be soldered individually to the inside of each opening, this feeling of separation, however tenuous, would be more difficult to achieve. Plate 124 illustrates this point with the now almost completed Royale bonnet. While Plates 125 and 126 illustrate the progress so far, these photos

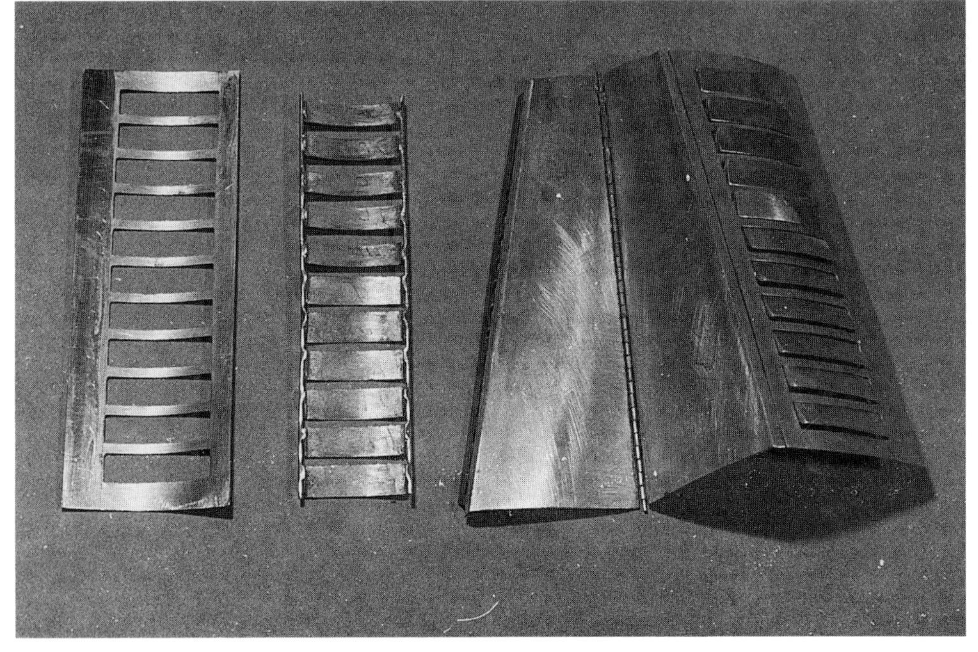

Plate 124

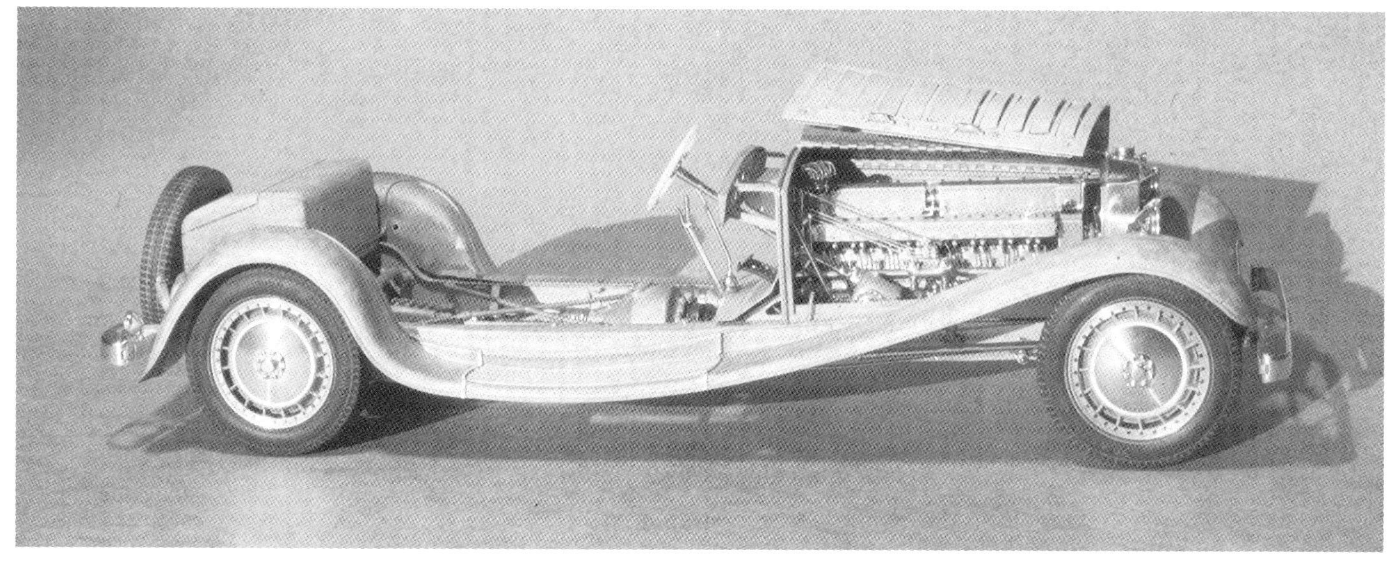

Plate 125

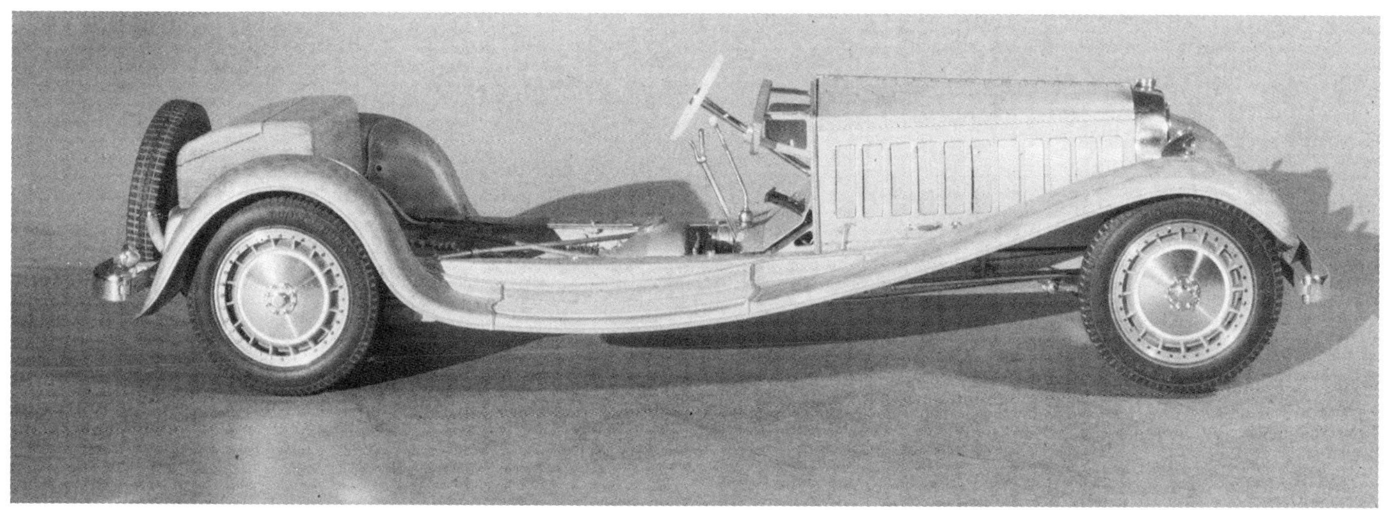

Plate 126

were actually taken a little later in the proceedings, hence the addition of several items not yet covered, but I do feel a need from time to time to sit back and view the progress, particularly in a long time-consuming project such as this. I particularly like these two shots because I think the grace and elegance of the full-size car is just starting to show through.

In the next six Plates, we see the Weinberger Cabriolet body starting to take shape. Although we are building the body panels in sheet metal and attaching them to a framework, in a similar way to that of the original, we do, by this technique, actually work in reverse. Rather than make and assemble the body frame and then make the panels to fit this, we first produce the sheet metalwork (with the aid of the hard wood patterns) and then manipulate the body framing to match and stiffen it.

In Plate 127, can be seen the master

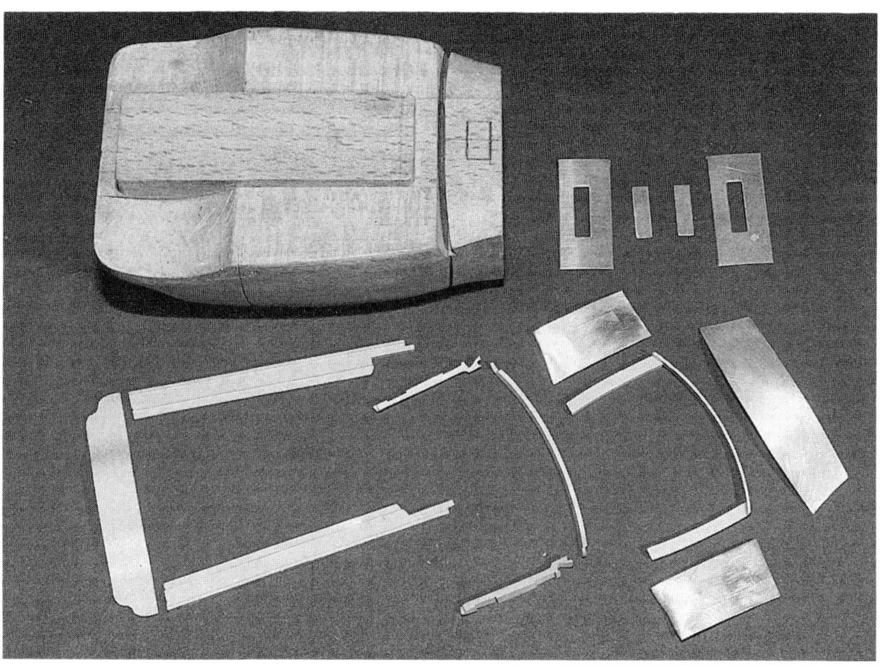

Plate 127

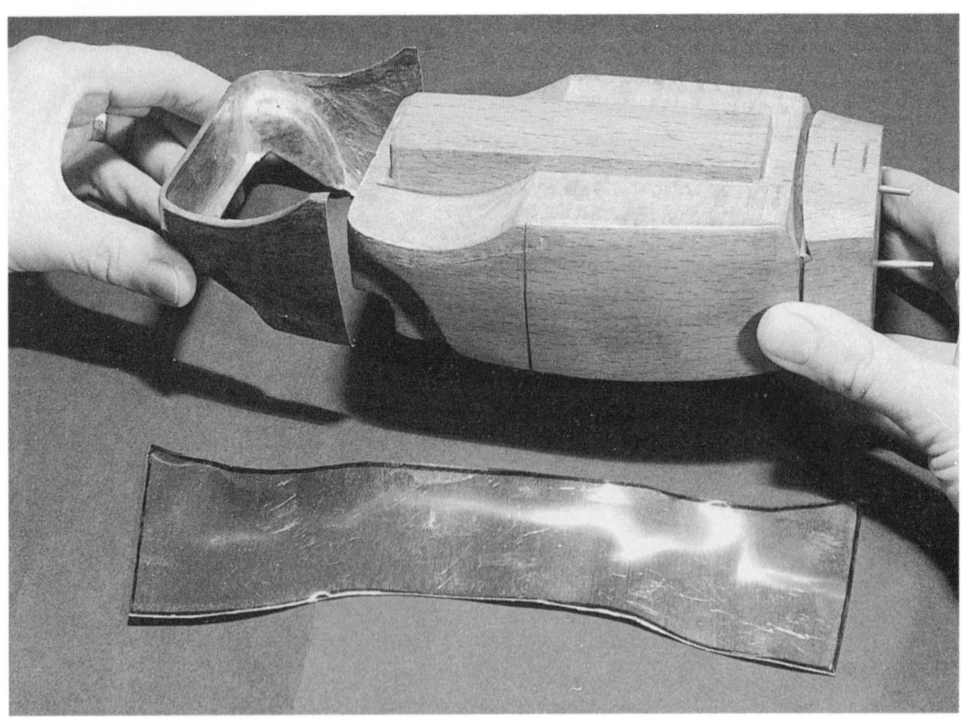

Plate 128

pattern together with the sheet brass for the scuttle. When these conform to the curves and shaping of the master pattern exactly, they are then used for marking out, and as a guide for bending the front end framing. This is made up from $\frac{1}{16}$ in (1.5 mm) and $\frac{3}{32}$ in (2.36 mm) thick strip material obtainable up to about two inches wide in machining-quality brass. Purchased in this form, a variety of widths can be cut to suit the job in hand. The two bottom strips and the near cross piece, to be seen at the lower left of Plate 127, are made as wide as practical to take the six small bolts that secure the body to the chassis frame. Being made of $\frac{3}{32}$ in (2.36 mm) thick brass it also provides some much-needed stiffening for the body at the door opening. All nine body framing parts are first drilled and given small locating dowel pins before being assembled with silver solder. The body panels are later soft soldered to them as they become available. In Plate 128 we see the largest of these, the complete rear section, being removed from the hard wood pattern block around which it was formed. Because of the shaping involved, we have reverted to the use of copper for this piece. As with the wing parts, a paper pattern was first used to determine the size and shape of the piece of copper sheet from which to form this section. A second piece may be seen at the bottom of this Plate showing the shape before working.

In Plate 129 we see the fitting together of all these pieces. Note that the assembly is taking place actually on the chassis, which brings me to the most important point to bear in mind as we proceed to tailor-make each section to fit the previous one. Because much of this will be dismantled for final finishing, there can be up to four paint or plating layers between the parts at the final fitting. If consideration is not given to this at this stage, much trouble can be expected, because often one does not have the option of scraping the paint off the offending parts without spoiling the whole model. This body section is a case in point. By forming parts by hand and assembling them one at a time, one can quite easily make everything an absolutely perfect fit. Consider now the addition of chrome plating to the fire wall, and the paint to the front face of the scuttle, rear wings, and rear body section where it fits over the latter. The consequences of not taking this into consideration here would be, at worst, the body not fitting at all, or at best, its bending in the centre thus preventing the doors from closing. To overcome these problems at this late stage, would

Plate 129

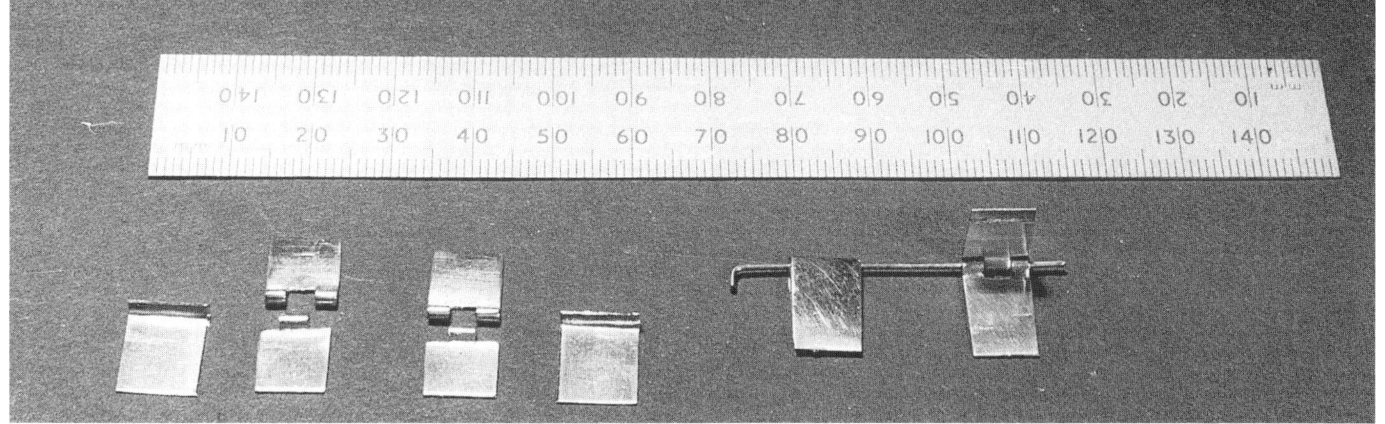

Plate 130

require stripping of the paint and the use of a large file, which are not to be recommended.

My solution to this is always to lay down several layers of Sellotape where a paint thickness may be expected to present a problem. This may get somewhat messy as work progresses, but it is a constant reminder of a vital provision that can be forgotten in the enthusiasm of work. The Sellotape, seen earlier with the assembly of the bonnet doors, illustrates how it will act as a barrier when we wish to soft solder two parts together while in contact with a third one, which is not part of the assembly.

In Plate 130, we come to the door hinges. These are made from nickel silver sheet and polished, because I prefer to make them a permanent fitting at this stage, rather than have them removable for electroplating. The minute size of screws needed to make these removable would greatly weaken a very vulnerable and vital part of the model, and I do not consider the risk worthwhile. The basic parts ('A' and 'B', Fig 10) are cut from 0.015 in (0.38 mm) thick sheet and bent around the shank of a $\frac{1}{32}$ in diameter drill to form a 'P'. Silver solder is run down the join, after which they receive the attentions of a small square file and are fitted together in pairs with a length of $\frac{1}{32}$ in nickel silver wire. The third part of the hinge, 'C', is cut and formed from 0.005 in (0.12 mm) thick sheet and soft soldered to one side of the hinge assembly, as indicated. This, when fitted correctly, should allow the hinge to open a full 90°. The double side of the hinge is fitted to the door and the single side fitted to the body. Plate 131 illustrates the fitting of the hinges to the body, the double sided one being clearly discernible in the opened position. To assemble, the sides of the hinges are tinned and, with the aid of an electric soldering iron, just 'spotted' in their correct position using the engineer's

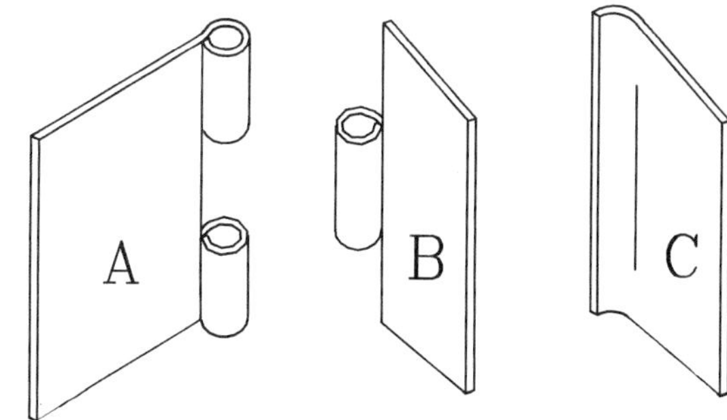

Fig. 10 The three-part door hinge with part C acting as the side cover.

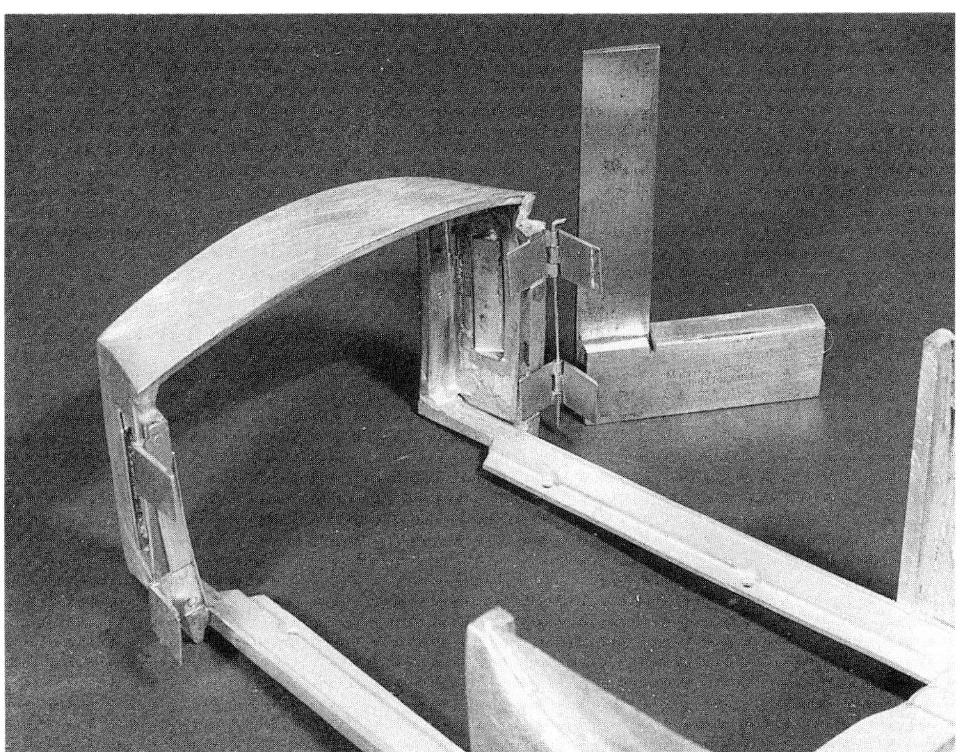

Plate 131

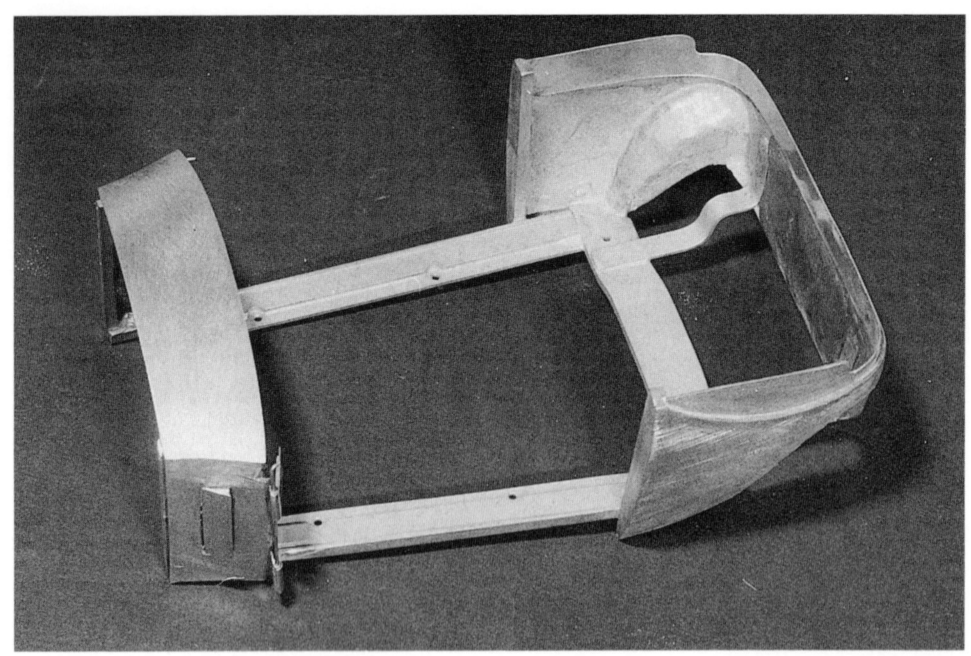

Plate 132

square to make certain that they are square with the body. To 'spot' something is to just touch the part with the iron sufficient to locate it for further working, rather than melt all the solder on the tinned parts to secure them permanently. Using the soldering iron in this way allows one to manipulate the various pieces with considerable freedom, using the iron in one hand while holding the part in the other with tweezers.

When the hinges have been correctly placed, they are drilled and riveted to their respective posts, reheated to allow the solder to run properly, then trimmed back to the framing. In Plate 132, is the basic body shape assembled. Note the stepped arm soldered from the cross piece to the rear body, and the strip of brass

Plate 133

Plate 134

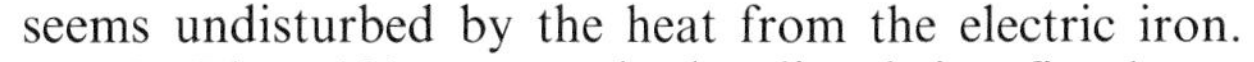

added to the top edge to form a step on the outside that will take the folding top. All these help to stiffen the rather fragile shell. To help further stiffen areas of sheet metal, such as that across the back and on each side between the door post and the rear wheel arch, I now add pads of the epoxy resin putty that we used earlier. These can be seen quite clearly in the following series of Plates. Provided that the resin has set properly and a little clearance is made between it and any soldered joints to be made at a later stage, it seems undisturbed by the heat from the electric iron.

In Plate 133 we see the beading being fitted between the rear body and wings. This is a strip of copper wire that is soft soldered to the wings. Put several layers of Sellotape on the rear body section, then bolt it to the chassis in its final position. Bend the wire to fit the shape as snugly as possible, then flux the immediate area of the rear wings that is to take the beading. Spot the beading in the centre with the iron, then feed solder to the wire as you gradually work your way along its length, fitting it tight into the corners and curves as necessary. Plate 134 shows the beading in place, with the body removed and the whole area cleaned up with the aid of abrasive rubber discs and cups (Plate 26) and the flexible drive.

Plates 135 and 136 illustrate two stages in fabricating the windscreen, the first stage of which is to make a pattern for

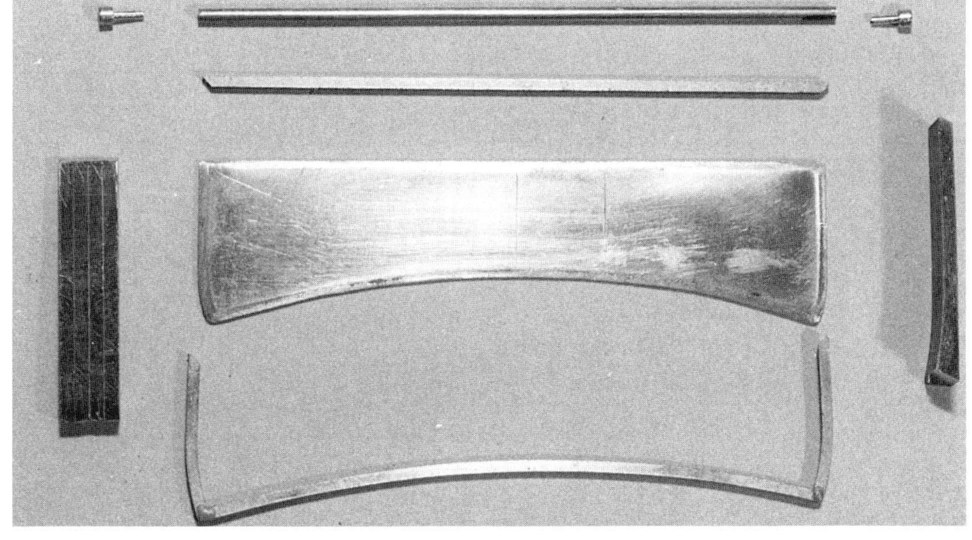

Plate 135

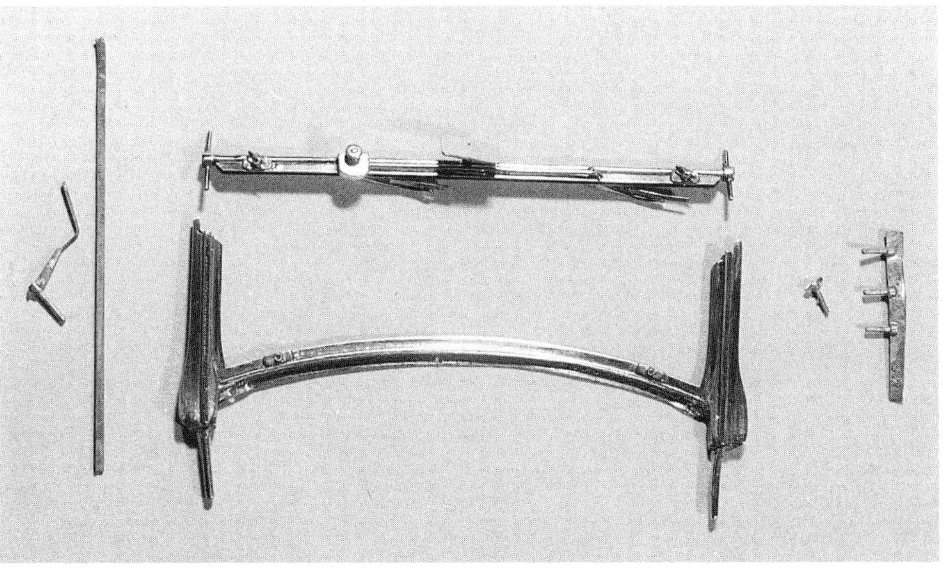

Plate 136

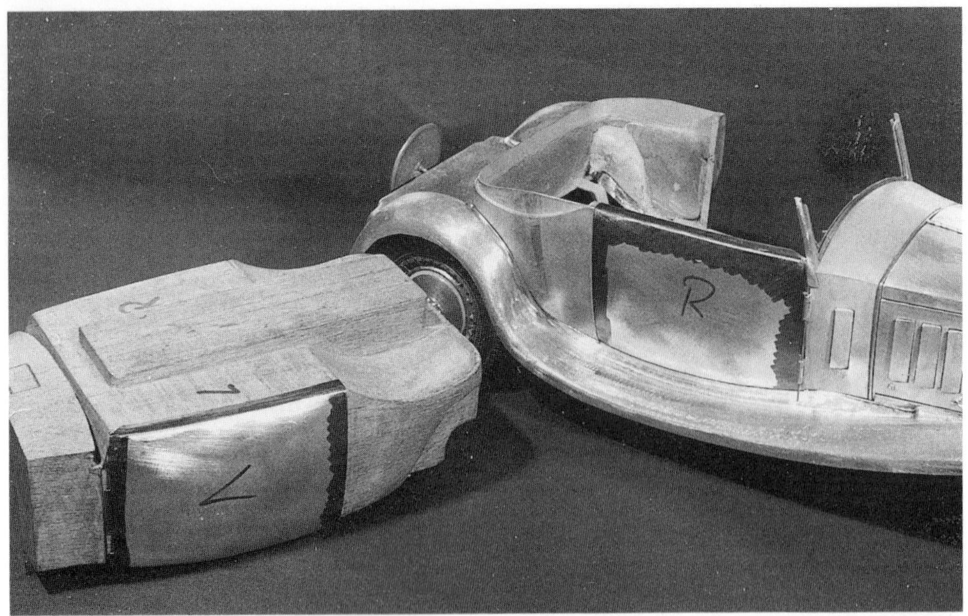

Plate 137

On this particular subject, the windscreen outer pillars and their fitting between the rear of the scuttle and the front top edge of the doors form a most intricate part of the design. When one finds a piece such as this, one should take as long as necessary to understand how and why it is shaped as it is. In this case, as can be noticed by the position of the slot across the front of the master pattern in Plate 128, the front corner of the scuttle is somewhat lower than the top of the door line. Also, in Plate 142, it will be seen that the outside shape actually follows the form of the moulding along the top of the door. The rear face of the pillar not only follows the angle of the side window, but also imperceptibly blends this into the vertical line of the door post. Because some of these vital parts of the jigsaw are not yet fitted, it is far better at this stage just to leave the outside shaping until they are. If the screen's outer posts fit the screen, fit the slot in the cowl and blend in with the vertical door post, then all the pieces can be soft soldered together. Much depends on the screen being positively and permanently secured.

To this end it can be seen in Plate 136 that I have soldered across under the U-section screen frame an angled securing piece of brass with three small holes in it. In addition two large pins extend down from the outer posts. Two vertical holes are provided in the tops of the door posts on which to locate the screen outer pins. The three holes in the cross piece are now provided with three small screws that thread into the brass frame work under the cowl to secure the screen assembly at the correct angle. The three small screws are later hidden behind the moulding that fits above the dashboard, shown as the top piece in Plate 157.

Plate 137 illustrates the next stage of body construction: the shaping of the doors. These are formed from brass sheet and have a very shallow convex surface. I have found this all but impossible to beat into a sheet with a hammer; if, however, the metal is first annealed, then laid flat on the iron block and the surface worked over vigorously with the flat of the hammer (as in Plate 116) from the centre outwards, the convex shape will in time start to develop. A second method is to sand blast it at about 80 psi. For some unaccountable reason, rather than developing a concave surface directly in the path of

the shape of the glass. The inner frame is made from a brass U-section, ie a brass bar that has already been formed to the shape of three sides of a rectangle but with sharp corners. This can be obtained in a range of sizes, the one used here being 1.5x1.5 mm. It is also possible to obtain this material as an angle, just two sides, and in the form of a 'T' and an 'H', each with its own range of sizes down to 1.0x0.5 mm. Never having come across this in Imperial sizes, I conclude it originates in Continental Europe, probably Germany.

To return to Plate 135, whenever a frame is required to encircle a piece of glass, it inevitably presents the problem of how you are going to get the glass into it. If the frame is of a U-section, one side at least will need to be removable, and if this is so, now is the time to determine how it will be secured in the final assembly. Small bolts are the ideal, but on this scale, unless you can hide them somewhere, they are difficult to place. Second best is the use of pins which can be fitted and removed as many times as necessary, yet be secured with a spot of instant glue at the final fitting. It was this later solution that I decided upon here and they can be seen at each end of the top bar in Plate 136. The two pieces carrying these together with the top bar, brass tube, and the top piece of U-section frame, are shown separated in the previous Plate. The corners of the bottom three sides of the main frame have been mitred and silver soldered together. The top assembly just mentioned, will also be assembled with hard solder while the outer frame and fittings will be added to these with soft solder.

A number of wing nuts are called for on this screen assembly. My method of making these can be seen down the left-hand side of Plate 136. These are turned on the lathe as short two diameter pieces, a larger short one at the head, with a thinner longer one for the tail (which would be the threaded end). Holding the tail in some pliers, the slitting disc can be used to put a slot across the head, which is then slipped over a short length of thin brass or nickel silver and silver soldered in place. Three pieces are shown here having just been assembled. These are then separated and filed to the required shape.

Plate 138

the spray, the surface appears to spring forward and develop a convex shape. By experimentation, or trial and error, one can find new ways of solving all these problems, and I find it is half the enjoyment of using tools.

As with the wings, the aim should be to overdevelop the curved surface, anneal the metal, then work it back on to the hard wood pattern with the flat of the hammer. When it matches the desired shape, the framework is made up from brass strips (Plate 138) and soft soldered to the door panel. This was undertaken by Sellotaping the door panel in place in the body, after first tinning the inner surface, and then shaping the two principal framing pieces, front and rear, until they fitted their allotted places before finally soldering them to the door panel. Note in Plate 138 a strip of metal standing to the left of the rear door post on the left-hand side of the model. This was cut from $\frac{1}{16}$ in (1.57 mm) thick aluminium sheet and fitted between the door post and the new door framing piece so that the latter could be precisely soldered at that point. The reason will become apparent in Plate 140 where it will be seen that we have yet to fit a pair of locating plates in this position.

Before that, a special moulding was cut out from a pattern taken directly from the scale plans (bottom item in Plate 139). This was formed in copper and cut and soft soldered as shown to become the moulding at the top of the door and around the rear of the body. With this in place, the final shaping of the outer windscreen pillar can be completed by marking out the exact shape directly from the door moulding just fitted. After this the remaining door framing

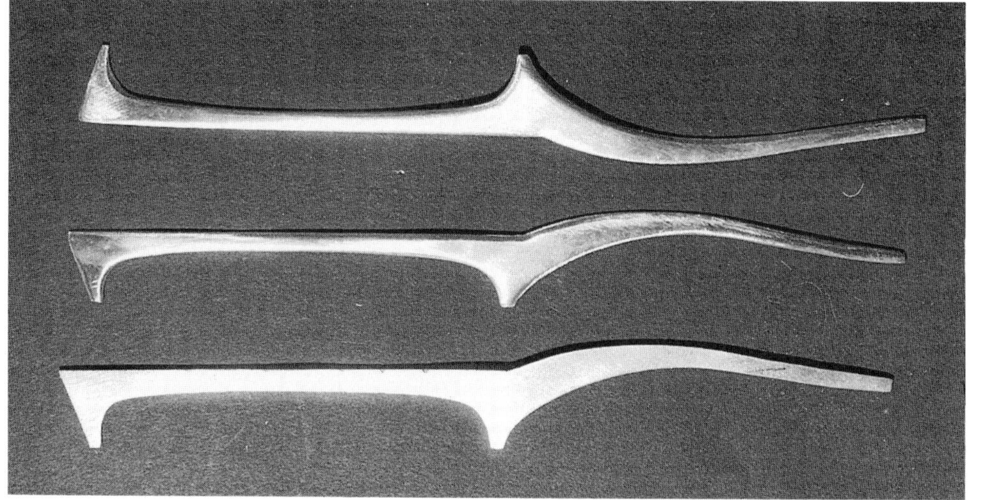

Plate 139

Plate 140

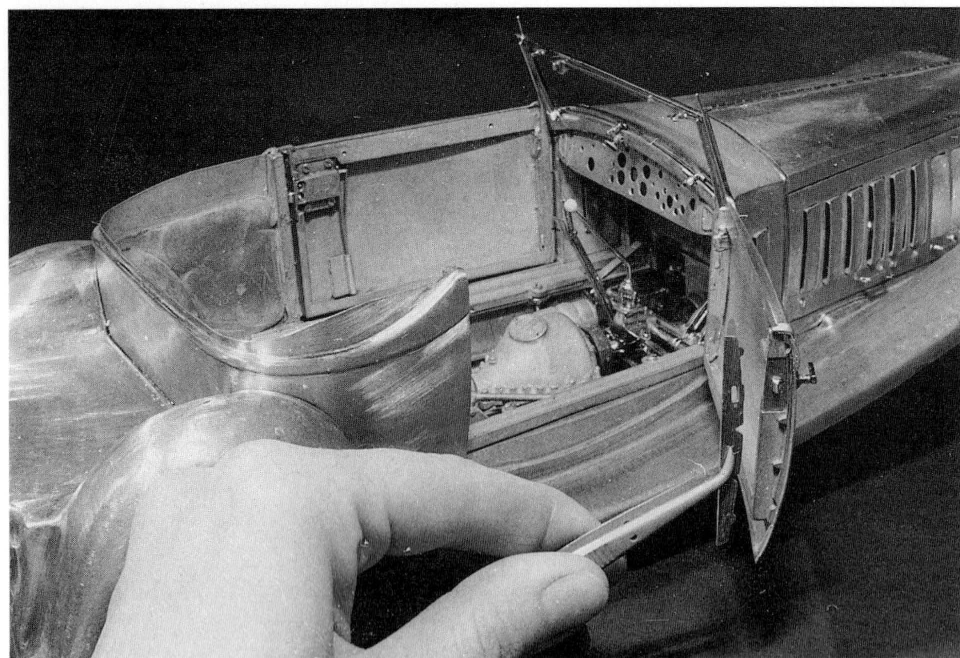

Fig. 11 The miniature operating door latch fitted to the Bugatti Royale.

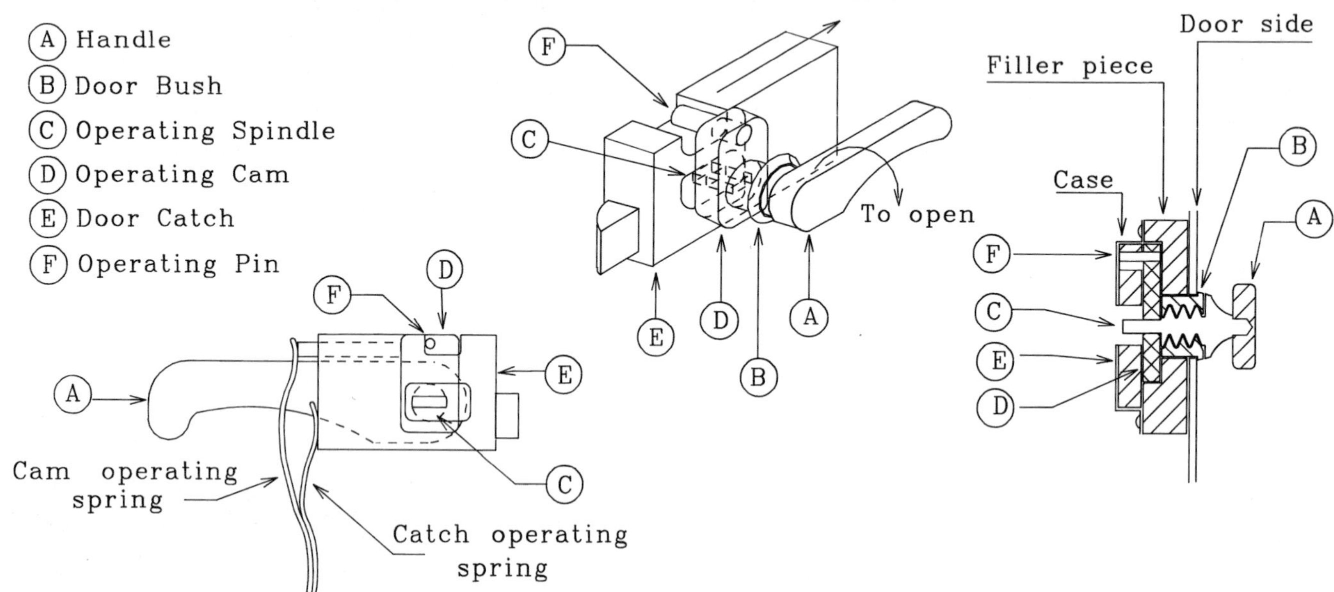

is attached together with the catch mechanism and door locating plates. The latter, Plate 140, are made as a pair, male and female. The male is soft soldered to the door, while the female has the rear surface tinned. The front surface (the one facing the door catch) is provided with a layer or two of Sellotape, and then slipped over the door catch and the door closed flush with the body and taped in place. The carbon rod soldering tool was then used to heat the rear door post sufficiently to solder the female locating plate to it. With the operation undertaken in this way, we can be certain that all parts fit exactly.

There is one point worth noting about fitting doors; for the outside sheet metal, we should ignore the requirement for a paint allowance. Doors should be made as exact a fit as possible, but due allowance should always be made for paint thickness in the framing. It will be found much less of a problem to locate hinges, catches and mouldings, etc on these working parts if they are made a tight fit until all fittings are attached. When complete, the edges of the door and frame can be filed back for the clearance.

I do not attempt to make my door catches emulate the workings of the original, but they do operate from the door handle and the actual catch is provided with a separate spring so that it moves independently of the handle when the door is closed. As the door catches need to be designed to fit in the space available, they will be different for each subject. The only other common feature is that the spindle from the handle to the mechanism is provided with a thread. This eliminates the problem of how to retain it in the door, because the amount of space that is left, on this scale, can be minimal in the extreme, although in this case it is quite spacious. The point about the threaded spindle is that although the handle is revolved to screw it in place, the lever attached to this on the inside, that actually moves the catch, now restricts the handle movement to just the quarter-turn necessary to open the door. Fig 11 shows a breakdown of this

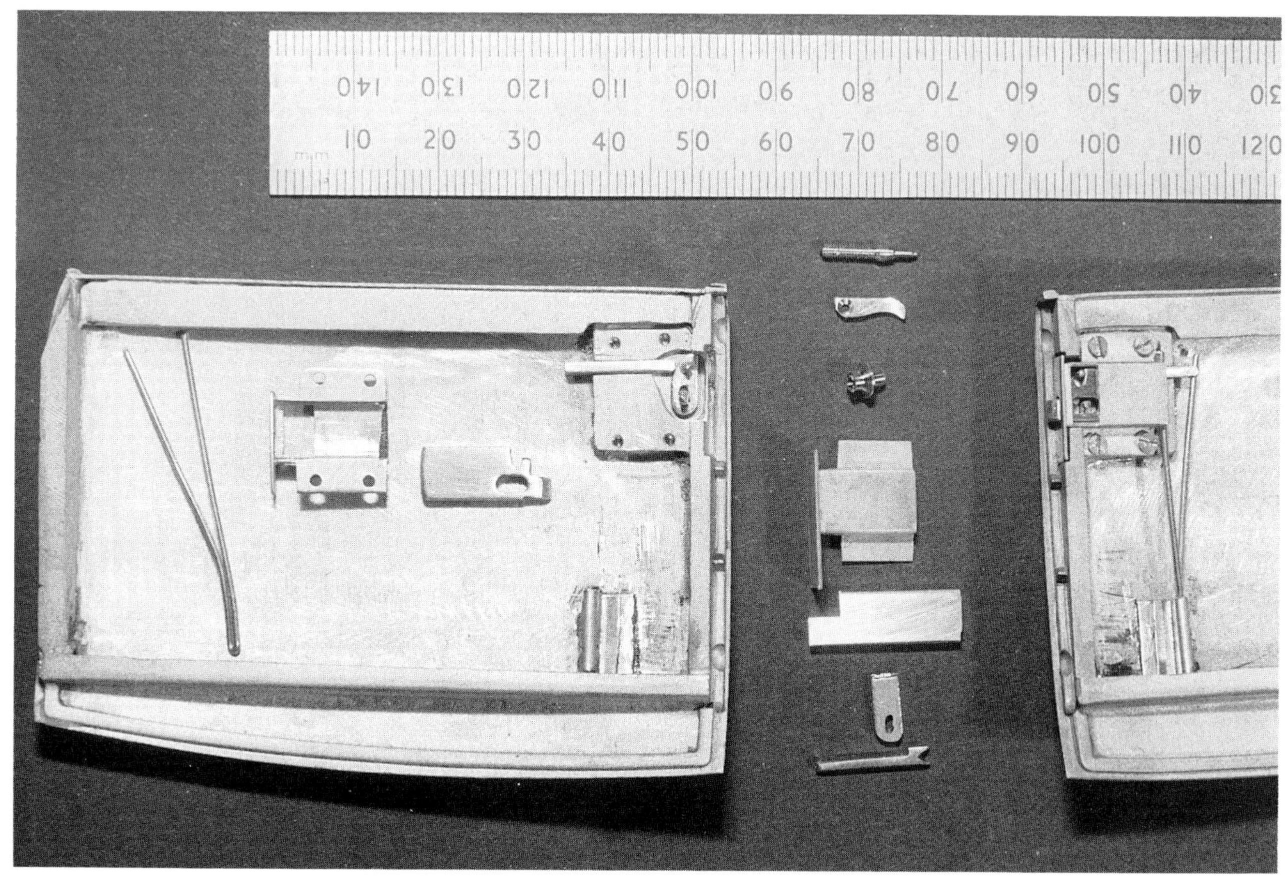

Plate 141

particular mechanism, while in Plate 141, we see in the centre, from top to bottom, the spindle, outside handle, threaded bush which is soft soldered to the door, fabricated housing for the working parts, the door catch, operating lever, and lastly the spring-loaded pin. All are made from nickel silver and are shown assembled in the door on the right, and opened to view on the left.

Plate 142 shows the door window frame in place with the pattern for the glass around which it was made. Note the scribed line and two holes along the bottom edge. The frame, formed in brass U-section stock, is in the shape of an inverted 'U'. The two ends are joined together by a strip of flat brass sheet, soldered to the outside face of the U-section at the points indicated by the scribed line on the pattern, which is provided with the same two holes. The strip cannot be seen on the window frame because it sits just below the top edge of the door. A second strip, also cut and drilled, has soldered to its top edge a strip of U-section brass which, when assembled, forms the bottom frame of the window. The complete frame is secured in the door by the two small screws visible on the right side door in Plate 142. This fixing is hidden by the inside door panel, two of which can be seen in Plate 143, one fitted on the left-hand side, the other removed.

Brass is used to form all the window parts, and also the door panel trim and pockets. Along the bottom edge of the trim panel is a strip of brass sheet

Plate 142

Plate 143

made to form a lip which slips over the bottom framing of the door, which is also made from sheet brass in the form of a lip, thus securing the bottom edge. The panel is actually held in place by the inside door handles, each of which is provided with a screw thread that passes through the panel to a threaded block soldered to the inside of the door.

The folding hood presented a number of problems, not least of which was to decide from what material it should be made. In *The Complete Car Modeller*, I describe the making of a fabric hood that can be folded. The design of the Weinberger hood is such that when folded, it is not a pretty sight. Very few of the German-style hoods of this period were visually pleasing in this configuration, being about as far removed from the 'disappearing hood' as it is possible to get. The hood is large, and it is expected to last forever, yet still look as though it were made yesterday. It was decided that relying on a fabric alone would be no answer. My experience is that on seeing a soft-top on a model for the first time, the ill-informed invariably stick their finger in the centre of it just to prove it is soft. In this case, they would have a surprise, for this soft-top is very hard, being made from sheet copper, as we will shortly see.

Another problem was the design of the folding bows, the framework that supports the fabric. Our research told us that originally the bows were visible from the inside of the vehicle, while today they are hidden behind a headlining. It was important then, if we were to show the correct configuration, that we should attempt to design an arrangement that matched the creases in the raised top as we know it today, and match the folding top arrangement of which we have just one photograph. The two-dimensional working model to be seen in Plates 144 to 147 shows the result of this effort. This formed

Plate 144

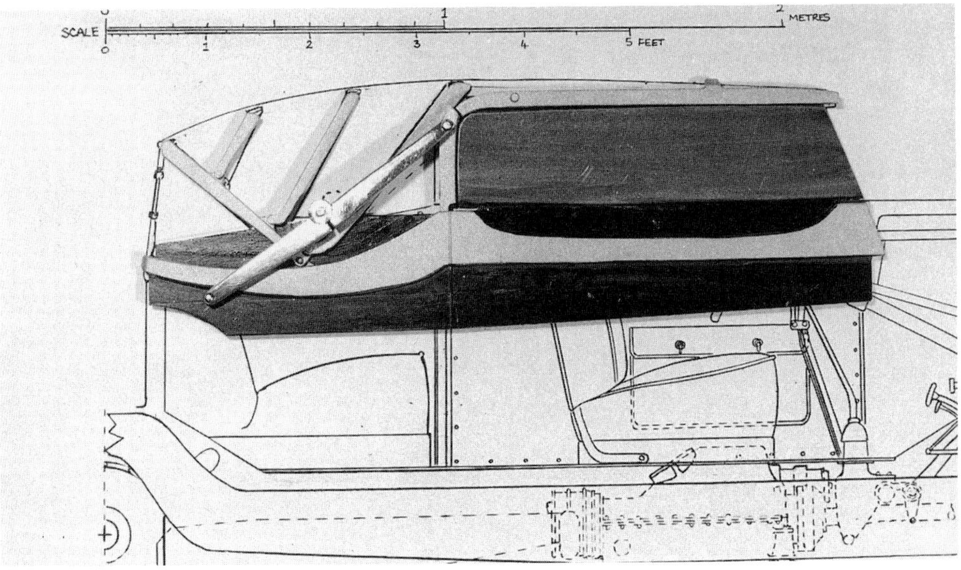

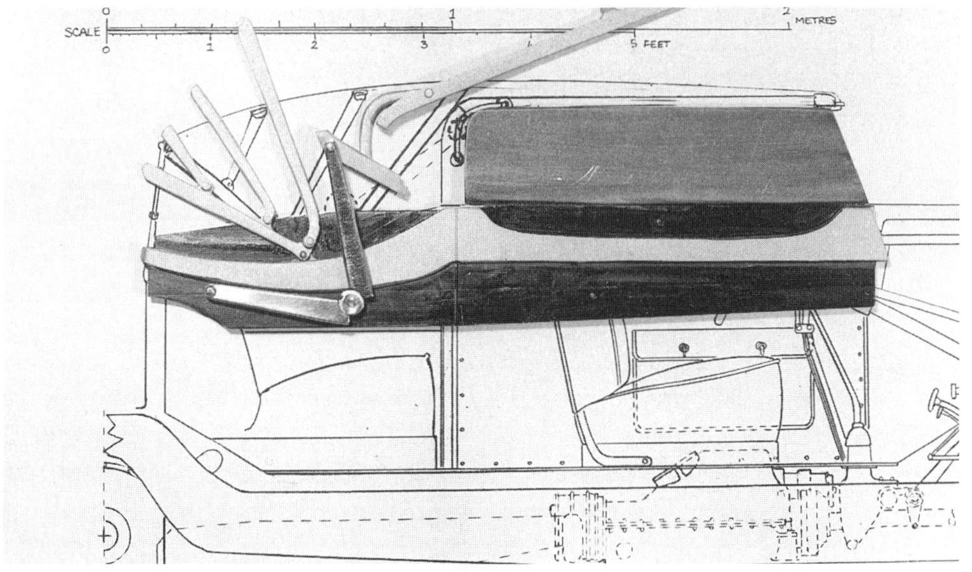

Plate 145

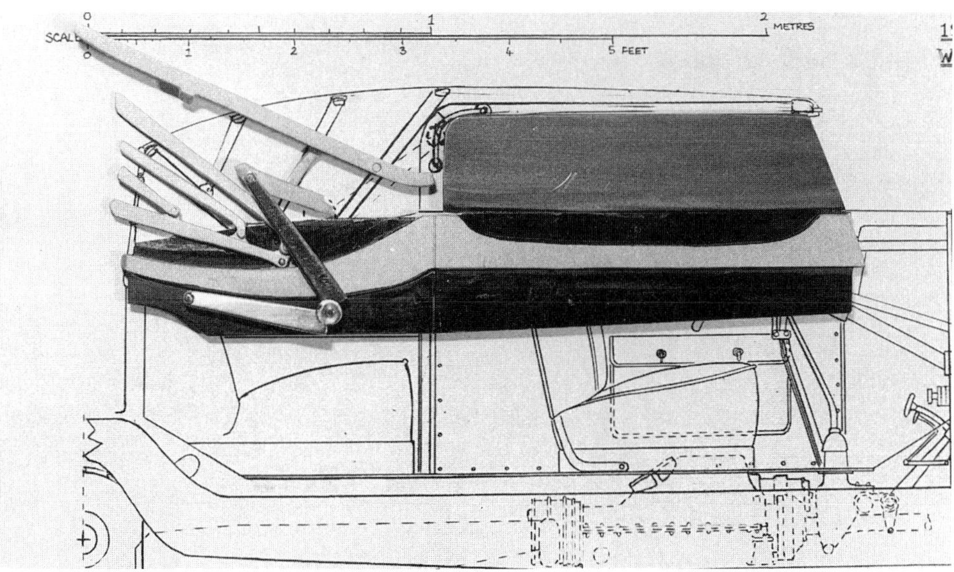

Plate 146

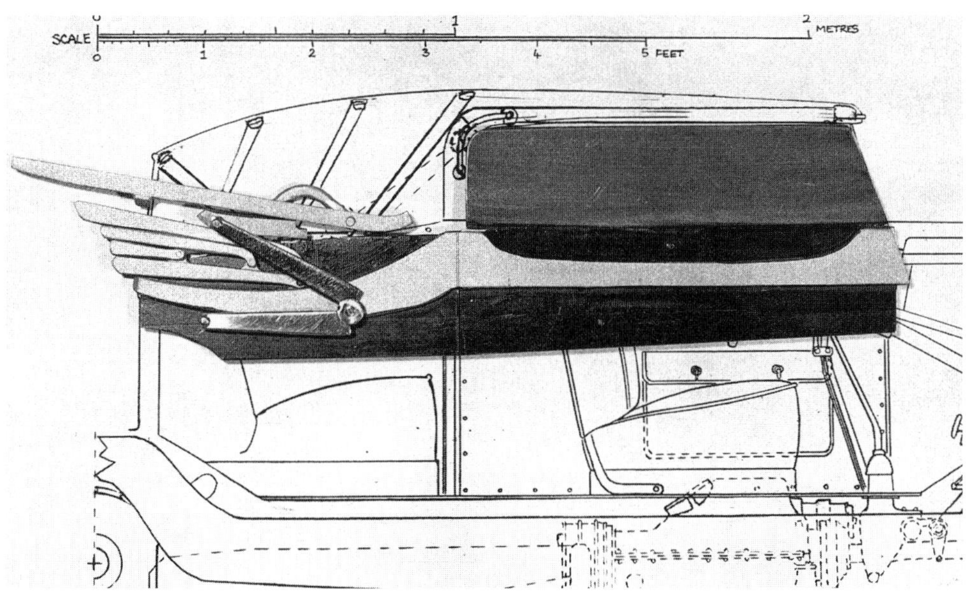

Plate 147

the basis of the folding top detail included in the actual model, and that fitted on the actual car. Museums are not keen to take these treasures apart for model makers, particularly when they are valued in millions of dollars.

Plate 148 illustrates the preliminary stages of the hood being worked in sheet copper, while Plate 149 shows the hard wood pattern and the finished shell. Note the bow positions worked into the top; because of the slight sag in between, these did take on quite a soft look. The hood received a covering of fabric; details of which are included in the final section of this book, together with paints and finishes, etc.

In Plates 150, 151 and 152, we see the assembled bows as fitted in the model, raised in the first Plate and lowered in the other two. Also included at the bottom of Plate 150 is a strip of brass bent in the flat state to the angles necessary to accommodate the curved corners when formed into a bow. The extreme example of this is the forward bow of the set, shown in the up position in Plate 153. Although the bow is at an angle of about 45 degrees, the top part must be flat to the lay of the fabric and should follow this over the radius at the corners. A strip of sheet metal is marked out and bent to the bow positions, then fitted as shown here to locate them for fitting the straps. On the model, these are two thin strips of brass that will connect all the folding top framework together. On the full-size hood these would be made of strong webbing and would position the individual bows as the hood was raised. As this is

Plate 148

Plate 149

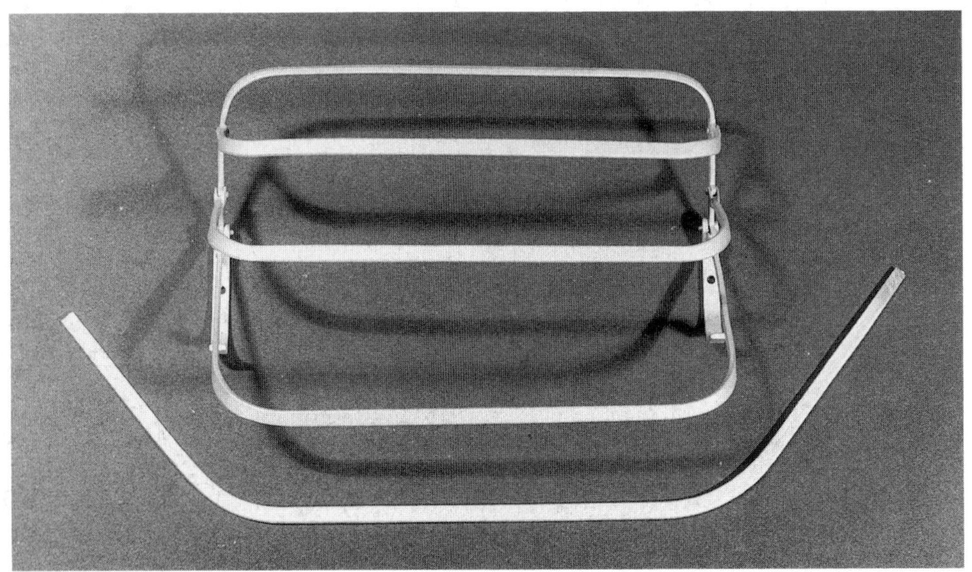

Plate 150

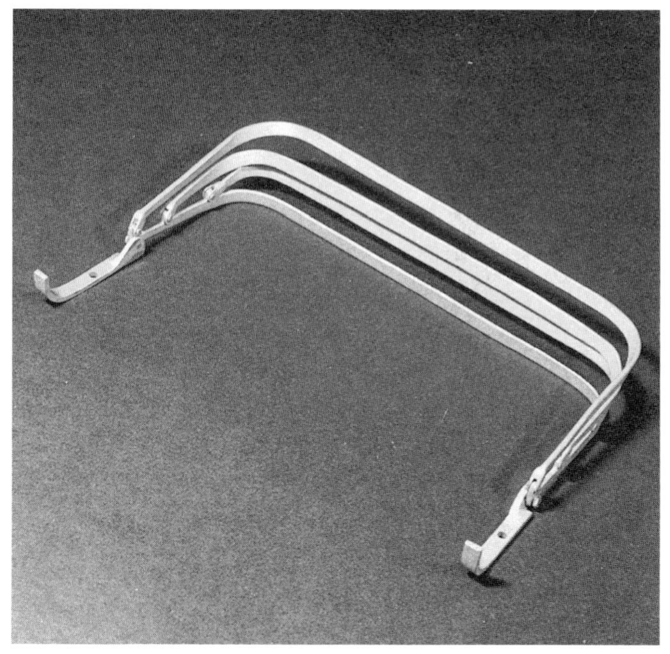

Plate 151

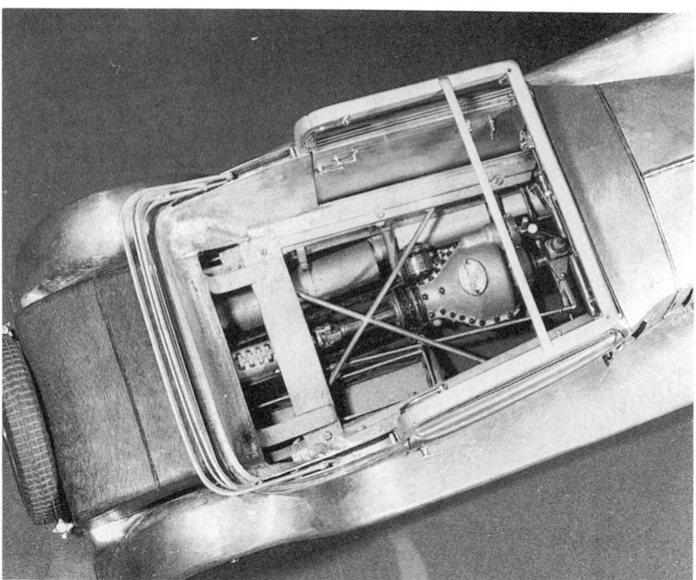

Plate 152

to be fixed in the up position, these brass straps are soft soldered to each of the components from front to rear with an extension down to meet, but not to be attached to, the rear body. In Plate 154, is the complete folding hood assembly including the two straps sitting in the soft-top shell. Note that due allowance has been made between the copper shell and the inner assembly to accommodate the fabric layer on the inside to be fitted later.

Plate 153

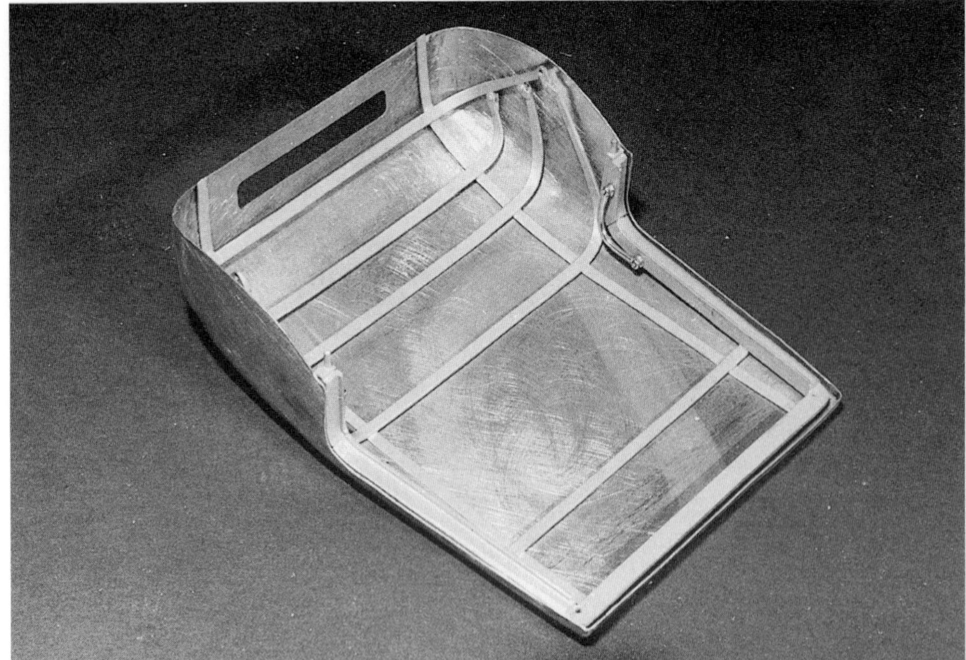

Plate 154

Plate 155

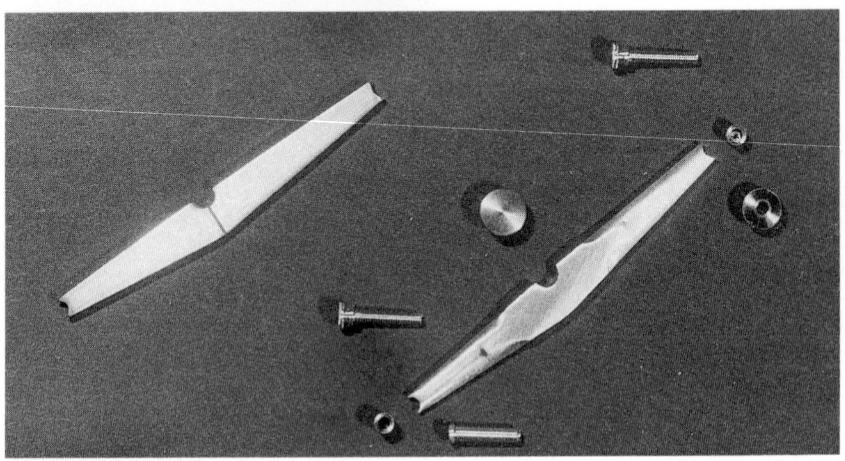

All that we now need to complete the top mechanism are the landau irons (Plate 155). These are fitted to the outside of the folding hood, and in full-size practice brace the assembly in the up position. Because these are not required to fold, they are made from a single length of brass strip with a bush silver soldered to each end, and a boss hard soldered into the half-circular space provided near the centre. The large-diameter bush on the far right is fitted to the top, while the long thin bush at the bottom is soft soldered into the rear of the body. Two of each are needed and they take the four hand screws that hold the landau irons in place, two of which are also shown here.

Now for the fitting out of the Royale's interior. First the clocks. These are drawn up ten times the finished size with as much detail as one wishes to include. In Plate 156, we see the set produced for the Weinberger Royale. Sitting on the thumb nail on the far left is the largest of the clocks, reduced to 1/15 scale. Under a magnifying glass, all the detail is still readable, even to the recorded mileage from the day I photographed the original. To reduce the drawn detail to this size, I photographed it with a 35 mm camera. After much trial and error, it is possible to arrive at a distance between camera and drawing that will provide an image on the negative

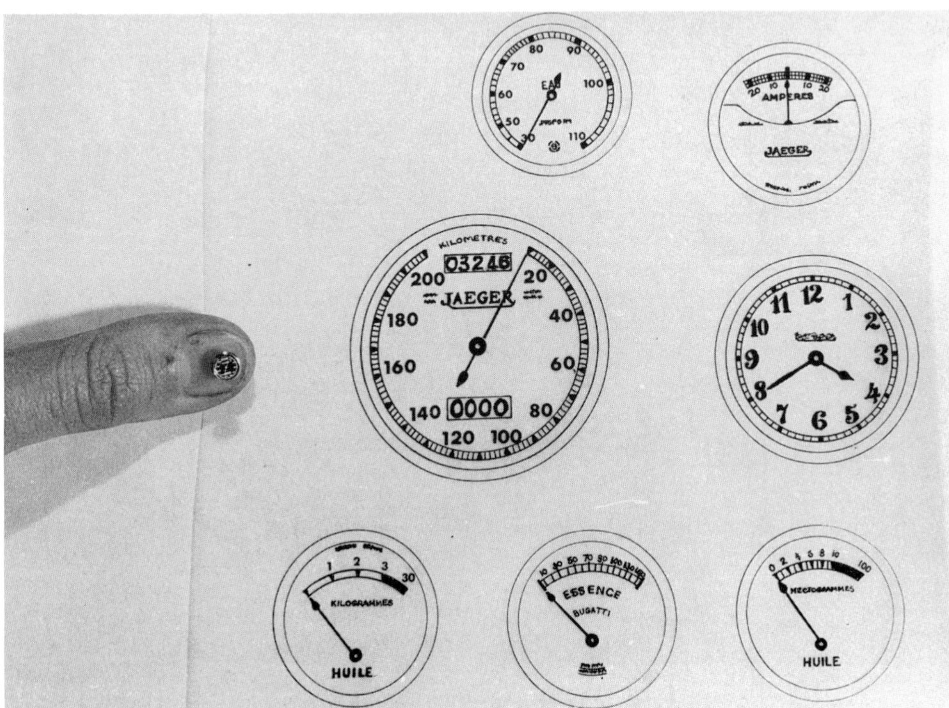

Plate 156

Plate 157

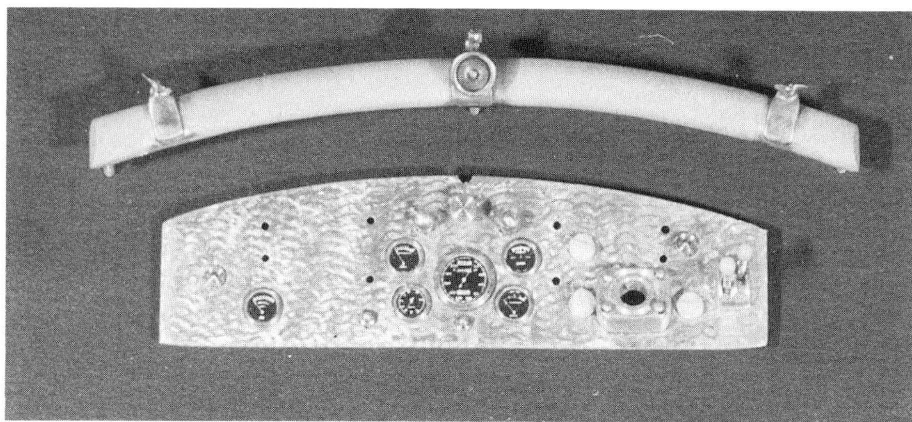

Plate 158

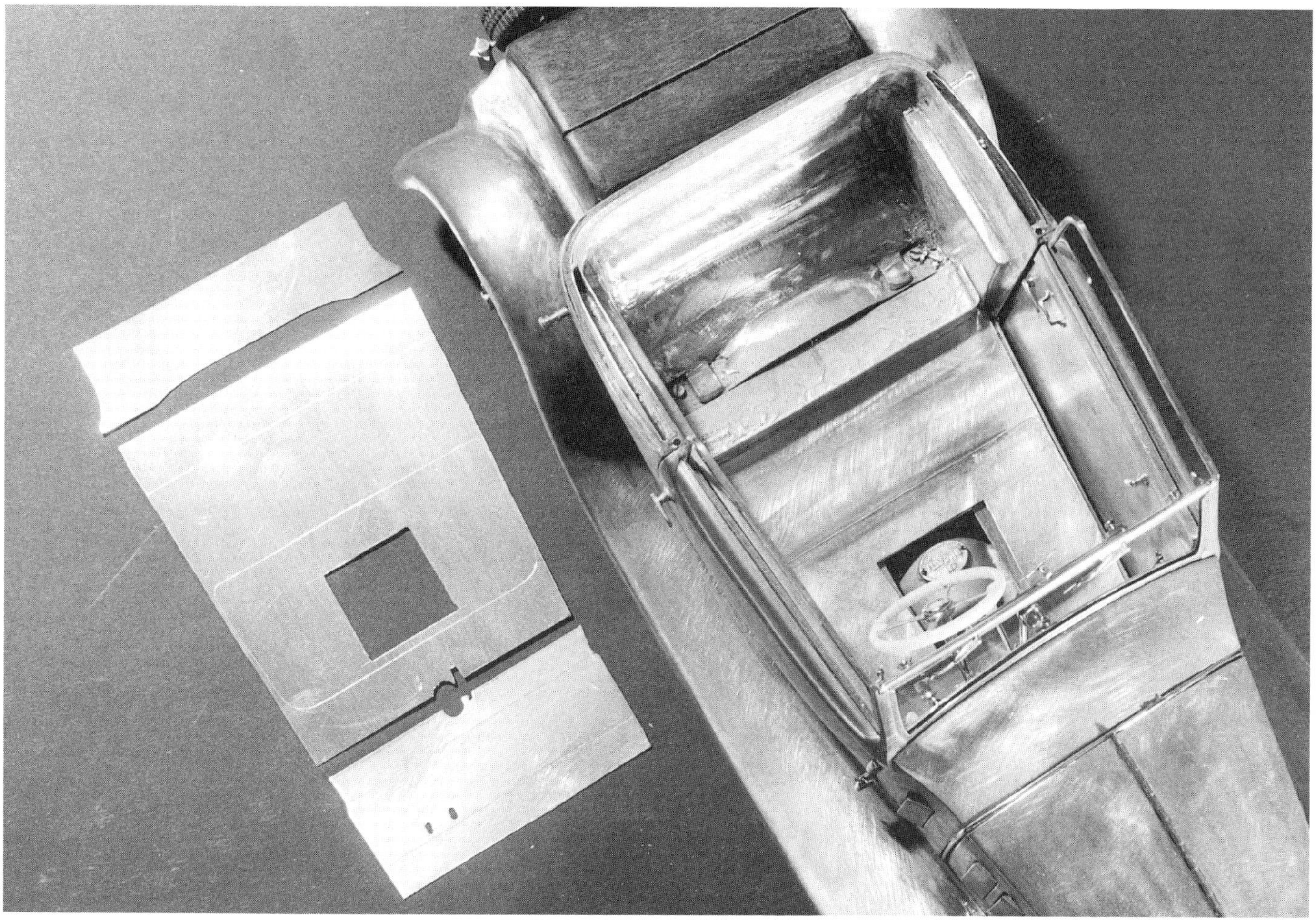

that will fit the 1/15 scale clock face. A contact print is then made from the negative that can be pressed or cut out with a simple tool turned to the required size on the lathe. The face can be glued into the nickel silver instrument space on the dash. To make white figures on a black face, either draw out the original on scratch card, or make (or have made) a direct film positive from the 35 mm negative just discussed. A print from this will produce a black face with white numbers.

The dashboard, Plate 157, like the steering wheel, was in contention even after the first model was completed. I have a letter from Ludwig Weinberger who designed this body in 1931/32 stating that 'the instrument panel was originally Bugatti, ie, mottled aluminium' and so this is what we have here. It was, however, only at the end of our research over twelve years that I discovered a photograph of the interior taken in about 1937 that showed clearly that the dash and steering wheel were, at that time at least, of polished wood. Although Ludwig Weinberger might be correct in his recollections, we feel that it is most unlikely that this aspect would have changed between 1932 and 1937. I do feel, however, that the mottled aluminium dash and the ivory steering wheel do fit so much better with the air of opulence conveyed by the cream-coloured Hungarian pigskin interior that was the original specification. The detail fittings on the dashboard are, for the most part, turned from nickel silver, although the large square bush that accommodates the steering column is machined from aluminium, and the white knobs are turned from ivory.

Plates 158 and 159 show the various parts of the

Above: **Plate 159** *Below:* **Plate 160**

Plate 161

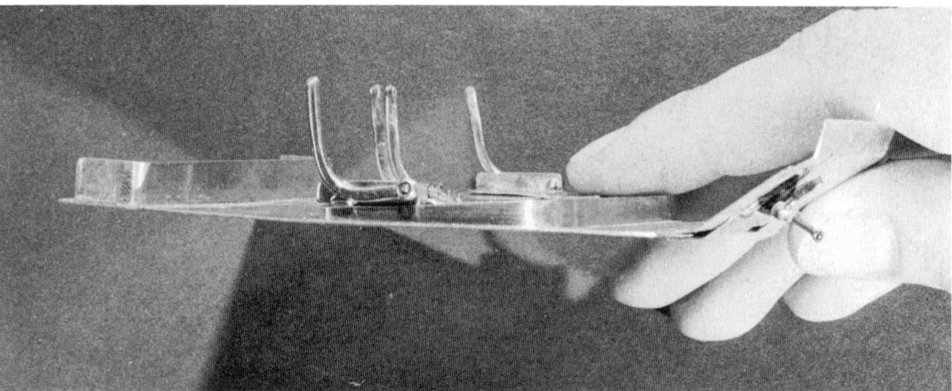

Plate 162

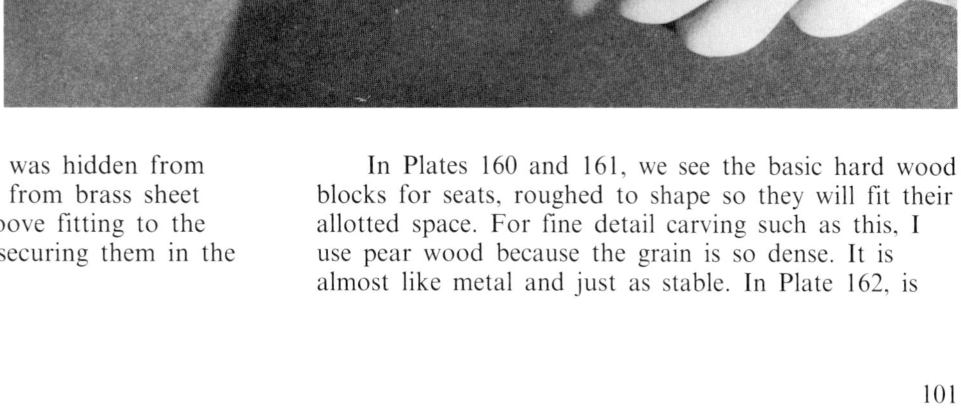

floor, and illustrate a common problem that always arises, of how to fit the floor parts around the gearchange and hand-brake levers without it showing. In this case, the floor was split into two parts at this point, but later provided with a carpet made from very fine velvet that was attached to the forward section and brought back over the join to the front seat base. This had two small holes in it to accommodate the protruding controls, so the join was hidden from view. The floor sections were made from brass sheet and provided with a tongue-and-groove fitting to the underside to assist in locating and securing them in the final assembly.

In Plates 160 and 161, we see the basic hard wood blocks for seats, roughed to shape so they will fit their allotted space. For fine detail carving such as this, I use pear wood because the grain is so dense. It is almost like metal and just as stable. In Plate 162, is

Plate 163

the floor section together with its various fittings attached. The arms that allow the front seat backs to fold forward are soldered to a single plate so that they can be chromed as one piece. This also makes for ease of assembly regarding the front seat squab and the two back sections, all of which can be seen with the rear seat parts in Plate 163. Note that the front seat backs are not of equal width, an unusual feature of this particular interior.

We conclude the manufacture with the final detailing. It may be noticed, with few exceptions, that the order of work I have discussed has actually followed the order of work shown in the model. The exceptions were, for the most part, because I had to re-photograph certain stages a second time to show the detail better. I find the sequence of building of the utmost importance particularly when approaching the subject with the eye of an artist looking for an impression of the original, rather than as an engineer making a perfect miniature copy. One needs to move through the various building stages setting out boundaries and then filling in the detail throughout the course of construction. This is so because, at the earliest stage possible, one needs to get a feel for the character of the subject and build on that as one moves forward. I felt that as soon as I had the first wheel complete, I had the essence of a Bugatti Royale, particularly when I stood this next to another car modelled to the same scale.

In Plate 164, are the wood strips that form the running board together with a drilled plate used as a guide. The strips are cut from pear wood on the milling machine with the aid of an engineer's slitting saw and held in place with very short lengths of aluminium wire of 0.030 in (0.76 mm) diameter. This

Plate 164

Plate 165

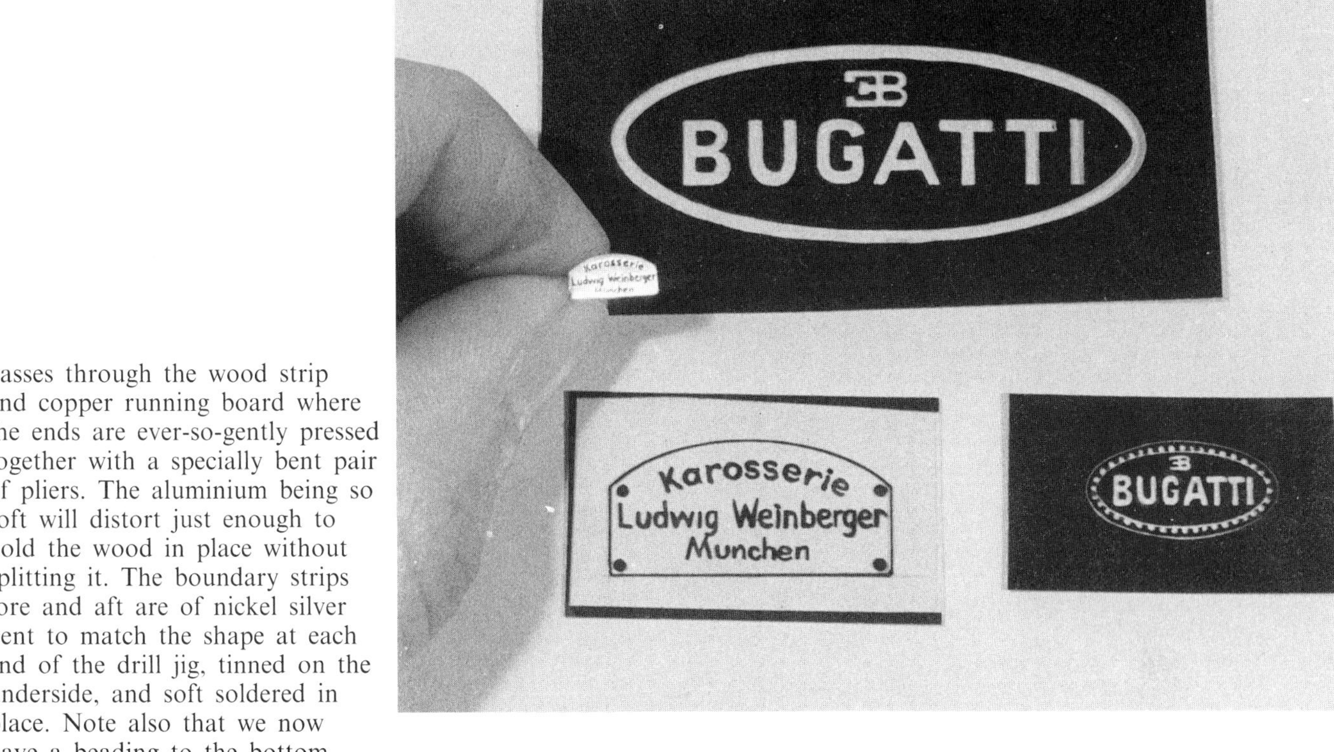

passes through the wood strip and copper running board where the ends are ever-so-gently pressed together with a specially bent pair of pliers. The aluminium being so soft will distort just enough to hold the wood in place without splitting it. The boundary strips fore and aft are of nickel silver bent to match the shape at each end of the drill jig, tinned on the underside, and soft soldered in place. Note also that we now have a beading to the bottom edge of the wings and running board. This, in full-size, would actually be formed in the metal of the wings and turned under with perhaps a thick wire enclosed within it to strengthen the edge. While part of this can be done on this scale, I prefer to add this as a separate item, so giving even more stiffening to this part. The beading in this case is formed from a 0.060 in (1.52 mm) diameter copper wire flattened between rollers to approximately 0.080x0.030 in (2x0.76 mm), tinned on one side and soft soldered to the lower edge all round.

The 1/15 scale body builder's nameplate is shown in Plate 165 etched in brass sheet to the back of which two small pins have been hard soldered for fitting to the body, just forward of the door front hinges. Also shown here is the artwork (masters) for the nameplate, together with that produced for the radiator nameplate and engine side plates.

In Plates 166, 167 and 168 we see the three stages of making a headlamp. On the left of the first of these can be seen the rough dimensioned drawings. Fig 12 shows this more clearly. As can be seen here, almost all the work is completed in a single operation, including what will pass as the bulb. A slight recess is formed at 'A' to take the glass. The second operation can be seen in Plate 167 where the now 'parted' headlamp is pressed on to a hard wood (pear wood) spigot for completing the shaping of the back with a file and fine abrasive paper. This is completed by first drilling, and then fitting a pin (hard solder) to the underside, and a small decoration (soft solder) at the top.

Plate 166

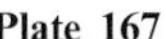

Plate 167

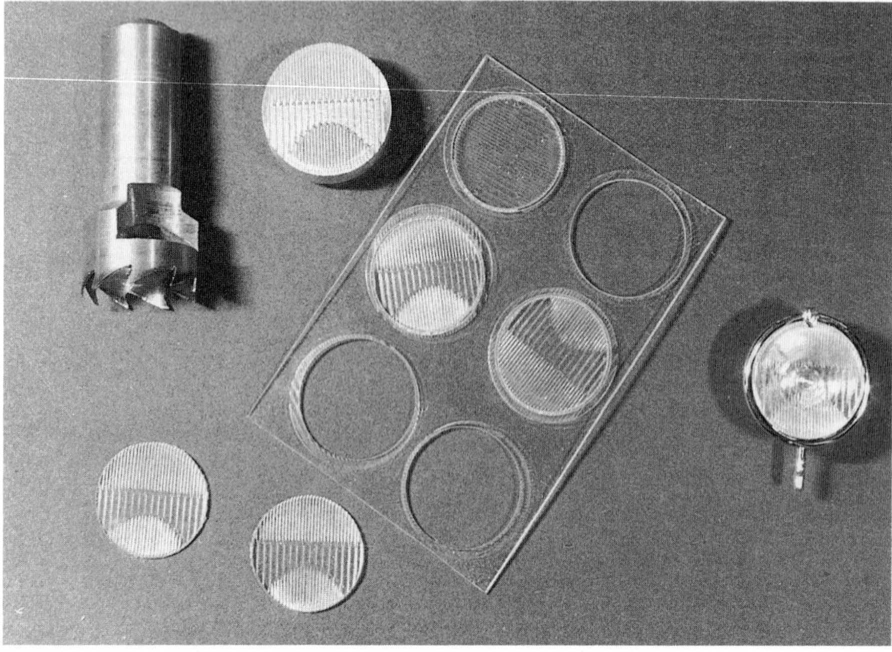

Plate 168

Glass has been mentioned several times, first in relation to the windscreen and side windows, and just now regarding the headlamp. In fact, I use perspex (acrylic sheet) also known by the trade name Plexiglass. This can be obtained in sizes down to $\frac{1}{32}$ in (0.81 mm) thickness or less, but this is the size I use for all my work here. Plate 168 shows, in the centre, a small rectangle of this material with six lens impressions, three having been cut out. The cutter is the tool at the top left which was machined on the lathe from mild steel, the teeth being filed to shape and a small cut-out milled on one side to assist in removing the lens from the cutting tool. This is not required to undertake a great deal of hard work so it is not necessary to make it in a hard tool steel. The inside diameter of the cutter should be about 0.010 in (0.002 mm) larger than the diameter at 'A', Fig 12, this size being worked down to with a

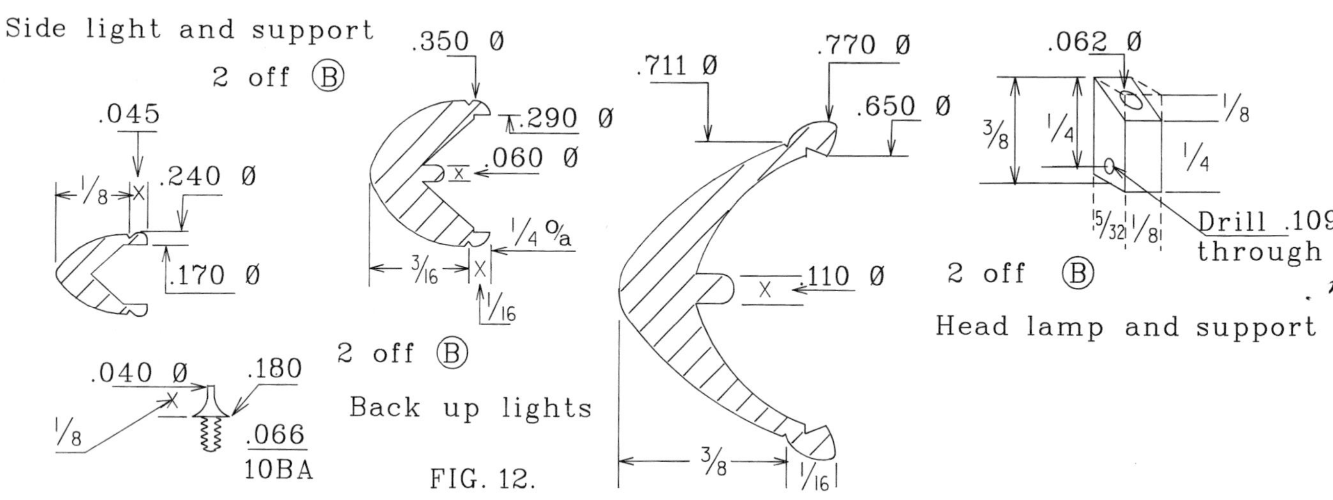

Fig. 12 Rough sketches for the Royale's lights.

Plate 169

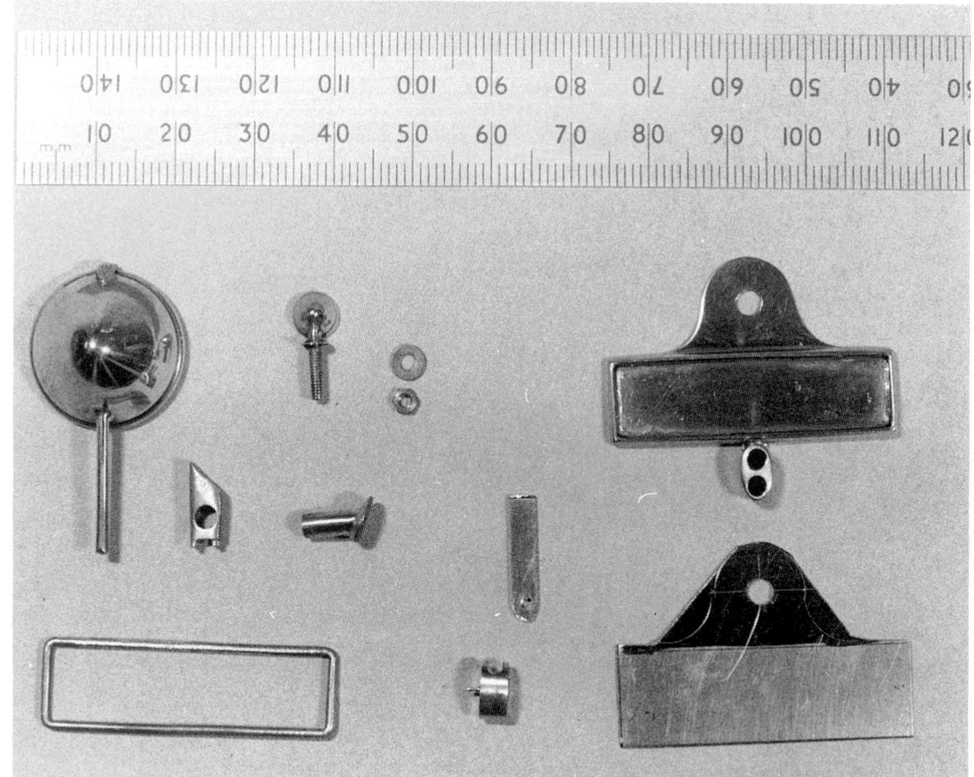

file on the individual pieces. Even then it will be found that the flexibility of the perspex will allow a lens of perhaps two or three thousandths of an inch larger than this to be pressed into the recess at 'A'. Once in though, it cannot be got out in one piece.

To the right of the cutter is a round block of brass (the die), into the top surface of which has been worked the design of the lens markings. These can be milled, scratched or otherwise carved to whatever complexity you desire, for when the die is heated and placed on the surface of the perspex sheet, it leaves the perfect imprint as can be seen here. The back of this block has been drilled and tapped so that a length of rod can be screwed in place to act as a handle. As a guide to the temperature needed for it to work, heat gently until a wet finger, when dabbed on it, will make it hiss. At this point, place the die on the perspex for a few seconds; if you have a smoking hole, you were too hot, if only a faintly marked sheet, not hot enough. Practice makes perfect. On the right of plate 168 is a completed headlamp with lens fitted.

Plate 169 shows some further parts of the headlamp assembly. Note the length of the pin attached to the underside of the lamp. This, as we will see later, is used for soldering the lamp to the wire frame for chrome plating and will finally be cut to length after that. The parts along the bottom and to the right form the number plate. A rectangular shape of brass is filed up to the inside dimensions of the number plate and has bent around it a length of nickel silver wire of about 0.050 in (1.27 mm) diameter, the ends of which are then silver soldered together. This is laid on the fluxed brass sheet and held over a flame with tweezers until silver soldering temperature. At this point a rod of solder is applied and the frame secured in place.

The next three Plates, 170 to 172, illustrate the fabrication and fitting of the rear bumper, a most unusual fitting for Bugatti. The reason I make that point is because a feature of all Bugatti rear ends is the high chassis dictated by the half-elliptic forward-facing rear springs. With this configuration, there is no conventional fixing place for a rear bumper.

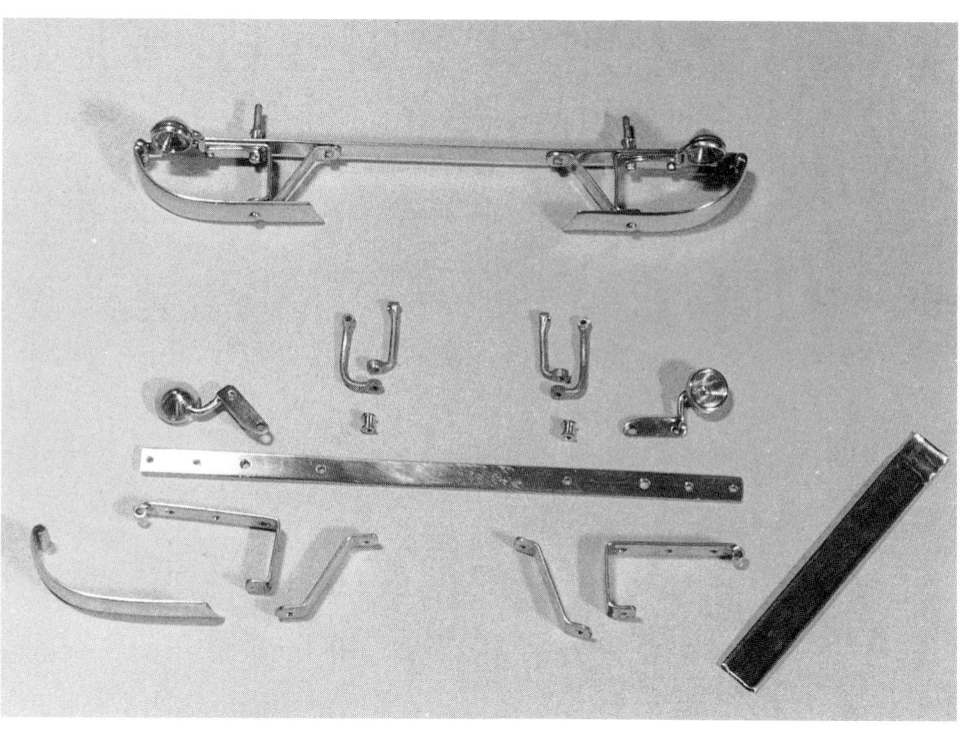

Plate 170

Above: **Plate 171**

Below: **Plate 172**

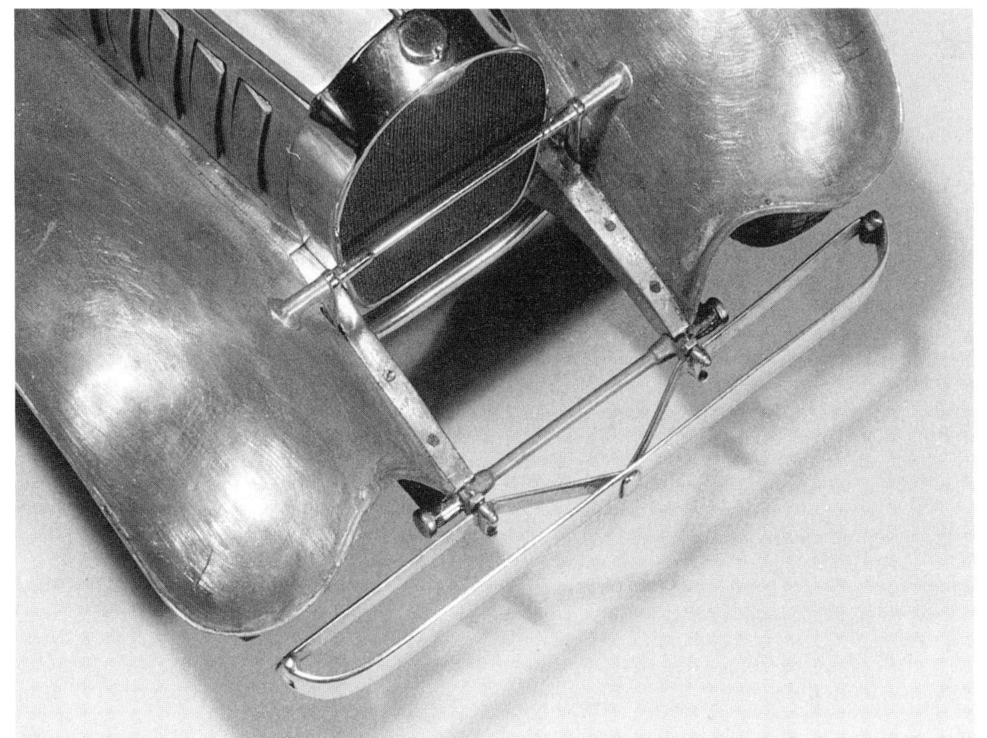

Plate 173

Weinberger overcame the problem in a most 'unengineering' way, by extending the end of the U-bolt that holds the rear spring leaves together, and fitting two forged arms from this back to the rear body. From here, a large bolt was taken through the bodywork to the rear bumper assembly. A not too sharp bang to the rear bumper would sheer these bolts off and upset the rear suspension seriously; not an ideal design for an otherwise brilliant engineer.

Two pairs of bent arms can be seen in the centre of Plate 170, and in place in the model in Plate 172. Plate 171 is a more conventional view of the rear-end fittings. Materials are brass throughout with the actual bumper made from a wide strip of $\frac{1}{16}$ in (1.57 mm) thick brass that has received the attentions of an end mill down the centre of the back face, and a file on the outside edges of the front face. This produced a form that looked as though it had been formed between convex and concave rollers. A section of this can be seen at the lower right corner of Plate 170. Plate 173 is of the front bumper made from the same material as just described.

Plate 174 shows an array of the smaller fittings that are added at the same time as the bumpers. With the exception of the two trafficators on the far right, there are the handles and catches for the bonnet, all of which are made from nickel silver wire. Plate 175 shows another collection of small parts, this time assembled into the levers and controls fitted to the engine side of the firewall. The centre four have been made up from the parts immediately to the right of each set. On the far left are the two parts of the horn, also one of the firewall fittings. In Plate 176 we have the wing inner liners, four strips of copper sheet formed over the original wing patterns, tinned and spot soldered to the centre of each wing on the inside. In full size, these give some protection to the wings proper against stones being thrown up from the wheels. Plate 177 returns us to the use of the louvre press, for fabricating the two panels that fit each side of the engine between the sump and the chassis frame. These are pierced by conventional louvres. For those not able (or willing) to make such a sophisticated tool as this to perform louvre forming, small single-width louvres can be pressed into this 0.010 in (0.25 mm) thick aluminium sheet with the

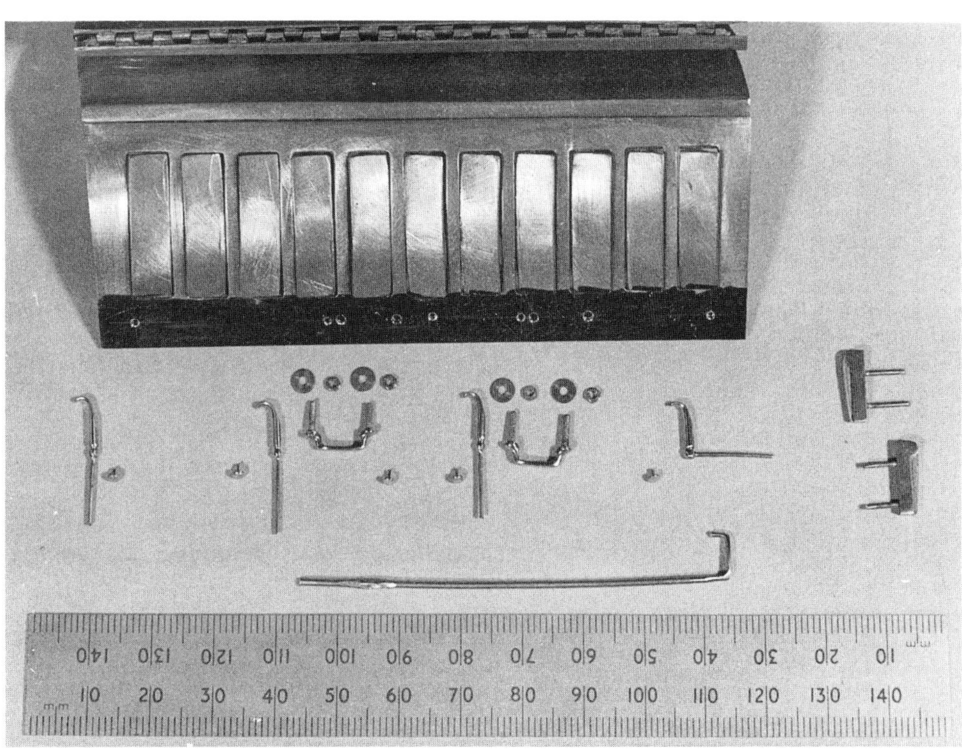

Plate 174

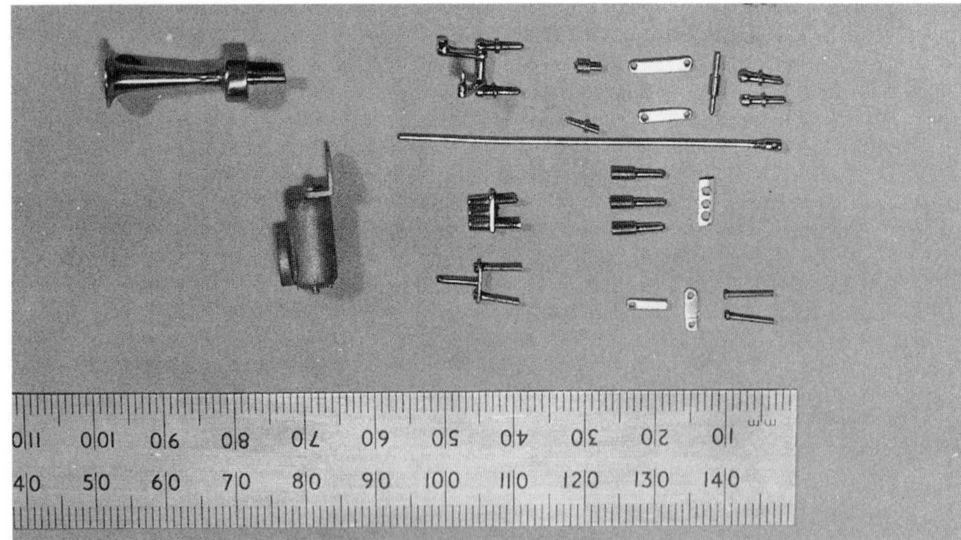

Plate 175

Plate 176

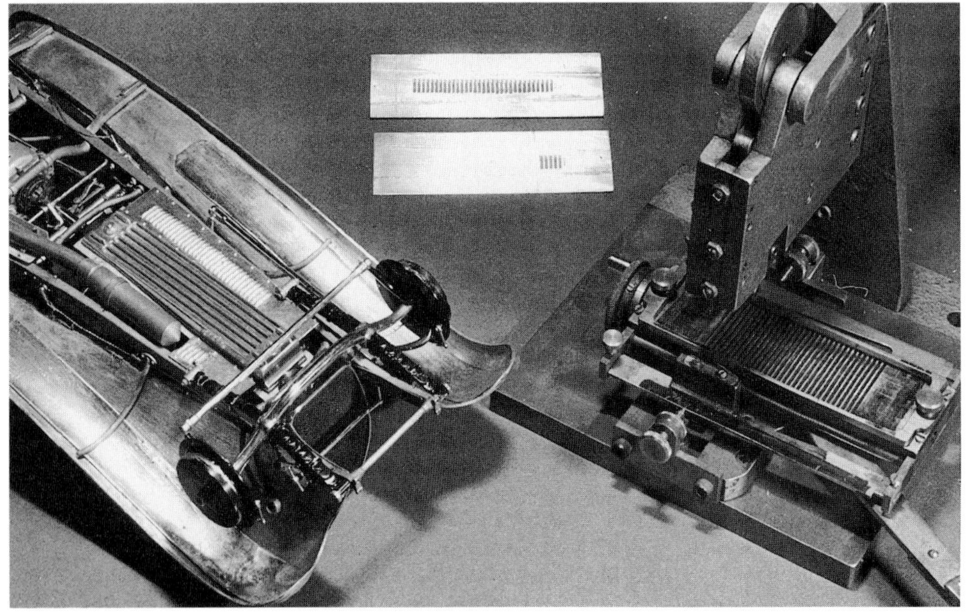

Plate 177

simplest of hand tools, provided adequate marking out is undertaken.

In Plate 178 we have at last arrived at the completed model, although there is also fitted a trunk which has had no mention as yet. I have endeavoured to leave all finishing operations to the last section, and the trunk is one piece that, when fully assembled, needed no finishing, but more on this later.

Plate 178

PART FIVE
The Finishing

HAVING NOW built and assembled almost every part, we proceed to take it all apart, clean it up, and separate those pieces for painting, plating of various sorts, and those needing no further work at all (Plate 179). This done, the parts for electro-plating are wired together on what is termed a 'tree'. Chrome plating is one operation that is best not attempted at home. It is a highly skilled operation that makes use of some very expensive equipment and some rather nasty chemicals. Your local yellow pages is the first place to look for electro-platers; they are to be found in most parts of the country. There is no substitute for a good electro-plater, so treat him well. Do not present him with a handful of minute parts and expect him to do everything.

First inspect each piece and provide it with the finish that you want; if it is to be highly polished, then use fine abrasive paper to remove all the marks, followed by metal polish to impart the shine. Neither chrome nor any other plating will change the finish on a surface, it will only deposit a very thin coating of the new metal – chromium, nickel, etc. – on what is

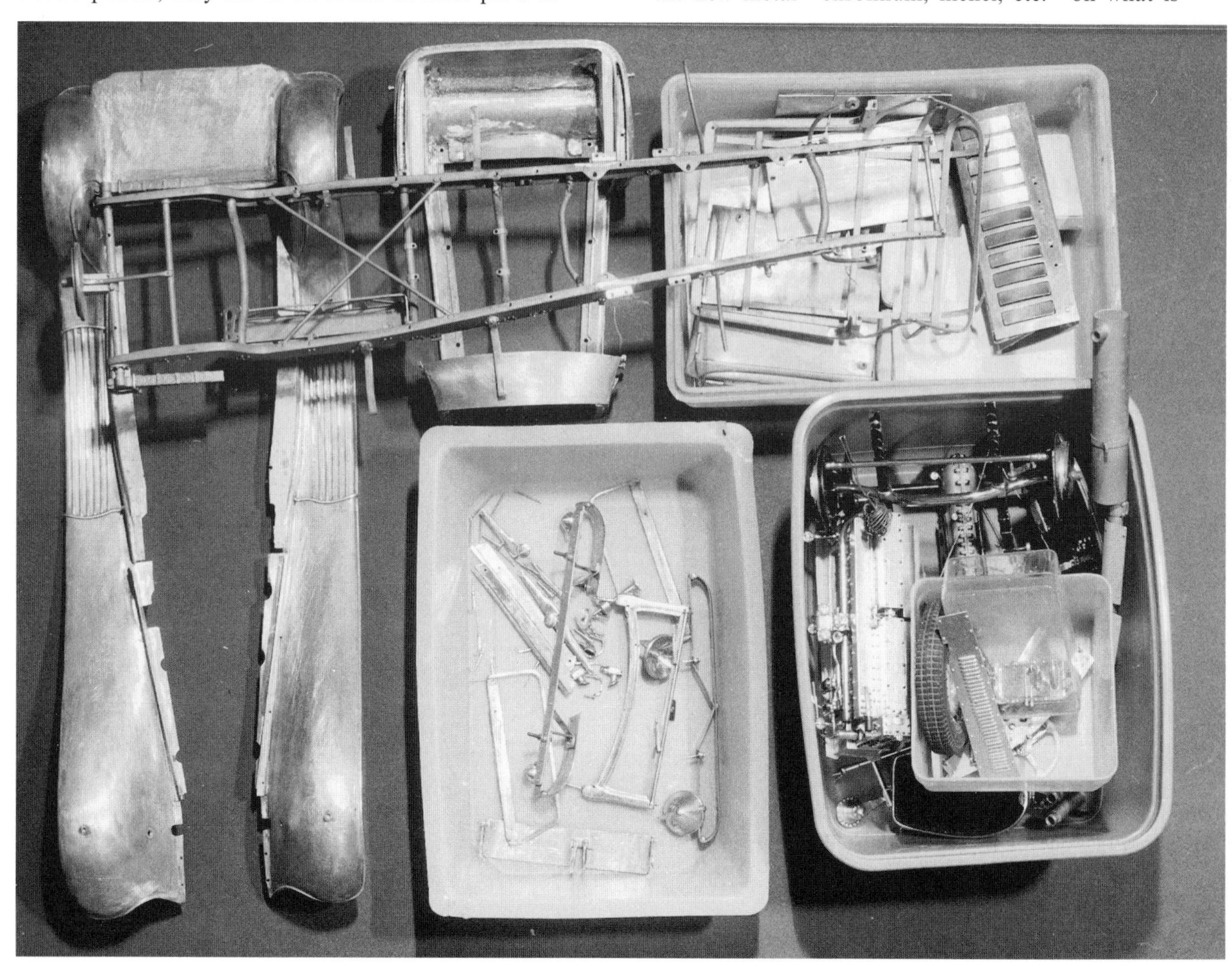

Plate 179

Plate 180

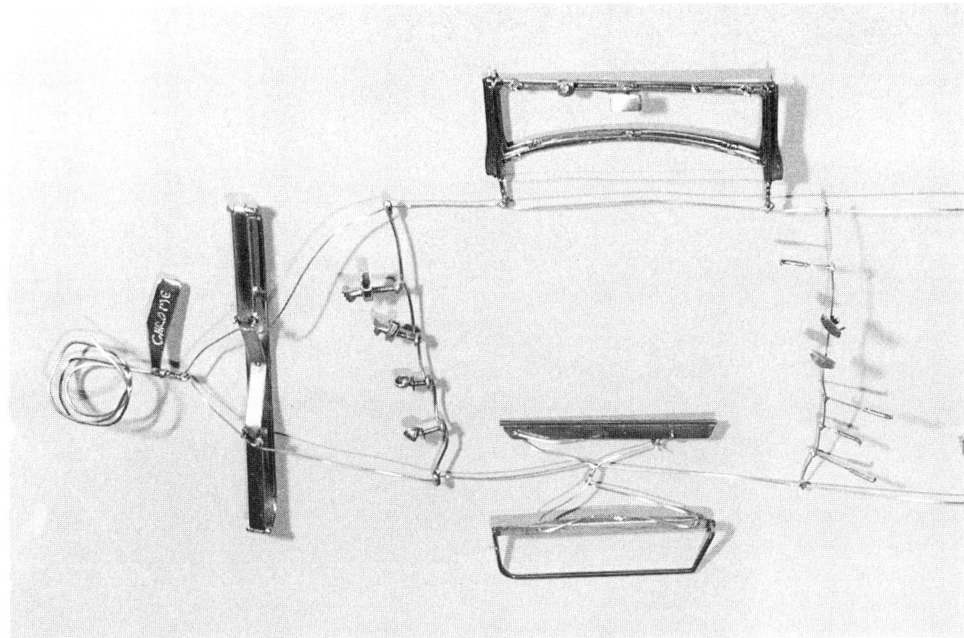

already there. If the part is rough now, it will be rough when it returns from the platers, albeit a rough chrome rather than a rough brass, and there is no way that you will be able to rectify the situation other than by removing the chrome (an extremely hard metal) from the brass and starting again. Next, make certain that every piece is provided with some means of attaching it to a wire tree. If it has been provided with dowel pins, then these can be soldered to the wire; if not then look for holes. If it has a thread in it, a long screw threaded tightly home can also be soldered to the wire. If it has a blind hole, (hole only partly drilled through a part) check if it is possible to tap a thread into this; in most cases it will be, depending on the stock of taps and dies you happen to have in your workshop. If it has a hole right through, perhaps this can also be threaded. If not, and it is on a part of the piece that is hidden in the final assembly, it may be possible to put a bolt and nut in it, or even thread a length of wire through in such a way that positive contact is made when it is attached to the tree. An example of the latter can be seen in Plate 180 at the bottom, where the two parts of one side window frame are attached by passing a wire through both (screw) holes on both pieces, and soldering this to the wire tree. The remaining parts have all been provided with extended pins and soldered to the tree via these. The screen at the top is the only piece here needing special attention. The top bar, you will recall, is attached to the frame by two pins that fit in holes drilled in the tops of the outside posts. One could solder this part to the tree via these pins, but there is a good chance that during the plating process these pins would increase in size, possibly by quite a large amount. As the tops of the pillars are, of necessity, quite small in size, there may not be room to increase the size of the holes to accommodate the now oversized pins. Where this is critical, the parts should be assembled for plating; in this case, a length of 0.004 in (0.10 mm) diameter stainless steel wire was wound around one of the pins attached to the tree, taken around the back of the driving mirror several times, and then secured to the second bottom pin. This was sufficient to allow the complete screen frame to be plated as a single piece. A tree of parts should be no longer than about 20 in (500 mm) with a 6 in (152 mm) length of free wire at each end for the plater to attach it to the plating frame. Parts soldered to the tree should be spaced no closer than you see here, the larger the part, the more isolated it should be on the tree. I have used two wires here with cross pieces, but a single wire with parts soldered down its length on alternate sides can also work.

With all the parts attached to the wire tree, double check them for marks and polish out anything that is doubtful; once plated you are stuck with it.

I mentioned earlier that there is a process for electro-depositing a black finish on brass. There is a company in New York, USA that produces a series of small kits for electro-plating various metals, including gold, silver, copper and black, on brass, copper and nickel silver. The kit consists of a battery holder (2AA size) wired to a paint brush and a clip. This comes with a bottle of polish and a small bottle of plating solution. I have used this for a number of years, the black finish being the best and most permanent that I have come across. The product is called JNT APPL-I-COTERS made by JNT Mfg Co. Inc., Box 870, Stormville, New York 12582, USA. I give this address as it is the only supplier I have come across, although I have been told that it is a product that dates back very many years when a number of such accessories were offered to the public. It is for this reason that the 6 to 12 volt DC transformer is used (mentioned in Chapter 1), wired up to replace the batteries to give flexibility in the voltages available.

With the plating taken care of, let us now turn to the painting. All parts should first be cleaned of all trace of flux residue, sanded smooth with abrasive paper or the sand blasting spray gun, and then provided with a handle. Like the plated parts, this can be by soldering or otherwise attaching them to a very stiff wire frame, as in Plate 181. Alternatively, they can be bolted to a twisted wire handle as in Plates 182 and 183. If you possess locking forceps, also shown in Plate 181, then you have yet another holding device. This, incidentally, shows the now chromed bumper that is about to receive a spray coat of black paint directed to all except the actual bumper bars on each side, and

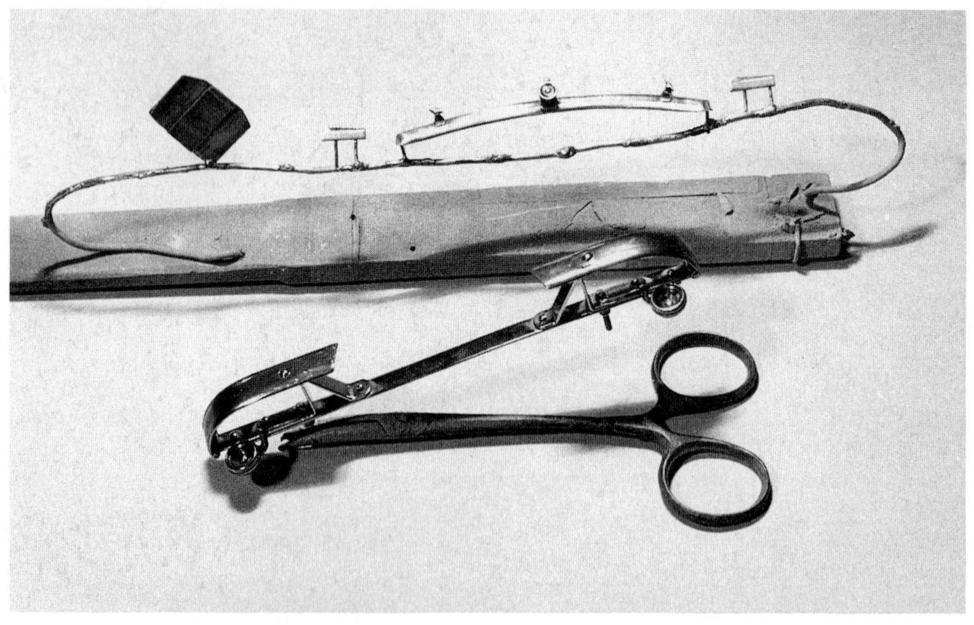

Plate 181

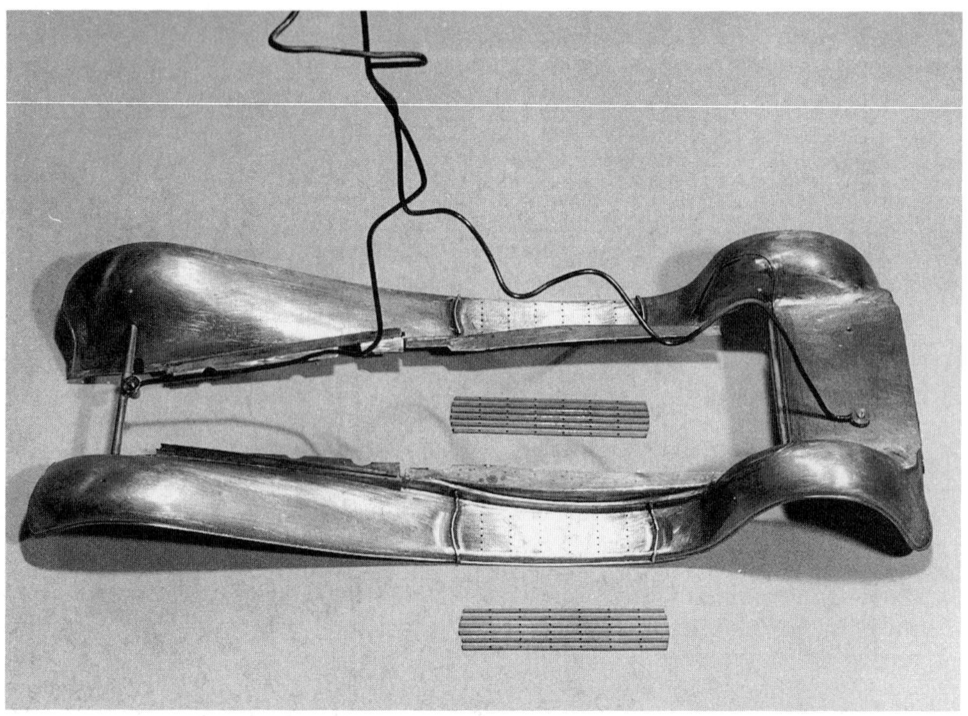

Plate 182

systems of this on the market. As it will need thinning before passing through an airbrush, and not all systems are provided with a thinning medium, find one that is, and try it. Another point to bear in mind is that it does apparently have a restricted shelf life, so purchase the smallest size available from a large supplier who can sell you new stock. Again, check with the dealer you are purchasing it from. As the name implies, this is not only a primer but also a filler, and very thick coats can be built up in a short time if care is taken. Because it dries very fast, the applications can be added to in quick succession. When I feel the deposit of filler is sufficient, I let the piece stand overnight. This is then rubbed down with fine abrasive papers to the desired finish and given a coat of grey cellulose primer, which is completely compatible with the polyester filler. After rubbing down again and checking for imperfections, the first colour coats are sprayed on, cellulose (lacquer) being used throughout (Plate 183).

Colour is applied, rubbed down and resprayed until the desired depth and finish have been attained, after which the parts are left to stand for a day or so to harden properly. If all is in order, and the chrome parts have returned without problems, the final assembly can be started. Plate 184 illustrates this stage with the chassis.

Another item ready for final assembly is the fabric hood and its fittings. The first of these is the rear window frame (Plate 185). Made from flattened nickel silver wire, it is bent to shape around a brass former, two identical pieces being called for. One is drilled with the required number of holes, and this used as a master to drill the second. One of these is provided with a nickel silver pin for each hole which is hard soldered in place. The diameter of these pins should be

the two reversing lamps which remain with the chrome finish. These four items are first painted with a masking medium that, when dry, resembles a rubber latex. After painting, this is rubbed with the fingers and can be peeled away to reveal the original chrome, or even paint, finish.

Spray painting is done with a medium-size air brush at a pressure of about 35 psi (except for special finishes). It is always undertaken in a ventilated spray area, wearing a special-purpose face mask equipped with the correct filters, and with rubber gloves on. The primer I use (always the first coat) is a two-part polyester spraying filler (catalyst and resin). It is used in the auto repair trade, and I find it sticks to absolutely everything you aim at. There are several

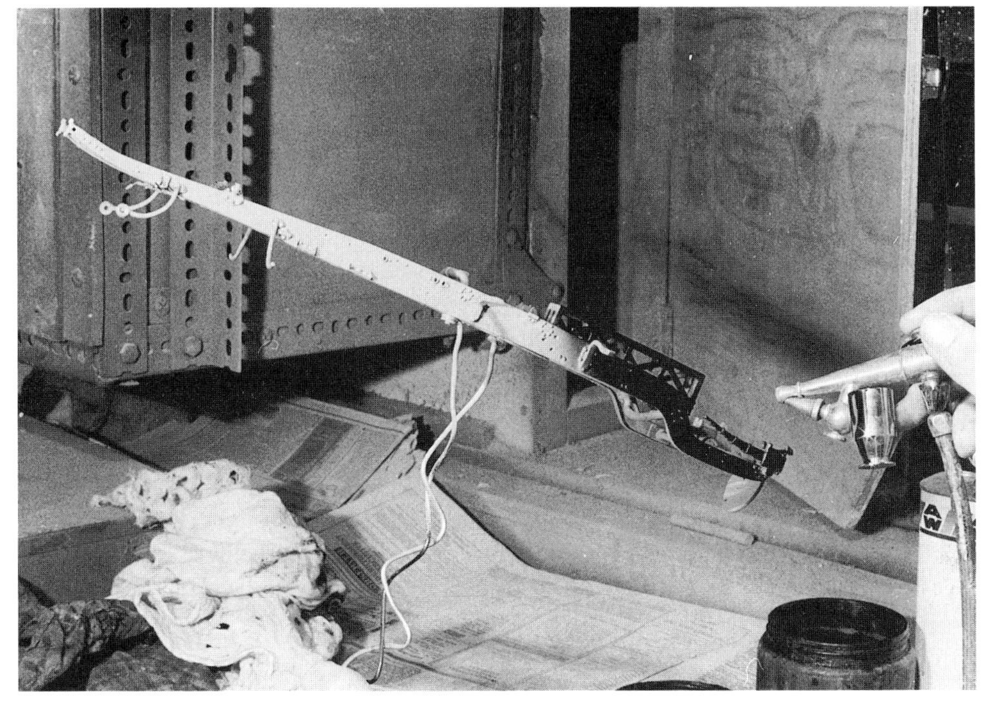

Plate 183

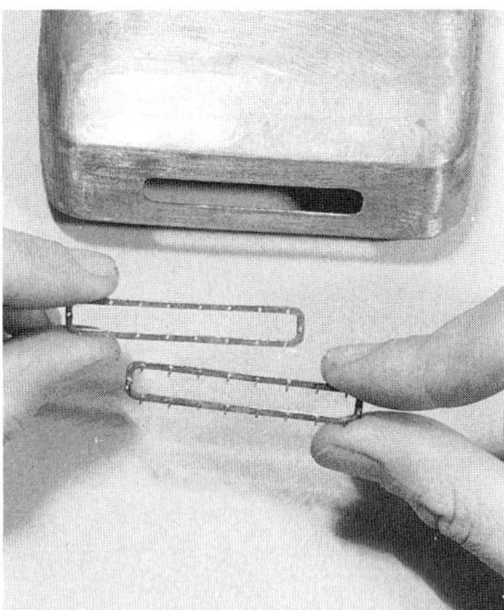

Plate 185

Plate 184

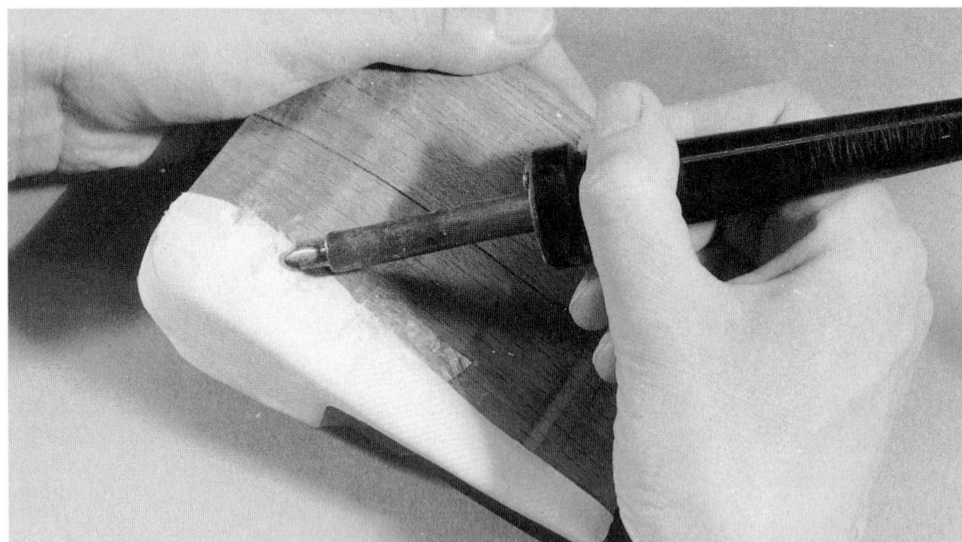

Plate 186

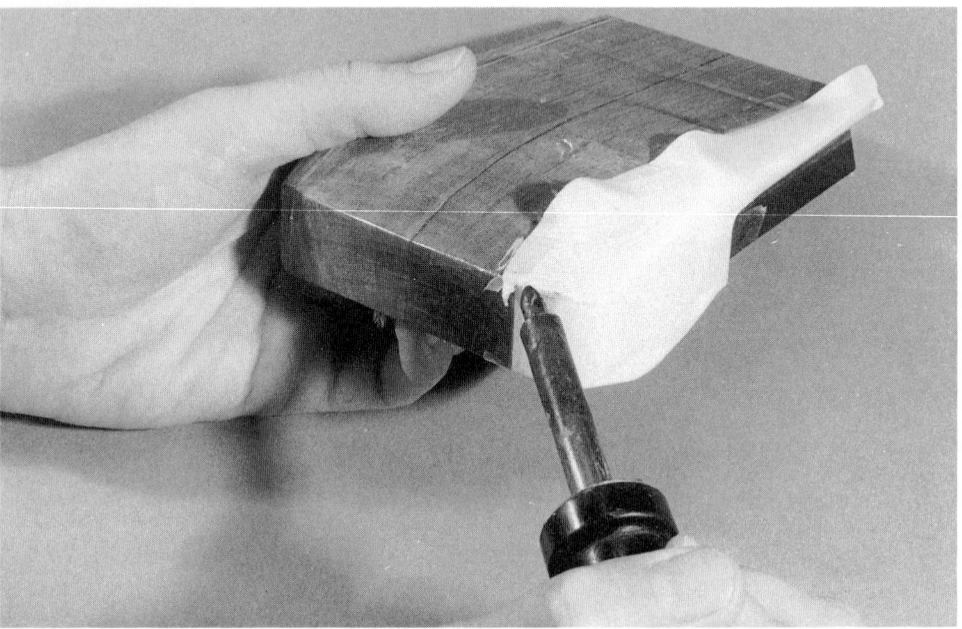

Plate 187

just less than a third of the width of the strip metal from which the frame is made. When assembled, the glass (perspex) will fill the inner third while the outer third will locate the frame within the opening at the rear of the folding top. As much fitting and manipulation is required, this is better undertaken well before the fabric is applied. The pins are cut back till they just protrude through the second frame when all is in place.

The fabric used for bonding to the copper is a very fine weave polyester (Plates 186 to 190). Because it is a man-made fibre, it has the advantage that it can be manipulated with heat, being moulded either with heat from a soldering iron held close by (Plates 186 and 187) or, better still, using the 'hot blow' torch shown in Plate 16. Cutting is undertaken with a sharpened heated bit as in Plate 188, or the 'hot knife' from the above kit, which will melt and fuse the ends of the fibres together. As can be seen in the previous two Plates, Sellotape is again utilised to hold the parts in place until they are where you want them. In Plate 189, we see the four side pieces formed to shape; two rectangular pieces are also needed to complete the set necessary to line the inside and cover the outside. Incidentally, it is here that the variable resistance to control the

Plate 188

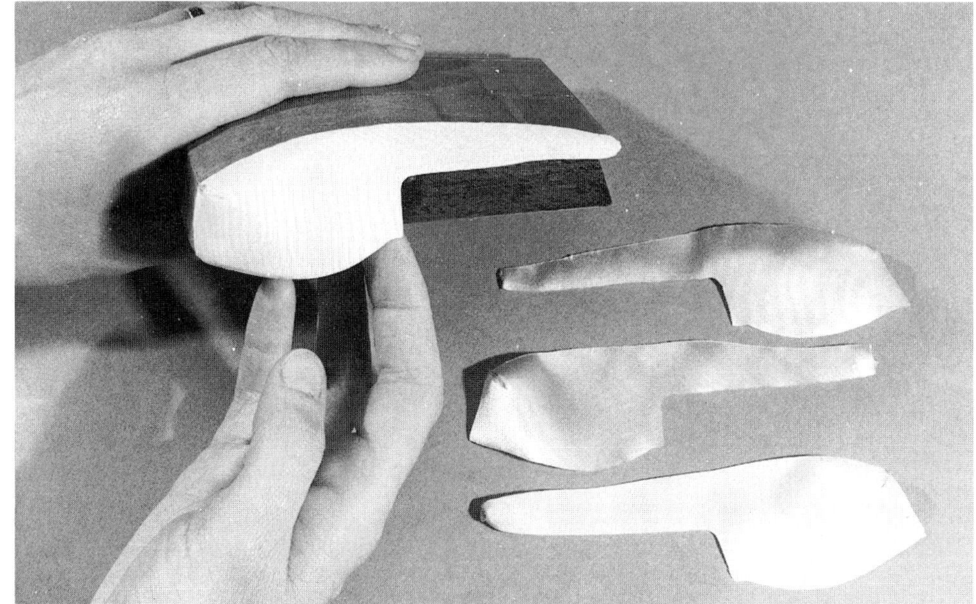

Plate 189

Plate 190

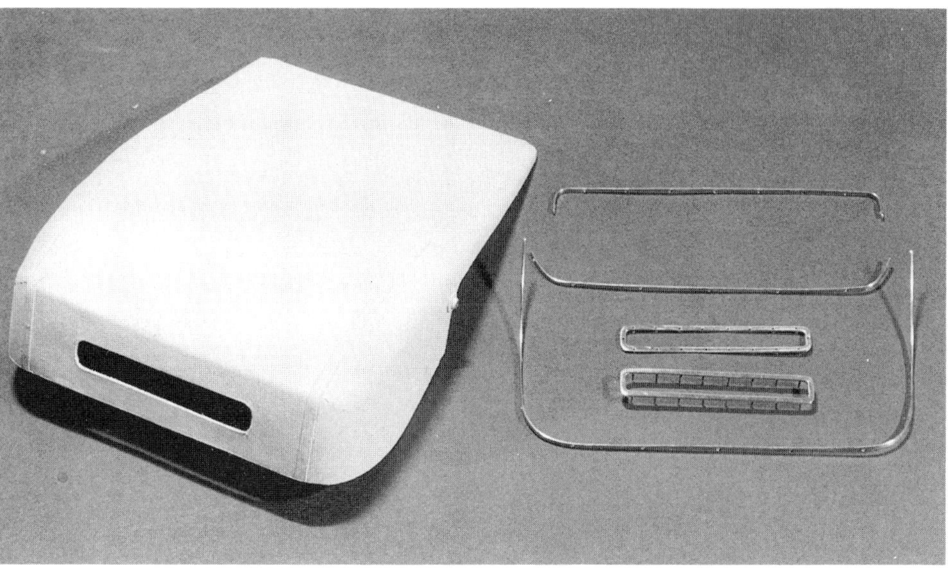

soldering iron (mentioned in Part One) comes into its own, as only half the heat output of this tool is needed to manipulate the fabric in this process.

The next stage is very messy, and if it does not work the first time, it is best to clean off, scrap the fabric pieces and start again. It is also best done in two separate stages, first the inside, and after that has thoroughly set, the outside. The procedure is to spray one side of the hood with quite a thick coat of polyester filler, and while still wet, press into this the fabric pieces. First the two sides should be fitted making certain it is pressed down into the filler with no air bubbles, then the centre piece is laid in and pressed home. As the filler dries so quickly, there is not much time to relocate the pieces if they do not go down right the first time. Once in place, a thin coat of the filler is sprayed over the fabric sealing it in place for good. If you do decide to have a second go, clean off everything with thinners as soon as possible.

With both sides covered, the nickel silver beading strips can be made up, taped in place and drilled for pinning (Plate 190) after which they should be removed and the hood sprayed with cellulose colour as necessary. If the colour is first mixed with a cellulose matting agent, (obtainable from the same supplier as the paint) then the hood will start to take on the authentic dull cloth-top finish.

The last of the chassis fittings to be made are the four batteries (Plate 191). Invariably, if I have a set of identical parts to be made such as this, I find it quickest to make one (far left), then produce a rubber mould (centre block), and mould the remainder in a pigmented resin (far right), thus not obscuring the detail with paint. The white caps were turned up on the lathe in white perspex and fitted in drilled holes, as was the wiring. Plate 192 shows them fitted into the battery box. Although little of this detail can be seen on the finished model, great satisfaction can be derived from the fact that you have put it all in.

In Plate 193 we see the underside of the finished chassis. In painting the chassis, we are working with a single colour, but with the wing and body parts we will be using three colours, so considerable masking will be necessary. As we saw with the rear bumper, one way to mask an area is to paint it with a masking medium, a sort of rubberised paint. Another method is to use masking tape, several varieties of which are available. The most common of these is a tough crêpe paper adhesive tape obtainable from hardware stores in reels of various widths. For the work discussed here, this is only really useful as a backing tape to prevent overspray, as the crinkly nature of the tape is not conducive to masking the sharp edged line we need here. In Plate 194, this tape is used to prevent the yellow getting under the wings (shown here being removed). It was also used to hold old newspaper around the edge and behind the tape actually used to

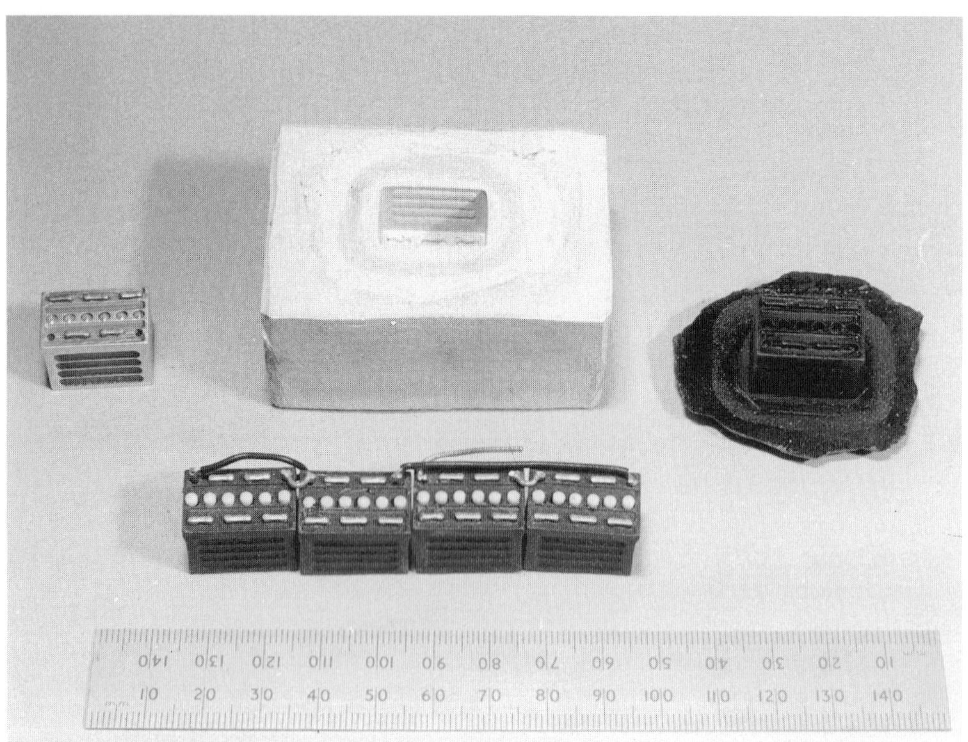

Plate 191

Plate 192

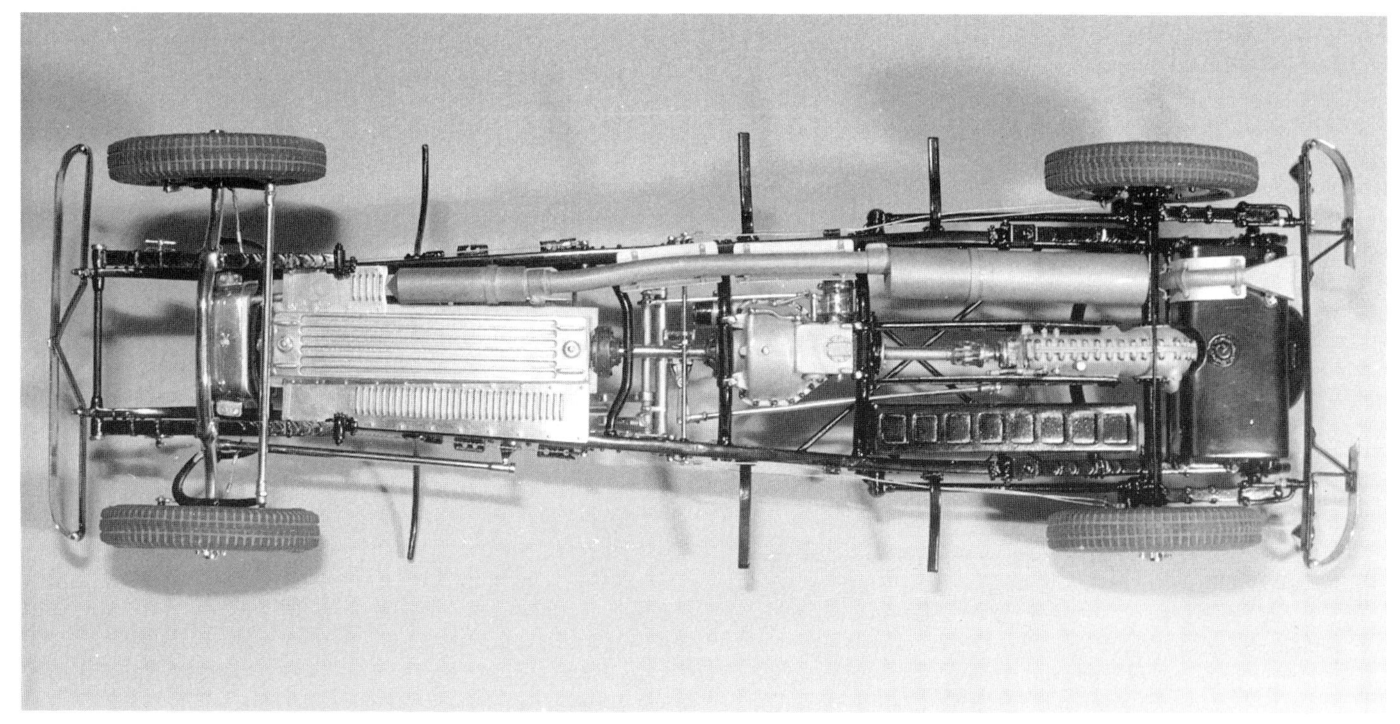

Plate 193

mask the outside of the yellow beading. This tape, seen partly peeled back over the front and rear wings, is obtainable in large diameter reels but of only $\frac{1}{8}$ in (3.17 mm) width. It is a smooth, flexible plastic masking tape, and because it is so narrow, it will with ease accommodate all the curves presented here. Because it is made from a flexible plastic, paint will not stick to it, and the smooth surface gives it a sharp edge which will be seen to cut the surplus paint as it is being removed.

One word of warning when using masking tapes, particularly the crêpe paper variety. Make certain that the underlying paint is not just dry, but really hard (several days old) before applying masking tape to it. The one attribute that you want in a good masking tape is that it will stick. Should the underlying paint be anything but rock hard, you have every chance of seeing an impression of the tape in it when you remove it. A hot thumb pressed on crêpe masking tape will inevitably leave an imprint on all but the hardest

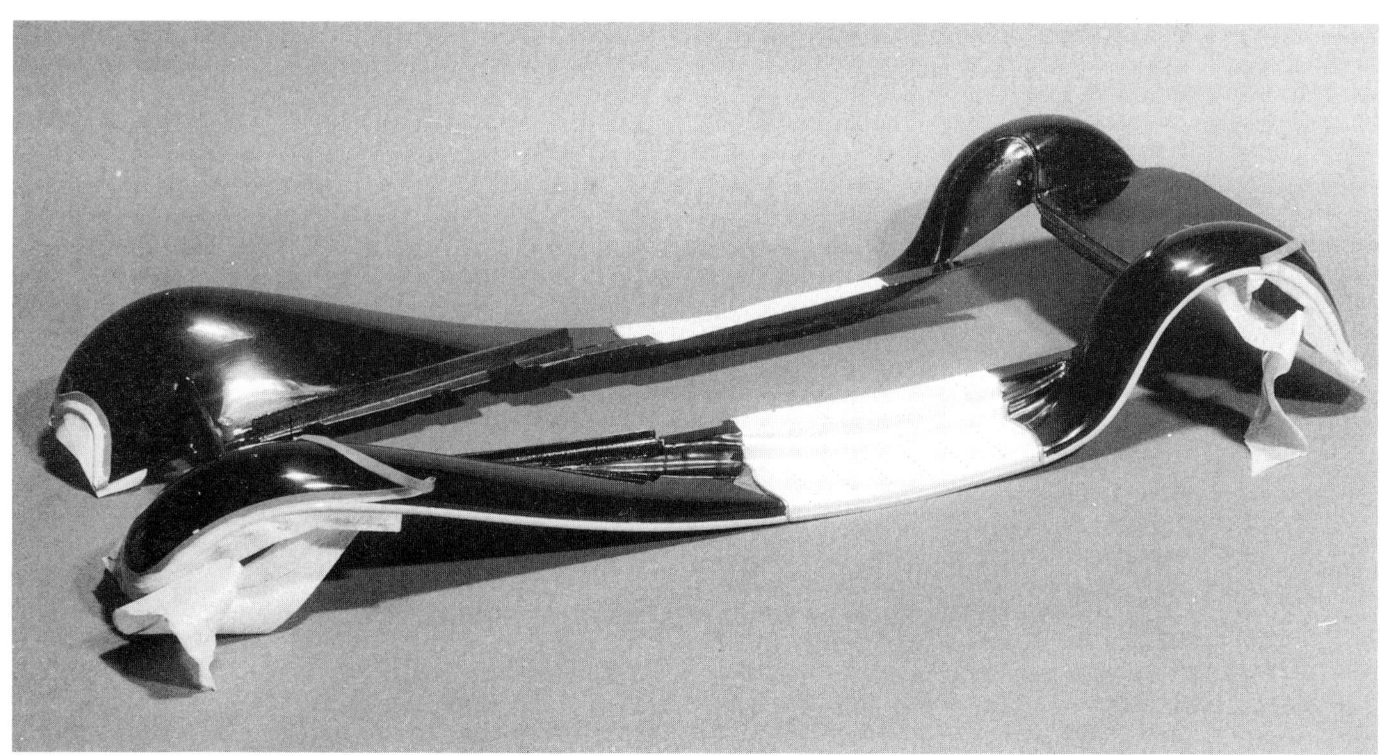

Plate 194

set finish, which is why I use newspaper to cover the large areas, with the tape used to hold it down on the edges only.

A point to take into consideration when deciding which to mask first is whether the colours need to be on the same level. If not, which should be on the top? If we take the wings in Plate 194, we have a white running board, black wings and yellow beading around the edge. Between the white and black is the nickel silver edging strip. To add the white on top of the black would double the thickness of paint. As we still have the wooden strips to fit here which need to be kept below the top edge of the nickel silver edging to look correct, the least paint used the better, so this was painted first. The white here represents a sheet of white rubber that was a feature of this design, so a small amount of the previously mentioned matting agent was added to the paint mix to take off the gloss finish. I did not feel it necessary to mask the rest of the wings other than the nickel silver strips because it was the first coat on, and the negligible amount of overspray was sanded off when dry.

A part like the nickel silver strip will need to be masked for the primer filler coat as well as for the white, black and yellow colour coats, because it is already in its finished polished state. If the original masking is left on throughout this, there is every chance that some, if not all the colours, will be seen as a thin line along the edges, when the masking is finally removed. By far the best plan is to remove it after each application of primer and colour, tidy up the edge where necessary, and mask anew each time.

Returning to the wings, the white and nickel silver parts were masked with a combination of masking fluid and tape, and the assembly painted black, after which the black was masked and yellow applied. As the yellow follows the raised beading around the wing edge, it actually benefits from being 'on' the black.

In Plate 195, we see all the ingredients necessary to make the rear trunk. This starts life as a hard wood block cut and shaped directly from the scale plans. It could just as well have been built up from strip wood as was the original, and made to open, but my experience is that the less the working parts, the less the number of hands trying them out. I do not normally use actual leather in this work, even though the part being made calls for a leather finish, because we work to a scale of 1/15, while leather is to a scale of one to one. As with all things in life, there has to be an exception, and this is it. The large rectangle is a piece of very fine quality bookbinding leather of only 0.004 in (0.10 mm) thickness. It was obtained from a book binder's supplier, which in this mass produced age is becoming quite a rare breed, for they principally

Plate 195

Plate 196

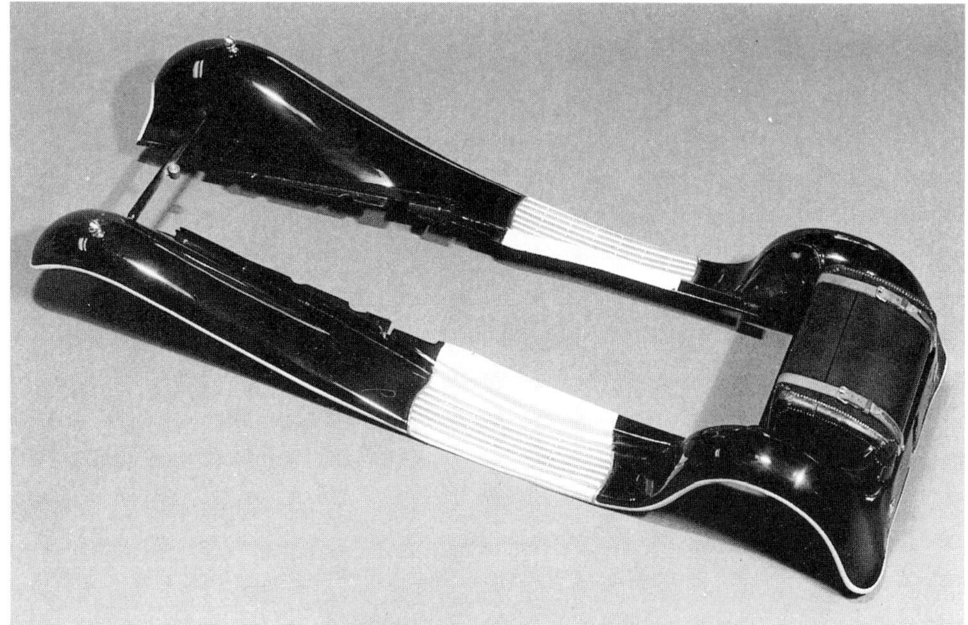

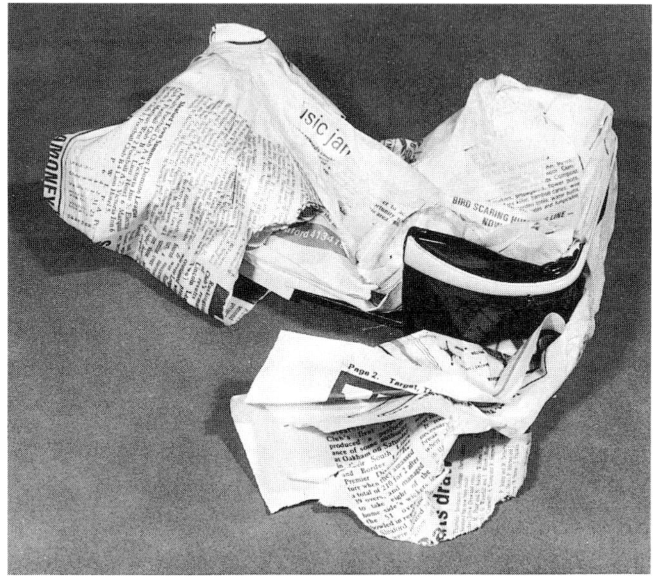

Plate 197

supply the craftspeople who hand-make book covers. Also, I am given to understand that this type of material is not a regular line, so one might have to wait some time even after locating a supplier, before one can lay hands on the right stuff. I managed to obtain a skin, which is the whole piece, of several square feet about twenty years ago, but only in black. I obtained a further two undyed skins of almost the same thickness about six years ago. That is the measure of the problem.

The straps were cut from a smooth fine leather that is 0.020 in (0.50 mm) in thickness, which is quite easily obtainable from most leather suppliers. The best place to look for these materials is the makers of leather goods, gloves, handbags, as well as bookbinders, for they invariably keep a scrap bin that could quite well supply your fairly small needs at minimal expense.

PVC adhesive was used to glue the leather to the wood. This is the same as the white liquid wood glue sold in plastic bottles, which if left to set as a blob will harden into a translucent, slightly flexible, plastic-type material. With the wood block shaped to size, any joins, lid to box for example, are marked out as a $\frac{1}{32}$ in wide and deep groove into which the leather can later be pressed. Leather this thin can be joined together almost invisibly. On a trunk such as this, however, where rows of nails can be seen, these are usually around the edge of a strengthening strip or corner, ie a second layer of leather. This will cover the joins at the corners. Also to be seen in Plate 195 are the buckles, (one is shown bent on the end of a length of wire) at the bottom, and the trunk catches, all of which are made from nickel silver. The buckles on the original trunk were for show, the actual catch being of the suitcase type at the bottom end of the strap assembly, on the far right. The pins (nails) on the left were made from nickel silver wire of 0.020 in (0.50 mm) diameter cut into short lengths, polished flat at one end, and clipped at an angle at the other to provide a point. With the leather in place on the wood block together with the strengthening corners and strips, etc a sharp pointed tool such as a sewing needle glued into a wooden handle, was used to locate each pin exactly, which was then pressed home to almost flush with the surface of the leather. The straps and catches were then glued in place, and the completed trunk screwed to the platform between the wings from the underside. In Plate 196, this was assembled with the running board woodwork and the side lights on top of the wings, and fitted to the chassis.

In Plate 197, we have the body emerging from the final painting operation, that of applying the yellow to the body moulding, and in Plate 198 we see the interior showing itself. This was a case where the first application of masking was left in place until all painting had been completed, the reason being that the cream interior borders only on the black and not the black and yellow, as with the running board edging. With the body, the interior was painted first with a colour mixed to match the original. To represent the Hungarian pigskin, the matting agent was added to give the desired dull finish, and the parts were sprayed at a low (15 psi) pressure at 18 to 30 in (450 to 760 mm) distance to simulate the grainy texture. With practice and patience, all manner of texture and finishes can be coaxed out of a spray gun using

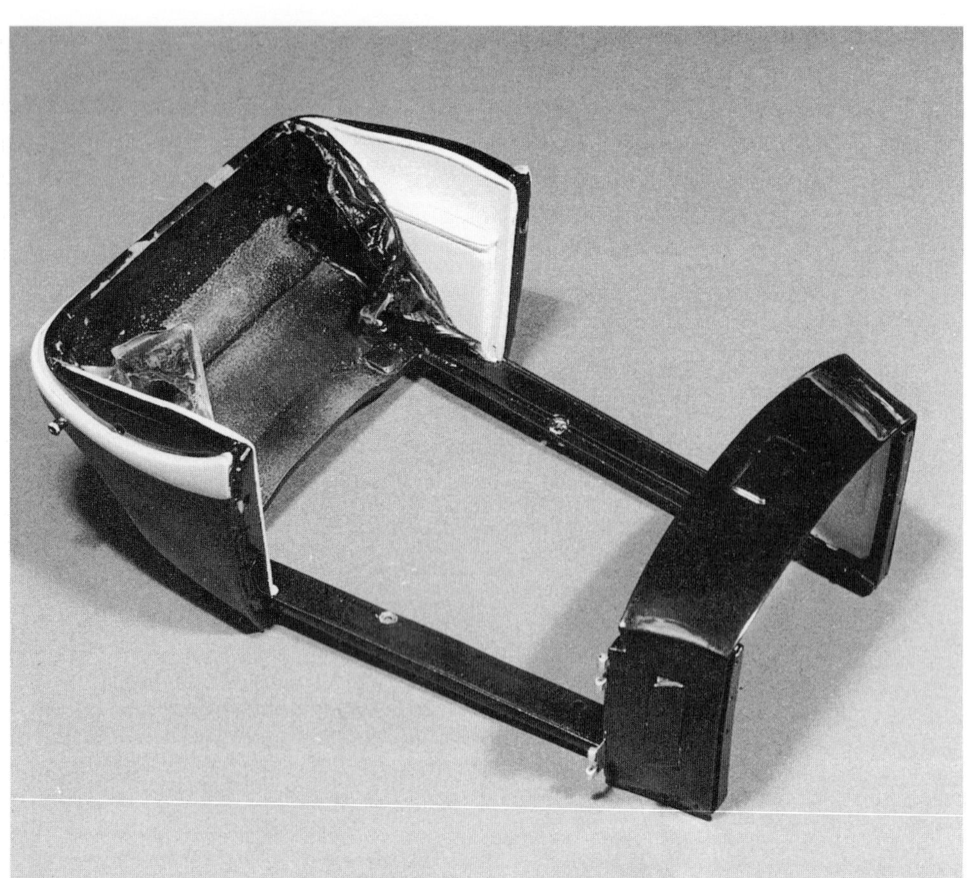

Plate 198

Plate 199

cellulose paint over and above the high gloss that one usually associates with them.

In Plate 199 we have the body in place ready for the completion of the interior. The final part to be fitted was the complete folding top assembly.

The following portfolio of photographs shows the completed model, the ones in a natural setting having been taken by Phyllis and me with a 28 mm lens on a single-lens reflex camera. The wide angle and great depth of field obtained with this lens, and the ability to set up exactly what you want that a single lens camera allows, is well worth the added expense that this equipment may cost. My feelings are that it is only by photographing the finished subject in this way that you will actually see you have captured the character of the original, which, after all, was the purpose of the exercise.

The photographs show two of the models mentioned in the text; I leave you to decide whether or not you feel that we have achieved our goal. The two models shown here differ only in that one is fitted out as recollected by Ludwig Weinberger with mottled aluminium dash and ivory steering wheel. The second has the polished wood steering wheel and instrument boards that we now know were in place in 1937, and were quite possibly the original ones.

Good luck with your model making!

Plate 200

Plate 201

Plate 202

Plate 203

Plate 204

Index

List of Figures

Contentious Terminology

American	**English**
Bumper	Fender
Fender	Wing
Hood	Bonnet
Top	Roof
Trunk	Boot

Mitutoyo
DIGIMATIC